CAMBRIDGE LIBRARY COLLECTION

Books of enduring scholarly value

Travel and Exploration

The history of travel writing dates back to the Bible, Caesar, the Vikings and the Crusaders, and its many themes include war, trade, science and recreation. Explorers from Columbus to Cook charted lands not previously visited by Western travellers, and were followed by merchants, missionaries, and colonists, who wrote accounts of their experiences. The development of steam power in the nineteenth century provided opportunities for increasing numbers of 'ordinary' people to travel further, more economically, and more safely, and resulted in great enthusiasm for travel writing among the reading public. Works included in this series range from first-hand descriptions of previously unrecorded places, to literary accounts of the strange habits of foreigners, to examples of the burgeoning numbers of guidebooks produced to satisfy the needs of a new kind of traveller - the tourist.

The Discovery and Conquest of Terra Florida

The publications of the Hakluyt Society (founded in 1846) made available edited (and sometimes translated) early accounts of exploration. The first series, which ran from 1847 to 1899, consists of 100 books containing published or previously unpublished works by authors from Christopher Columbus to Sir Francis Drake, and covering voyages to the New World, to China and Japan, to Russia and to Africa and India. This volume is an eye-witness account by an anonymous Portuguese 'Gentleman of Elvas, describing Ferdinand de Soto's four-year expedition to Florida which landed in Tampa Bay in 1539 and marched hundreds of miles north-west through present-day Florida, Georgia and Alabama. De Soto died of fever in May 1542, and the survivors made their way back to Mexico in 1543. The text of this translation, by Richard Hakluyt himself, was published in 1611, and first appeared in this annotated edition in 1851.

T0382235

Cambridge University Press has long been a pioneer in the reissuing of out-of-print titles from its own backlist, producing digital reprints of books that are still sought after by scholars and students but could not be reprinted economically using traditional technology. The Cambridge Library Collection extends this activity to a wider range of books which are still of importance to researchers and professionals, either for the source material they contain, or as landmarks in the history of their academic discipline.

Drawing from the world-renowned collections in the Cambridge University Library, and guided by the advice of experts in each subject area, Cambridge University Press is using state-of-the-art scanning machines in its own Printing House to capture the content of each book selected for inclusion. The files are processed to give a consistently clear, crisp image, and the books finished to the high quality standard for which the Press is recognised around the world. The latest print-on-demand technology ensures that the books will remain available indefinitely, and that orders for single or multiple copies can quickly be supplied.

The Cambridge Library Collection will bring back to life books of enduring scholarly value (including out-of-copyright works originally issued by other publishers) across a wide range of disciplines in the humanities and social sciences and in science and technology.

The Discovery and Conquest of Terra Florida

*By Don Ferdinando de Soto
and Six Hundred Spaniards His Followers*

RICHARD HAKLUYT
EDITED BY WILLIAM B. RYE

CAMBRIDGE
UNIVERSITY PRESS

CAMBRIDGE UNIVERSITY PRESS

Cambridge, New York, Melbourne, Madrid, Cape Town, Singapore,
São Paolo, Delhi, Dubai, Tokyo, Mexico City

Published in the United States of America by Cambridge University Press, New York

www.cambridge.org
Information on this title: www.cambridge.org/9781108008068

© in this compilation Cambridge University Press 2010

This edition first published 1851
This digitally printed version 2010

ISBN 978-1-108-00806-8 Paperback

WORKS ISSUED BY

The Hakluyt Society.

DISCOVERY AND CONQUEST OF
TERRA FLORIDA.

M.DCCC.LI.

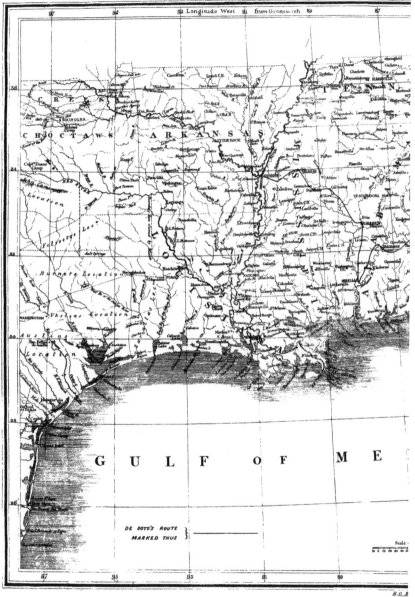

DE SOTO'S ROUTE
MARKED THUS

Buxton, Ao 1831.

THE

DISCOVERY AND CONQUEST

OF

TERRA FLORIDA,

BY

DON FERDINANDO DE SOTO,

AND SIX HUNDRED SPANIARDS
HIS FOLLOWERS.

WRITTEN BY A GENTLEMAN OF ELVAS, EMPLOYED IN ALL THE ACTION, AND
TRANSLATED OUT OF PORTUGUESE,

BY RICHARD HAKLUYT.

REPRINTED FROM THE EDITION OF 1611.

EDITED,

With Notes and an Introduction,

AND A TRANSLATION OF A NARRATIVE OF THE EXPEDITION
BY LUIS HERNANDEZ DE BIEDMA, FACTOR TO THE SAME,

BY

WILLIAM B. RYE,

OF THE BRITISH MUSEUM.

LONDON:
PRINTED FOR THE HAKLUYT SOCIETY.
M.DCCC.LI.

THE HAKLUYT SOCIETY.

INTRODUCTION.

The first account of Fernando de Soto's travels through the southern portion of North America, was written by one of the Portuguese adventurers who accompanied the expedition throughout, and returned to his native country. It was published at Evora, in 1557, under the following title: "Relaçam verdadeira dos Trabalhos q̄ ho Gouernador dō Fernādo d' Souto & certos Fidalgos Portugueses passarom no d'scobrimēto da Provincia da Frolida. Agora nouamēte feita per hū Fidalgo Deluas". Copies of this work are extremely rare. The price of one, mentioned in Mr. Rich's "Catalogue of Books relating principally to America", is stated at £31. 10s. It is a small octavo, in black letter. There is a copy in the collection of the Right Honourable Thomas Grenville, recently bequeathed to the British Museum.

The translation by Hakluyt, here reprinted, of this narrative by the "Gentleman of Elvas", has been already brought under the notice of the Hakluyt Society by Mr. Winter Jones, in his Introduction to the "Divers Voyages touching the discoverie of America". The reader will have there seen, that Hakluyt's intention in making this translation, was evidently to encourage the young colony in Virginia, and to procure an increase of support for that undertaking, at a period when its chances of prosperity were but precarious. The work first appeared in 1609, under the following title: *Virginia richly valued by the description of the maine land of Florida her next neighbour ; out of the foure yeeres continuall travell and discoverie for above one thousand miles east and west, of Don Ferdinando de Soto, and sixe hundred able men in his companie. Wherein are truly observed the riches and fertilitie of those parts abounding with things necessarie, pleasant, and profitable for the life of man ; with the natures and dispositions of the inhabitants. Written by a Portugall gentleman of Elvas, emploied in all the action, and translated out of Portuguese by Richard Hakluyt. At London, printed by Felix Kyngston for Matthew Lownes,* 1609 ; small 4to.[1]

[1] Among the poems of Michael Drayton, the celebrated author of the Polyolbion, is an " Ode to the Virginian Voyage", which was most probably written at this period (1609), and in a warm tone of sympathy with Hakluyt's praiseworthy exertions. We quote from the collected edition of his poems published in 1619-20 :

You brave heroique minds,
Worthy your countries name,
　That honour still pursue,
　Goe, and subdue,
Whilst loyt'ring hinds
Lurk here at home with shame.

And cheerefully at sea,
Successe you still intice,
　To get the pearle and gold,
　And ours to hold
Virginia,
Earth's only Paradise,

Britans, you stay too long,
Quickly aboord bestow you,
　And with a merry gale,
　Swell your stretch'd sayle,
With vowes as strong
As the winds that blow you.

Where nature hath in store
Fowle, venison, and fish ;
　And the fruitfull'st soyle,
　Without your toyle,
Three harvests more,
All greater then you wish.

Your course securely steere,
West and by south forth keepe ;
　Rocks, lee-shores, nor sholes,
　When Eolus scowles,
You need not feare,
So absolute the deepe.

And the ambitious vine,
Crownes with his purple masse
　The cedar reaching hie
　To kisse the sky,
The cypresse, pine,
And usefull sassafras,

The losses and mismanagement of the Virginia colony during the following year, had produced so much discouragement, and Hakluyt, as one of the chief patentees under the charter granted by King James for establishing this first settlement of the English in North America, naturally felt so much interest in its success, that as a fresh temptation to adventurers, and to stimulate the exertions of the colonists themselves, he in the year 1611 altered the title of the " Virginia richly valued", to that which we have adopted for our title-page.

Our reason for giving preference to the later title, is not only that it is much more scarce, but that it precludes the chance of a mistake, into which the earlier title might lead an unprepared reader, of concluding that the work itself treated of Virginia, and not of Florida.

This little volume is extremely rare, not being included in either of the editions of Hakluyt's cele-

To whose, the Golden Age
Still natures lawes doth give ;
  No other cares that tend,
  But them to defend
From winters age,
That long there doth not live.

When as the lushious smell
Of that delicious land,
  Above the seas that flowes
  The cleere wind throwes
Your hearts to swell,
Approching the deare strand.

In kenning of the shore
(Thanks to God first given)
  O you, the happy'st men,
  Be frolike then ;
Let cannons roare,
Frighting the wide Heaven,

And in regions farre,
Such heroes bring yee foorth
  As those from whom we came ;
  And plant our name
Under that starre
Not knowne unto our north.

And as there plenty growes
Of lawrell every where,
  Apollo's sacred tree,
  You it may see,
A poets browes
To crowne, that may sing there.

Thy Voyages attend,
Industrious HACKLVIT,
  Whose reading shall inflame
  Men to seeke fame,
And much commend
To after-times thy wit.

brated collection, though reprinted in the supplement
to that of 1809.

In America, it has been reprinted by Mr. Peter
Force, in the fourth volume of his collection, entitled,
" Tracts and other Papers relating principally to the
origin, settlement, and progress of the colonies in
North America"; published at Washington in 1846,
but without any notes; and in " Part II" of the " Historical Collections of Louisiana" (Philadelphia, 1850),
also without annotation, in which the spelling is
modernized, and Hakluyt's preface, and his marginal
notes, with the exception of three, omitted.

An abridgment of Hakluyt's translation is inserted
in " Purchas his Pilgrimes", fol. 1625. Part IV, pp.
1528-1556.

Another English version,—but very inferior to that
by Hakluyt, and erroneous as to numbers, distances,
and names of places, — was published anonymously
in 1686, in 8vo., under the title of " A Relation
of the invasion and conquest of Florida by the Spaniards, under the command of Fernando de Soto,
written in Portuguese by a gentleman of the town
of Elvas. Now Englished. To which is subjoyned,
Two Journeys of the present Emperour of China
[Kang-He] into Tartary, in the years 1682 and
1683, with some discoveries made by the Spaniards
in the Island of California, in the year 1683". This,
however, was merely a translation from a French
version, anonymous also, but by Citri de la Guette,
which appeared in Paris the year before, in 12mo.,
entitled, " Histoire de la Conqueste de la Floride par

les Espagnols, sous Ferdinand de Soto, écrite en Portugais par un gentilhomme de la ville d'Elvas."

The Preface to this second English translation says : " This Relation now published has the preference in Spain, not onely for its rarity, but for the merit of its author also. As to its rarity, there was but one manuscript of it in Spain, which was taken out of the library of the Duke of Sessa to be printed, and but few copies of the impression in any other country besides. It hath the advantage to be an original, and to come from the first hand ; whereas that of the Ynca Garcilasso de la Vega came abroad but since,[1] and, how pompous soever it may appear in language, has no greater authority than the bare report of a private trooper, and by consequent cannot be compared to this, since the trooper who served Fernando de Soto in that expedition, might, for want of good intelligence, have in many things been mistaken, as well as Garcilasso, for want of memory and application. The truth of this seems more than probable, seeing Garcilasso, in the beginning of his Florida, affirms confidently, that Soto went thither accompanied with thirteen hundred men ; whereas our author says, and that upon better ground, that he had but six hundred ; whereupon, it is to be observed, that a gentleman, as he was, hath

---

[1] Garcilasso de la Vega's History of Florida was completed in 1591. It was first printed at Lisbon in 1605, under the title of "La Florida del Ynca. Historia del Adelantado Hernando de Soto, Governador y capitan general del reyno de la Florida, y de otros heroicos cavalleros Españoles è Indios." We shall presently have occasion to offer some remarks on the relative merits of the Portuguese and Spanish works.

commonly more knowledge, and a greater respect for truth, than a private souldier. The title of the relation informs us, that our author was a Portuguese gentleman of the town of Elvas, and that he accompanied Soto in all that expedition. He is certainly one of those who are named in the second chapter, though he cannot be particularly known, since he has been unwilling to name, or any other way distinguish himself from the rest. It is very probable that his birth and quality made him to be admitted into the most important councils and deliberations; and the particular account he gives us of them, is sufficient to confirm this opinion. It is not at all to be doubted then, but that his information was good; and they who take the pains to examine his book, will be convinced of it, by his way of writing. His stile is natural, plain, and without any ornaments, such as the stile of a discourse ought to be, which hath truth onely for its object. He never wanders from his subject into useless digressions, as Garcilasso de la Vega doth, who seems to have had no other scope but to relate the exploits of Gonsales Sylvester, whom, in a manner, he makes the heroe of his romance; and who, nevertheless, is not so much as named by our author."

A Dutch translation is in Van der Aa's voluminous collection of voyages and travels, " Naaukeurige versameling der gedenk-waardigste Zee en Land Reysen na Oost en West-Indien", published at Leyden in 1706, in 8vo., accompanied by a map, and beautiful (?) engravings—" schoone kopere Platen".

The same map is inserted in the French translation of Garcilasso de la Vega's " Florida", by Pierre Richelet, published by Van der Aa, at Leyden, in 1731.

The Appendix to the present edition consists of a translation of another narrative of Soto's expedition, written by Biedma, or Viedma, a Spaniard, who accompanied it in the capacity of factor. This translation we have made from Ternaux-Compans' *Recueil de Pièces sur la Floride*, published at Paris in 1841, and forming part of his collection of " Voyages, relations et mémoires originaux pour servir à l'histoire de la découverte de l'Amérique". An abridgment of this narrative is given in the Historical Collections of Louisiana, before quoted, as " A translation of a recently discovered Manuscript Journal", and in the Preface to the volume, we are informed that this manuscript was discovered in Spain ; the natural assumption from which would be, that the version in question had been made from the original Spanish document: we are, however, at a loss to account for the occasional introduction of French words, such as *Facteur de sa Majesté*, *Pamfile*, *Saint Esprit*, etc.[1]

The question, as to whether England or Spain may claim the priority in the discovery of Florida, has given rise to many contradictory statements. By the English, the honour has been claimed for Sebastian

---

[1] It is only a few days since, and after the text had been printed off, that an opportunity was afforded us, through the obliging attention of Mr. Henry Stevens, of inspecting the volume of the Historical Collections above alluded to.

Cabot; and by the Spaniards, for Ponce de Leon.
Upon this subject, the historian De Thou, in his
" Historia sui temporis", lib. xliv, 12mo., 1609, has
the following remark :—" Floridam, qui primus inve-
nerit, inter scriptores ambigitur. Hispani ... gloriam
Joanni Pontio Legionensi deferunt... verum quod et
certius est, plerique affirmant, jam ante Sebastianum
Gabotum ... primum in eam Indiarum provinciam
venisse."

Mr. Biddle, in his " Memoirs of Sebastian Cabot",
thus treats the matter :

" The question, how far Cabot, on quitting the
north, proceeded along the coast of the continent, has
been the subject of contradictory statements. By
some, his progress is limited to a latitude corresponding with that of the Straits of Gibraltar, while others
insist on carrying him to the extreme point of the
Atlantic sea coast. We can hardly be at a loss to
decide, when it is recollected that while there is no
direct authority for the latter opinion,—and it is one
which would readily be adopted, in mistake, from the
vague use originally of the title *Florida*,—the former
has the direct sanction of Peter Martyr, (*Dec.* iii,
cap. vi), ' Tetenditque tantum ad meridiem, littore
sese incurvante, ut Herculei freti latitudinis *fere* gradus
equarit; ad occidentemque profectus tantum est ut Cu-
bam insulam a læva longitudine graduum *pene* parem
habuerit.' ' He was thereby brought so far into the
south, by reason of the lande bending so much south-
warde, that it was there almost equall in latitude with
the sea called *Fretum Herculeum*, having the north pole

elevate in maner in the same degree. He sayled likewise in this tract so farre towarde the west, that hee hadde the iland of Cuba on his left hande, *in maner*, in the same degree of longitude.'" (Peter Martyr's *Decades*, translated by Lok, p. 125.)[1]

Gomara, more definitely, but perhaps only determining by conjecture the circumstantial statement of Peter Martyr, names 38°. Hakluyt, in the dedication of his second volume to Sir Robert Cecil, boasts of the universal acknowledgment, even by foreigners, " that all that mighty tract of land, from sixty-seven degrees northward, to the latitude *almost* of Florida, was first discovered out of England, by the commandment of King Henry VII"; and again, in a marginal note of his third volume (p, 9), he states, that Cabot discovered "the northern parts of that land, and from thence as far *almost* as Florida."

Peter Martyr informs us, that a failure of provisions at this point compelled an abandonment of the further pursuit of the coast, and a return to England.— (Biddle's *Memoir of Seb. Cabot*, pp. 79-80.)

It has, however, to be observed, that while it is difficult to decide how far Cabot may have sailed in his southward track along the eastern coasts of America, before he was compelled from want of provisions to direct his course towards England, it is equally difficult to decide how much of the southern portion

---

[1] Peter Martyr, in the same page of his *Decades*, speaks of the great navigator in these terms :—"Cabot is my very friende, whom I use familiarly, and delight to have him sometimes keepe mee companie in my owne house."

of North America at that time bore the name of Florida. We learn from Sanford's *History of the United States*, that " Florida then included an indefinite extent of territory north and west of the present Floridas"; and in Williams's *Territory of Florida*, it is said that " The name Florida was at one period applied to all that tract of country which extends from Canada to the Rio del Norte. This extent has in a course of two hundred years been curtailed by various political arrangements, until it was finally settled by the treaty with Spain, in 1795."

Whatever may have been the southernmost point reached by Cabot in coasting America on his return; it is certain that he did not land in Florida, and that the honour of first exploring that country is due to Juan Ponce de Leon. This cavalier, who was governor of Puerto Rico, induced by the vague traditions circulated by the natives of the West Indies, that there was a country in the north possessing a fountain whose waters restored the aged to youth, made it an object of his ambition to be the first to discover this marvellous region. With this view, he resigned the governorship, and set sail with three caravels on the 3rd of March 1512. Steering N. $\frac{1}{4}$ N., he came upon a country covered with flowers and verdure; and as the day of his discovery happened to be Palm Sunday, called by the Spaniards Pasqua Florida, he gave it the name of Florida from this circumstance.[1]

[1] Peter Martyr says (*Dec.* iv, Lok's transl. p. 163), " Joannes Pontius called it Florida, because he founde that *iland* on the day of the resurrection; the Spaniard calleth Easter the flourishing day

He landed on the 2nd of April, and took possession of the country in the name of the king of Castile.
The warlike people of the coast of Cautio (a name
given by the Indians to all the country lying between
Cape Cañaveral and the southern point of Florida)
soon, however, compelled him to retreat, and he pursued his exploration of the coast as far as 30° 8′ north
latitude, and on the 8th of May doubled Cape Cañaveral. Then retracing his course to Puerto Rico, in
the hope of finding the island of Bimini, which he
believed to be the Land of Youth, and described by
the Indians as opposite to Florida, he discovered the
Bahamas, and some other islands, previously unknown.
Bad weather compelling him to put into the isle of
Guanima to repair damages, he despatched one of
his caravels, under the orders of Juan Perez de
Ortubia and of the pilot Anton de Alaminos, to gain
information respecting the desired land, which he
had as yet been totally unable to discover. He
returned to Puerto Rico on the 21st of September,
and a few days afterwards, Ortubia arrived also with
news of Bimini. He reported, that he had explored
the island,—which he described as large, well wooded,
and watered by numerous streams,—but he had failed
in discovering the fountain. Oviedo places Bimini at
forty leagues west of the island of Bahama. Thus

of the resurrection". But according to Purchas, it was so named
" because it was first discovered by the Spaniards on Palm Sunday,
or on Easter Day, which they call *Pasqua Florida ;* and not, as
Thevet writeth, for the flourishing verdure thereof" Herrera says
that Ponce de Leon had regard to both reasons.

all the advantages which Ponce de Leon promised himself from this voyage, turned to the profit of geography: the title of "Adelantado of Bimini and Florida", which was conferred upon him, was purely honorary; but the route taken by him in order to return to Puerto Rico, showed the advantage of making the homeward voyage to Spain by the Bahama Channel; and science became indebted to him also for the first exploration of the small islands, and numberless rocks and shoals, which render this arm of the sea so dangerous to navigation.

Many authors have spoken of the miraculous fountain, whose waters effaced the wrinkles of age and restored departed beauty. Thus, in the old Romance of "Huon de Bordeaux", mention is made of it in these terms:—"Elle était située dans un lieu désert, et venait du Nil et du Paradis terrestre. Ses vertus étaient telles que si un homme malade en buvait ou en lavait ses mains, il était aussitôt sain et guéri; et s'il était vieux et décrépit, il revenait à l'âge de trente ans, et une femme était aussi fraiche qu'une pucelle." Edmund Burke also in his anonymously published "European Settlements in America", humorously remarks, that if this fountain had been discovered, "it would undoubtedly be the best commodity the country could yield, both for domestic consumption and for the foreign markets, and would be a far better basis for stocks and funds than the richest mines of gold or silver."

In the year 1519, Francisco Garay, Governor of Jamaica, sent out at his own expense four ships, with

skilful pilots, under the command of Alonzo Alvarez
de Pineda, with orders to search for some gulf or strait
on the continent towards Florida. They sailed during eight or nine months, without meeting with the
success anticipated, having seen only the same country
which had been already explored by Ponce de Leon.
After this, they endeavoured to coast eastwards; but
the numerous shoals and reefs which they encountered,
together with the contrary winds, and the violence of
the currents, compelled them to return. They then
held a westerly course, making a careful survey of all
the country, bays, rivers, and other objects worthy of
notice, till they fell in with Hernando Cortes, who
happened at that time to be engaged at Vera Cruz.
They made this the limit of their researches, having
ranged the coast for the distance of more than three
hundred leagues, and taken possession of the country
for the crown of Castile. On their homeward voyage,
they discovered a mighty river, at whose mouth dwelt
a considerable population. They sailed six leagues
up this river, on either shore of which they observed
about forty villages, situated in a province called
Amichel.[1]

The next visit to Florida by Europeans was made
in the year 1520, by the licentiate Lucas Vasquez de
Ayllon, described by Peter Martyr as a " grave man,
and of authority, and a citizen of Toledo". This man
wanting slaves to work the Spanish mines, entered
into an agreement with some of his associates to kid-
nap a number of Caribs from the neighbouring islands

[1] Navarrete. *Coleccion de los Viages,* etc., tom. iii, pp. 63, 148.

in lieu of those who were rapidly disappearing under the hard treatment of the Spaniards. He equipped two ships at San Domingo, and steering either by chance or design, or driven, according to Barcia, by a tempest in a north-westerly direction, he came to the most distant part of the Bahama islands, and thence to that part of Florida between 32° and 33° of north latitude. He then discovered and surveyed two provinces, one named Chicora; and the other, according to Barcia, Duharhe, but, according to Navarrete, Gualdape,—a river, which was named the Jordan,[1]

[1] Writers disagree as to the part of the coast upon which Vasquez landed, and as to the river called Jordan. Ribault believed Port Royal to be the same river. He says : "This is the river of Jordan in mine opinion, whereof so much hath been spoken." Laudonnière thought differently, and supposed the Jordan to be further north. (*Basanier*, p. 16.) The place of landing was called Cape St. Helen's, which in Charlevoix's map is placed near the Santee, making that river the Jordan. This is evidently a mistake. St. Helen's Sound is more than half a degree south of the Santee, and about twenty miles north of Port Royal. The Jordan was doubtless one of the large rivers emptying into this sound. There are three such rivers,—the Coosaw, the Combahee, and the Edisto. Of these the Coosaw is the largest, and is most likely to have been the Jordan. But the Coosaw is only an extension of the Broad river, or Ribault's western arm; the two uniting to encompass the island of Port Royal; so that Ribault, in his expedition up the western arm, [in 1562] may have entered the waters of the Jordan. It is singular, however, that so recent an event as that of the treacherous conduct of Vasquez,—his last voyage having been in 1525,— should not have been remembered by the natives, and caused them to view their new visitors with strong suspicion, if not to have met them with open hostility. But it would not seem, from anything that is written by Ribault or Laudonnière, that the natives had ever before seen or heard of Europeans. (*Note* by Mr. Jared Sparks, in his "Life of Ribault",—vol. xvii of *American Biography*.)

after the captain of one of the vessels,—and a Cape St.
Helena, so called because discovered on St. Helena's
day.   The Indians of Duharhe are thus described by
Peter Martyr, on the authority of Ayllon:—" These
people have a king of a gyantlike stature and height,
called *Datha*, and they say that the queene his wife
is not much shorter than himselfe.   This lord being
demanded, why he alone and his wife should attaine
to that talnesse and height of body, and none of the
people besides, says, that this gift is not hereditary
unto them by nature or from their birth, that they
should exceede others by that prerogative; but that
it proceedeth from violent art, after this manner:
While the infants are in the cradell, and under the
breastes of the nurses, the Masters of that Art are sent
for, who annoint the several members of the infant
for certayne dayes, with medicines of certayne hearbes
which mollifie the tender bones, so that the bones
being presently converted into the softnesse of luke-
warme waxe, they so stretch them out in length oftentimes, that they leave the poore miserable infant almost
halfe deade ; and after that, they feed the nurse with
certaine meats of powerfull vertue.   Lastly, the nurse
giveth it the brest, while it lyeth covered in warme
clothes, and refresheth and cheereth the infant with
milke gathered from substantiall meates: and after
some fewe days of refreshing, they returne to the
dolefull service of wresting and winding of the bones
againe."
    Another of Ayllon's strange stories refers to a
country called Inzignanin :—" The inhabitauntes, by

report of their ancestors, say, that a people as tall as
the length of a man's arme, with tayles of a spanne
long, sometime arrived there, brought thither by sea,
which tayle was not moveable or wavering, as in
foure-footed beastes, but solide, broad above, and
sharpe beneath, as wee see in fishes and crocodiles,
and extended into a bony hardness. Wherefore, when
they desired to sitt, they used seates with holes through
them, or wanting them, digged upp the earth a spanne
deepe or little more, they must convay their tayle
into the hole when they rest them."[1]

Ayllon treated these Indians with remarkable kindness, until he had gained their confidence sufficiently
to induce one hundred and thirty of them to come on
board, when he at once weighed anchor and sailed
for San Domingo with his prize. The greater part of
the wretched captives pined to death, refusing to par-
take of food, or were wrecked in one of the vessels
which foundered at sea. A few experienced perhaps
even a worse fate in Spanish slavery. This ungrateful
cruelty on the part of Ayllon met with loud expres-
sions of indignation even from the Spaniards in San

[1] The historian Andres Gonzalez Barcia, who writes under the
pseudonyme or anagram of "Gabriel de Cardenas z Cano", when
relating this "marvellous report" in his "Ensayo cronologico para
la historia general de la Florida", 1723, notes parenthetically that
"Polydore Vergil informs us that the Englishmen of the county of
Kent (—'los Ingleses del condado de Kent'—) are likewise born
with similar tails, [as a punishment] because their ancestors out of
derision cut off the tail of the horse which carried the illustrious
martyr Thomas à Becket." The tale may be seen at length in
Lambard's "Perambulation of Kent" 1576, under the division of
Stroud.

Domingo, and it was hoped that his villany would receive its merited punishment. The contrary however was the case. Instead of punishment, he obtained from the emperor upon his petition the government of the country. Peter Martyr, who was acquainted with Ayllon, makes the following statement upon this point of his history:—" We caused Licentiatus Aiglionus, the senator, to obtaine his desire: so that now he is sent away from us and from Cæsar's majestie [Charles V] through our perswasion. Hee determined to builde a newe fleete in Hispaniola, to passe over to those coastes, to plant a colonie; nor shall he want folowers: For all this Spanish nation is so desirous of novelties, that what way soever they be called with a becke onely, or soft whispering voyce, to any thing arising above water, they speedily prepare themselves to flie, and forsake certainties under hope of an higher degree, to followe incertainties; which wee may gather from that which is past." (*Decade* vii, translated by Lok, p. 256.)

In the document granting permission from Charles the Fifth to conquer the country,[1] there is, however, a passage to the effect that in the new province there should be no "repartimientos", or distributions of Indians, and that they should not do personal service except of their own good will and with wages, " as is done with our free vassals and the working men in these kingdoms". In 1524, Ayllon sent out a prelimi-

---

[1] Printed in Navarrete's *Coleccion de los viages y descubrimientos*, tom. iii, p. 153, etc.

d

nary expedition of two vessels, which returned with a favourable report, and in the year following he went in person with six ships, carrying five hundred men and between eighty and ninety horses. The expedition was most unfortunate. The pilot Diego de Miruelo could not find his way to Chicora, although he had piloted the first expedition in 1520, and died mad with vexation. At length Ayllon landed in a favourable spot, and was received by the Indians with every show of friendship and kindness. It was now their turn to be treacherous. Deceived by appearances, Ayllon sent two hundred men on an exploring expedition, about a day's journey from the coast; the natives entertained and feasted them for four days, and when they were thus put completely off their guard, murdered them in their sleep to a man. This slaughter was followed by an attack on those who remained in the ships, which compelled them to put to sea, and they only reached San Domingo after great sufferings. Accounts differ respecting the cause of Ayllon's death: some say, a broken heart, and others, disease brought on by cold and fatigue. We close our brief notice of him with the following extract from Galvano (Galvam). He says that " he was lost with all his companie, leaving nothing done worthy of memorie. And I cannot tell how it commeth to pass, except it be by the just judgement of God, that of so much gold and precious stones as have been gotten in the Antiles by so many Spaniards, little or none remaineth, but the most part is spent and consumed, and no good thing done." (Galvano's *Discoveries of the World unto the yeere* 1555. Published by Hakluyt, 1601, pp. 57 and 63.)

In 1524, Giovanni da Verazzano, a Florentine, who had been sent the year before by Francis I of France to prosecute discoveries in the northern parts of America, coasted from Florida as high as Cape Breton.[1]

In 1527, preparations were made in Spain for a fresh expedition to Florida. Pamphilo de Narvaez, having by interest obtained from the Emperor Charles the Fifth the somewhat vague grant of all the lands extending from the Rio de las Palmas to Cape Florida, with the title of "adelantado", and a commission to conquer and govern the provinces within the above limits, set sail from St. Lucar on the 17th of June of that year, with five ships and a force of about six hundred men. A hurricane at Cuba caused so much injury to the expedition, as to deter Narvaez from proceeding to Florida till the ensuing spring. He accordingly put to sea in February 1528, and landed his army at the bay of Santa Cruz in Florida. Having formally taken possession of the country and explored the neighbourhood, they were induced by

[1] Verazzano's Letter addressed to Francis I, is the earliest original account in existence of the Atlantic coast of the United States, nearly the whole extent of which was visited by him during the voyage described in it. (See *Reprint* in Hakluyt's "Divers Voyages", edited by J. Winter Jones, Esq.) A new translation of this letter, by Joseph G. Cogswell, Esq., made from a copy of the original manuscript in the Magliabecchian Library at Florence, accompanied by the Italian text, is printed in the *Collections of the New York Historical Society*. Second series; vol. i, 1841.

the accounts given by the natives, of the existence of great store of gold, to direct their course to the province of Apalache. After a wearisome march they reached the village or town which constituted the capital of the province and bore its name, on the 26th of June. They now made themselves masters of the place, but were so much harassed by the repeated attacks of the natives, as to be compelled to direct their course to the sea-coast. In their march towards the Bay of Aute (now called the Bay of St. Mark's), they lost nearly one third of their number by the arrows of the Indians, and of the remainder a great many suffered from disease induced by the hardships to which they were exposed. Here, while labouring under a degree of famine which compelled them to kill a horse every third day, they resolved upon constructing vessels, in the best manner that their scanty means afforded them, for encountering the dangers of the sea. They contrived in about five weeks to build five boats, capable of holding from forty to fifty men each. Stirrups, spurs, and every other species of iron they possessed, were converted into nails, saws, axes, and other tools. The ropes were formed of horse-hair, and the sails of the soldier's shirts. They put to sea in these frail barques, and moved along the coast in a westerly direction. In this trying position Narvaez resigned the command, and Cabeça de Vaca (who had in the first instance sailed as the treasurer to the armament), took charge of the small remnant of the expedition. Narvaez was lost with many others in a storm, about the middle of November, near the mouth of the Mississippi, and the whole undertaking was frustrated. In this expedition Narvaez is said to have discovered the Bay of Pensacola, and to have landed there. Cabeça de Vaca was kindly received by some of the Indians, but a scarcity of food occurring in the winter, the Spaniards were reduced to the necessity of eating each other,—an act which so horrified the natives that they could no longer regard them with favour. Cabeça de Vaca and his companions were reduced to a state of slavery, but afterwards escaped, through a variety of incredible hardships, to Mexico, whence he was enabled finally to set sail for Europe, and arrived at Lisbon on the 15th of August 1537.[1]

It has been very generally supposed that Soto was the first European who discovered the Mississippi. He crossed it in the year 1541, near the thirty-fifth degree of north latitude; and after his death the remnant of his companions descended it to its mouth. This view is supported by no less an authority than Mr. Bancroft, and also in an able review of Colonel Pickett's pamphlet on " Soto's invasion in Alabama", 1849, in De Bow's *Commercial Review*, vol. ix, 1850. There have not, however, been wanting learned investigators into this question, who are of opinion, judging from the account given by Cabeça de Vaca himself, that the honour of this discovery is due either to this latter adventurer, or to Pineda,

---

[1] The subsequent career of this remarkable man is admirably narrated by Southey, in chap. v of his *History of Brazil*.

who preceded him in 1519. That the reader may judge more fully for himself, we give at length the two following extracts, in confirmation of the latter view. The first is from a paper, " On the early voyages to America", in review of Robinson's Account of Discoveries in the West, published by the Virginia Historical Society (*Southern Literary Messenger* for December 1848):—

" It is among the adventures of the early Spanish navigators here recorded, that we would recommend all who require the seasoning of romance to search, in order to gratify their taste; and we doubt whether they will be disappointed in perusing the extraordinary narrative of Cabeça de Vaca's journey on foot from Florida to Mexico. Making all due allowance for the perhaps natural desire which Cabeça felt to magnify his exploit, there are too many intrinsic evidences of truth in this narrative to justify a disbelief of its general veracity; and it is conjectured with strong probability, that while we are in the habit of according to Ferdinand de Soto the discovery of the mighty Mississippi, the 'father of waters', it is to Cabeça de Vaca that this merit belongs. At all events, it is highly probable that he passed that river in his voyage along the coast of Florida, and this conjecture is strengthened by the fact, that in his long over-land journey from Florida to Mexico, he does not mention his having encountered it. Mr. Robert Greenhow, of Washington, in a letter addressed to the Historical Society of Virginia, communicating a very valuable memoir on the first discovery of the Chesapeake Bay, declares that 'proofs undeniable exist of the discovery of the Mississippi by the Spaniards many years before the expedition of Ferdinand de Soto in 1541'; and in Mr. Greenhow's forthcoming 'History of Florida, Texas, and Louisiana', we may expect to see this interesting speculation more fully developed."

Our second quotation is from a letter addressed by Mr. Greenhow to De Bow, the editor of the *Commercial Review*, October 1849, in which he says:—

" In order to show how imperfectly the early records relating to that part of America have been studied, I send you an extract of my work, containing the account of the *Second visit of the Spaniards to the mouth of the Mississippi*, made some time before the expedition of Hernando de Soto, who has been hitherto universally regarded as the discoverer of the great river, and in commemoration of whose supposed discovery, an artist of much talent is now employed by our government in painting a picture to adorn the halls of the national legislature.

(EXTRACT.)

" The mouth of the Mississippi was first discovered in 1519, by Alonzo de Pineda [Alonso Alvarez de Pineda, in *Navarrete*, iii, p. 64], who gave it the name of Rio del Espiritu Santo,[1] as clearly proved in the history of Florida, Louisiana, and Texas, from the official report of the voyage and the chart annexed to it, of which a fac-simile is preserved [in *Navarrete* iii, 148].

---

[1] See note in *Portuguese Relation*, p. 90.

In the spring of that year [1528], Panfilo de Narvaez
landed with several hundred men on the shore of a
bay, which was most probably the same now called
Charlotte Harbour, on the south side of the peninsula
of Florida; and thence they marched northward to a
country called Apalache, which can be satisfactorily
proved to have been the south-eastern portion of the
state of Alabama. After remaining for some time suffering from want of food, and undeceived as to the
hope of finding rich nations to be plundered, they built
boats on a bay named by them Baia de Cavallos, in
commemoration of the slaughter of their horses; which
appears to have been the same now known as Choc-
tahatchee Bay, communicating with Pensacola Bay
on the west by Santa Rosa Sound. With their departure from this place, begins the following extract
from the history, for which the only authority is the
narrative published by Alvar Nunez [Cabeça] de
Vaca, the treasurer of the expedition, and one of the
four survivors of the party engaged in it:—

" From the place of embarkation, the Spaniards
pursued their voyage towards the west for seven days
before reaching the open gulf, which they at length
entered, through a strait, between the mainland and
an island, — most probably through the entrance
of the Bay of Pensacola, which is just ninety miles
from the eastern extremity of the Bay of Chocta-
hatchee. Thence they continued their navigation
westward along the coast, suffering constantly from
insufficiency of food, and often from thirst, as thei
horse-skin bottles proved useless; and they were

obliged in many cases to have severe combats with the natives, in order to procure fresh water.

" Wending their way thus slowly along the coast, the Spaniards, at the end of a month, had reached a small cluster of islands near the mainland, where they were attacked by a numerous party of natives in canoes, who chased them during the whole day, and annoyed them considerably by volleys of stones and arrows. 'Thus' (writes Cabeza de Vaca in his narrative) 'we continued our voyage through that day (November 1st) until the hour of vespers; when my boat being the foremost, I observed a point of land, beyond which was a very great river, and I halted at an islet off the point to wait for the other boats. The governor (Narvaez), however, would not come up, but chose rather to remain in a bay very near, where were many small islands; and there we joined company, and *took up fresh water from the sea, into which the river poured in a torrent.*[1] As we had eaten our corn raw for two days, we landed upon the island to parch some; but finding no wood there, we agreed to go to the river beyond the point, *a league distant :* on going there, however, the current was so violent, that we were entirely unable to enter, and were driven away from the land, notwithstanding all our efforts and labour to reach it."

The original passage, which is not given by Mr. Greenhow, is as follows:—"Navegamos aquel dia hasta hora de visperas que mi varca que yva delante descubrio

[1] Compare *Portuguese Relation*, p. 157; and Biedma's *Narrative*, p. 199.

una punta que la tierra hazia, y del otro cabo se via un rio muy grande: y en una ysleta que hazia la punta hize yo surgir por esperar las otras varcas. El governador no quiso llegar, antes se metio por una baya muy cerca de alli, en que avia muchas isletas: y alli nos juntamos, y *desde la mar tomamos agua dulce, porque el rio entrava en la mar de avenida.* Y por tostar algun maiz de lo que trayamos, porque ya avia dos dias que lo comiamos crudo, saltamos en aquella isla, mas como no hallamos leña, acordamos de yr al rio que estava detras de la punta *una legua de alli;* y yendo era tanta la corriente que no nos dexava en ninguna manera llegar, antes nos apartava de la tierra: y nosotros trabajando y porfiando por tomarla." (*La relacion y comentarios del governador Alvar Nuñez Cabeça de Vaca*, 1555, 4to., fol. xv and xvi.)

" The river here mentioned," proceeds Mr. Greenhow, " could have been no other than the Mississippi, the only stream flowing into the Mexican Gulf, or into any other sea from North America, the waters of which remain so pure and unmixed with those of the sea, as to be potable at the distance of a league from their outlet. This outlet had been already seen in 1519 by Pineda, who represented it on his chart under the name of Rio del Espiritu Santo; or the merit of discovering the greatest river of North America, if not of the whole world, should have been assigned to Panfilo de Narvaez and Cabeza de Vaca."

Reference having already been made to the three accounts, directly or proximately given by parties engaged in the expedition of De Soto, we propose here to make an especial appeal to the reader's judgment as to their individual or correlative value, with the view of giving an answer to those who have attempted either to disparage, or altogether to annihilate, the credibility of our author. For this purpose, we shall commence by quoting first the statements of those who aim at attributing an apocryphal character to the entire narrative ; and secondly, those of Mr. Theodore Irving, who would assign to the Gentleman of Elvas a lower standard of credibility than to the Inca Garcilasso de la Vega. From these antagonistic statements themselves, we hope to prove the fallacy of the respective charges; and to confirm our proof by reference to two synoptical tables of such points in the three narratives, placed side by side, as mutually tend to establish the validity of the main story, and expose the extravagancies of the Spanish historian Garcilasso.

In the life of Father Marquette, in Mr. Jared Sparks' *American Biography*, vol. x, the following passage occurs :—" It is generally believed that the Mississippi River was first discovered by Ferdinand de Soto, as early as 1541. The accounts of his expedition in Florida are so highly exaggerated, so indefinite, and in many parts so obviously false, that little more can be inferred from them, than that he passed far into the country, had many combats with the natives, and finally died in the interior. The probability is so strong, however, that he and his party actually crossed the Mississippi, that it has usually been assumed as a historical fact. ...

" Soto died on the 21st of May; and his followers, under Moscoso, as the story says, constructed brigantines, in which they sailed down the river to its mouth....

" The first account of Soto's expedition purports to have been written by one of the Portuguese adventurers, who accompanied it throughout, and returned to his native country....The book was first published in 1557, more than fifteen years after the principal events it narrates. There is much show of exactness in regard to dates; but the account was evidently drawn up for the most part from memory, being vague in its descriptions, and indefinite as to localities, distances, and other points usually noted by journalists.

" The Inca Garcilaso de la Vega completed his work on Florida in 1591. It was first printed at Lisbon in 1605. The author's style is flowing and agreeable, but his fancy constantly takes the lead of his judgment, and no tale is too marvellous for his pen. ... A large portion of his work is taken up with the adventures of Soto. Although he wrote more than forty years after the death of his hero, yet he had no other written materials for his guidance than those which had been furnished by the ' Gentleman of Elvas'; and in fact the narrative of this unknown person is the only authority which can be considered of any value respecting the wanderings of Soto. In several points, Garcilaso differs from his original. Citri de la Guette says, that he took his account chiefly from the narration of a common soldier, who was in Soto's expedition, and this at least forty years after the events. Little could be gathered from such a source which is worthy of confidence. Both of the accounts are too romantic and vague for history; yet some of the names of places and of Indian tribes and descriptions of the country, in the narrative of the anonymous Portuguese writer, could hardly have been given, except from personal observation; and they render it in the highest degree probable that Soto crossed the Mississippi near the thirty-fourth degree of latitude.

"It may be doubted, at least, whether either of these works can be trusted as affording genuine historical materials. They have been cited by respectable writers in default of other authorities; but they border so closely upon the regions of romance, that they may as justly be ranked in this class of compositions, as in that of history. This is generally conceded in regard to Garcilaso. His predecessor, the Gentleman of Elvas, is thought to have higher claims, and perhaps he has; yet whoever follows him closely will be likely to run into ten errors in arriving at a single truth, with the additional uncertainty of being able to distinguish the former from the latter. The narrative is, moreover, disfigured with descriptions of atrocious acts of injustice, oppression, and cruelty. In short, if this narrative is worthy of credit, few readers will be inclined to dissent from the remark of Philip Briet, in his *Annales Mundi*, that it is difficult to decide whether cruelty or avarice was the predominant trait in the character of Soto."

Again:—in the *North American Review* for July 1847, in an article on Gayarré's *History of Louisiana*, the writer says:—" The first chapter of M. Gayarré's work is devoted to the apocryphal story of Hernando de Soto's overland expedition to the lower Mississippi, which he discovered in 1541, of his death the following year, and of a remnant of his followers descending the river to its mouth, and thence returning along the shores of the Gulf in safety to Mexico. All this is a romantic and interesting tale; but for how large a portion of it we are indebted only to the vivid fancy of the Spanish historian, it is impossible to say; exaggerations and imaginative details may easily be detected in it by internal evidence. Spain made no attempt to take possession of the country to which this expedition, if real, had given it a valid claim, nor did any of its subjects venture to follow the track of Soto's discoveries."

Mr. Theodore Irving, in the preface to his *Conquest of Florida*, draws the following comparison between the Gentleman of Elvas and the Inca Garcilasso de la Vega:—" The Inca is most to be depended upon,—the Spanish cavalier from whom he derived his principal information being more likely to be admitted to the intimate councils of his commander than one of a different nation, and being free from the tinge of national jealousy which may have influenced the statements of the Portuguese."

We have given these three quotations all together, because the charges contained in them are alike in character, though different in degree, and, as we hope to show, present powerful arguments in refutation of each other.

Now it is not only from a sense of the respect due to the high authority of Mr. Jared Sparks, but from our own conviction of the general correctness of his opinions on this question, that we welcome the statements above quoted from him in favour of the superior credibility of our author. While however we acknowledge that the investigation of the narrative justifies his remark, that " whoever follows it closely will be likely to run into ten errors in arriving at a simple truth",—a fact not to be wondered at when the toils of this laborious and perilous expedition are taken into consideration,—yet we deprecate the expression that " *both* of the accounts are too romantic and vague for history", as calculated, when coming from such an authority, to lead the reader into utter distrust of the whole story. We fear that the general consideration of the subject has led Mr. Sparks to blend the characteristics of the Spanish and Portuguese historians, and to transfer to the latter more of that tendency to romance for which the former is remarkable, than we believe the careful reader will be willing to concede ; and here we would refer to the table which follows, to show that three accounts, which, though written independently of each other and confessedly differing in minute detail, can present so many points of agreement in regular sequence, must have been founded on facts which are *not*, in so far as those points are concerned, " too romantic and vague for history."

*Table of Names mentioned either in two or in each of
the three Accounts.*

THE GENTLEMAN OF ELVAS.	GARCILASSO DE LA VEGA.	BIEDMA.
Paracossi.	Urribarracuxi.	Hurripacuxi.
Cale.	Ocali.	Etocale.
Caliquen.		Aguacalecuen.
Axille.	Ochile.	Veachile.
Vitachuco.	Vitachuco.	Ivitachuco.
Uzela.	Ossachile.	
Anaica Apalache.	Apalache.	Iniahico.
Capachiqui.		Acapachiqui.
Altamaca.	Altapaha.	Altapaha.
Ocute.		Ocute.
Cofaqui.	Cofaqui.	Cofoqui.
Cutifa-Chiqui.	Cofachiqui.	Cofitachyque.
Chalaque.	Chalaque.	
Xualla.	Xuala.	Xuala.
Guaxule.	Guaxule.	Guasuli.
Chiaha.	Ychiaha.	China.
Coste.	Acoste.	Costehe.
Coça.	Coça.	Coca.
Tallise.	Talisse.	Italisi.
Tascaluca.	Tascaluça.	Faszaluza.
Mavilla.	Mauvila.	Mavila.
Chicaça.	Chicaça.	Chicaza.
Alimamu.	Alibamo.	Alibanio.
Quizquiz.	Chisca.	Quizquiz.
Casqui.	Casquin.	Ycasqui.
Pacaha.	Capaha.	Pacaha.
Quigaute.	Quiguate.	Quiguata.
Coligoa.	Colima.	Coligua.
Tatalicoya.		Tatilcoya.
Cayas.		Cayas.
Tulla.	Tula.	Tula.
Quipana.		Quipana.
Autiamque.	Utiangue.	Viranque.
Nilco.	Anilco.	Anicoyanque.
Guachoya.	Guachoya.	Guachoyanque.
Aguacay.		Aguacay.
Nissoone.		Nisione.
Lacane.		Lacame.
Nondacao.		Nandacaho.
Soacatino.		Xuacatino.

The above table, as we have said, presents too
many points of agreement in the three accounts to
leave any excuse to those who would venture to

impeach the credibility of the main story; and if this be granted, the next inquiry will naturally be, which of the three contains the greatest number of details of a character serviceable to history and geography, but neither dictated by, nor catering to, an exaggerative spirit of romance. In this respect, not only Sparks and Bancroft, but every other critic that we have read upon the subject, unite in acknowledging the superior credibility of the Gentleman of Elvas.

Mr. Bancroft's observations are as follows (*History of the United States*, edit. 1834, vol. i, p. 66):— " On Soto's expedition, by far the best account is that of the Portuguese eye-witness. ... This narrative is remarkably good, and contains internal evidence of its credibility. The work of Vega is an extravagant romance, yet founded upon facts. Numbers and distances are magnified, and everything embellished with great boldness. His history is not without its value, but must be consulted with extreme caution."

For the rest, Mr. Sparks's criticism entirely disarms Mr. Theodore Irving of his arguments in favour of Garcilasso de la Vega. Any reader of the work will readily concede the correctness of the remark, that " the author's fancy constantly takes the lead of his judgment, and that no tale is too marvellous for his pen". Wisely did Mr. Irving, with the object he had in view, select it for the basis of his romantic and ably-written story. But if, as we believe, such charge is not to be fairly brought against the Portuguese narrator, the details here presented to the reader, difficult as they may be to follow, from the

f

hindrances which the perils and toils of the route must have opposed to constant journalizing, form a subject worthy of the attention of the Hakluyt Society, both in an historical and geographical point of view.

To assist the reader's judgment as to the extravagancies of Garcilasso, and the greater accuracy of the Gentleman of Elvas and Biedma, we here give another synoptical table, exhibiting the statements respectively given in the three accounts, with particular reference to numbers :—

PLACES MENTIONED.	GENTLEMAN OF ELVAS.	BIEDMA.	GARCILASSO DE LA VEGA.
Landed in Florida (Bay of Espiritu Santo).	600 men. 213 horses.	620 men. 223 horses.	1000 men. 350 horses.
...	John Ortiz came to meet us with 10 or 11 principal Indians.	9 Indians. (8 or 10, in Soto's letter to the municipal authorities at Cuba; printed in Ternaux-Compans's *Pièces sur la Floride*.)	50 Indians.
...	The Governor left Calderon at the port with 30 horsemen and 70 footmen.	26 horsemen. 62 foot soldiers.	40 horsemen. 80 foot soldiers.
Patofa.	The cacique gave the Governor 700 Indians to bear burdens.	800 Indians.	4000 ; and 4000 besides as an —— escort. 8000*[See note p.xxxv.]
Cutifachiqui.	They found 14 arrobas of pearls in a temple.	6 or 7 arrobas.	20 arrobas.

[*Table continued.*

PLACES MENTIONED.	GENTLEMAN OF ELVAS.	BIEDMA.	GARCILASSO DE LA VEGA.
Mavila (the battle).	2,500 Indians killed. 18 Christians killed. 150 Christians wounded, with 700 wounds. 12 horses killed.	20 Christians killed. 250 Christians wounded : — 660 arrow-shots.	Upwards of 11,000 Indians killed.* 82 Christians killed. 1770 Spaniards wounded. 45 horses killed.
Chicaça (the battle).	11 Christians killed. 400 hogs burnt.	13 or 14 Christians killed. 300 hogs burnt.	40 Spaniards killed. Nearly all perished.

* The following note is from the Hon. Albert Gallatin's valuable "Synopsis of the Indian Tribes" (*Archæologia Americana*, ii, 106). "If we were to place implicit faith in the accounts given by Garcilaso de la Vega of the number of Indians in various places, we should infer a greater population than was found to exist one hundred and fifty years later. Considering the sources from which he derived his information, the proneness of common soldiers to swell the number of enemies, and the habitual and notorious exaggeration of the Spaniards of his time, we will in that respect give the preference to the more sober statements of the Portuguese narrator, who kills only 2,500 Indians by the fire and sword, at the storming of Mauvila, whilst Garcilaso swells the number to 11,000. Yet Garcilaso did not intend to impose on his readers, or exceed, according to his knowledge, the bounds of credibility. Born in Peru, he was deceived by an erroneous analogy, and saw nothing extraordinary in the accounts given to him of eight to twelve thousand Indians collected together. In another place, at Cofaqui or Patofa, the last inhabited district before the arrival of the Spaniards at Cofachiqui, the cacique, who was very friendly, gave them, according to Garcilaso, 4000 warriors to escort them, and 4000 retainers to carry their supplies and clothing. It must be observed that the total amount of their baggage was such, that, on their departure from Anhayca, each soldier carried his supply on his back. On the seventh day of their march through an uninhabited country, the army was arrested by the termination of the path which they had followed

Mr. Theodore Irving, in the revised edition of his *Conquest of Florida*, published during the present year, remarks, that "nothing is more perplexing than to make out the route of De Soto in conformity to modern landmarks". It is only left to us in meeting this perplexity, to endeavour to reconcile the three accounts as far as possible with the various explanations which have been offered by learned and industrious American critics, aided by the personal observations of travellers. Of these investigators, the most careful and laborious have been Dr. J. H. M'Culloh (*Researches, philosophical and antiquarian, concerning the aboriginal history of America.* Baltimore, 1829); the Honourable Albert Gallatin (*Sy-*

thus far. They were then within twelve leagues of the first village in the province of Cofachiqui, and not one of the 8000 Indian allies could point out the proper direction, which at last was discovered by the Spaniards themselves. And the Indian chief assured De Soto that none of his followers had ever been in that place, and that in their wars with the Indians of Cofachiqui, those of Cofaqui had never passed over their own frontiers. Whether any one Indian warrior has ever been found ignorant of the way to an enemy's village, hardly one hundred and fifty miles distant, and through a country offering no particular obstacle, we are able to judge. According to the Portuguese narrator, De Soto had demanded only six hundred Indians; and when he found himself at a loss which way to pursue, he had no other guide but a young Indian they had brought from Appalache, and who confessed that he did not know where he was. 'The Indians of Patofa (or Cofaqui) had been sent back as soon as provisions began to be scarce', though the poor men showed a great deal of trouble to leave the Christians before they saw them in a good country. The numbers, as stated in the Portuguese relation, are not in the whole inconsistent with a population nearly the same as at this time. The greatest apparent exaggeration is, perhaps, that of the cacique of Ocute sending two thousand Indians to De Soto with a present of some provisions."

nopsis of the Indian Tribes, published in the second volume of the *Archæologia Americana*. Cambridge, 1836); Mr. Thomas Nuttall (*A Journal of Travels into the Arkansa territory during the year* 1819. Philadelphia, 1821); and Dr. J. W. Monette (*History of the discovery and settlement of the Valley of the Mississippi;* 2 vols. New York, 1846).

Mr. Irving also, who seems to have made use of all these commentators except Dr. Monette, has added to his revised edition of the *Conquest of Florida* some notes upon the route, which, aided as they are by the personal observations of Mr. G. R. Fairbanks, who travelled over the south-easterly portion of it himself, deserve particular respect and credence. The map which we have used in guiding us through these puzzling accounts and their various renderings, is that published in 1839 by David H. Burr, Geographer to the House of Representatives of the United States, on the scale of one-inch to ten statute miles.

De Soto arrived in the Bay of Espiritu Santo, on the western coast of East Florida, on the 25th of May 1539, and after four days spent in taking observations of the vicinity, landed his army probably in that part of it known as Hillsborough Bay. Six miles in a north-westerly direction brought them to an Indian village named Ucita by the Portuguese historian, but Hirrihigua by the Inca Garcilasso de la Vega.

Their onward route towards the north-east, passing through the province of Paracossi, or Urribarracuxi, is thus minutely described by Dr. Monette:—

" The army pursued an Indian trace, which traversed
the low, marshy region south and east of the Hillsborough River, towards the north-east.   Their guides
led them through thick woods, with tangled vines
and undergrowth ; through swamps, marshes, and
deep morasses, almost impassable for man or
horse. ... After several days of severe toil and great
perplexity, in threading their way through swamps
and bogs, they at length came to a deep river,
which was out of its banks from recent rains.
On each side of the stream, for a mile and a half in
width, was a low swamp, which was excessively boggy
when not completely covered with water.   Three
days were spent in continued and fruitless attempts
to find a firm crossing-place....A rude Indian bridge,
made by a tree felled in from each bank, and joined
by a floating raft, enabled them to cross, while the
horses were obliged to swim.   They were now, in all
probability, on the Withlacoochy River, in the region
of the Wahoo swamp ; and pursuing their route,
they crossed from the south to the north side, and
continued their march towards the north.   After
almost incredible difficulties, the army arrived at the
village of Acuera, about thirty miles north of the
Withlacoochy or Amaxura River, situated in a beautiful and fertile bottom, environed by extensive fields
of corn, and by gardens, besides beautiful copses of
fruit trees....Near the village of Acuera, De Soto
remained for twenty days....The Spaniards were now
about seventy or eighty miles distant from Hillsborough Bay, in a due north direction, and about

twelve miles south-west from Orange Lake....De Soto determined to march for the country of Ocali [Cale], about forty miles further north.   In the first thirty miles, they passed over a thin, barren region, and some fine forests, probably north-west of the present site of Fort Micanopy, before they entered the fertile region of Ocali.   For twenty miles further, they passed through a fruitful valley, thickly inhabited, and abounding in fields.   At length they arrived at the chief town, called, after the country, Ocali.   This was one of the most extensive towns in Florida, and contained six hundred houses.   It was situated upon the south side of a river, in all probability the Su-wanee, or the Santa Fé branch.   Here the Spaniards remained several days."

It were almost vain to attempt to trace the precise positions of the various so-called towns or villages which next occur, as referred to by the Portuguese narrator, and by him alone, until they arrive at the country of Vitachuco or Palache.   This province would seem to have extended northward, according to Dr. Monette, as far as the Suwanee river, which forms the southern limit of Hamilton County, Florida. Ochile was its frontier province ; and the town of Vitachuco itself is supposed by the same author to have been about twelve miles south-east of Suwanee river, or the northern verge of the province itself.

This account, however, we think carries the jour-ney too far north; and we incline to agree with Mr. Fairbanks, in placing Ocali in the neighbourhood of Fort King, and Vitachuco about fifteen miles west of

Fort Micanopy. He says that in this vicinity are numerous lakes and prairies, which might be taken as the scene of a battle, described very fully by Garcilasso de la Vega.

Their route thence brought them to a large and deep river, doubtless the Suwanee, which they crossed on rafts, and came to the village of Uzela or Ossachile, which Mr. Fairbanks takes to be Suwanee old town. In journeying hence towards the country of Apalache, they crossed a " great morass", and after a dangerous and toilsome march came to a deep river bordered by dense forests, which was in all probability the Oscilla, and about twelve miles beyond was the town of Anhayca. The swamp crossed is thought by Mr. Fairbanks to be that at the head of the Estauhatchee, a river emptying into the gulf. He remarks, that it could not have been the Okefenokee, as supposed by Mr. M'Culloh, as that is nearly one hundred and fifty miles from Apalache, and is altogether unlike the morass, and no Indian highway goes through it; its diameter being twelve or fifteen miles. Almost any wet Florida swamp at the head of a river would answer the description given of the morass crossed by De Soto. He adds, that from his *personal* knowledge of the country, he feels confident that the course we have thus far marked out must be nearly, if not exactly the one taken; and the fact, that the Seminoles kept the whole army of the United States at bay for seven years, and now require to be bought out, is itself an evidence of the nature of the country.— *Vide* Kerr's *Voyages and Travels*, vol. v, page 466; M'Culloh's *Researches*, page 524; Darby's *Florida*, pp. 19-20.

Upon the position of the town of Anhaica or Anhayca, and of the Bay of Aute, in its vicinity, Mr. Gallatin makes the following observations :—" This was situated in the vicinity of a port into which he [De Soto] ordered his vessels, and which, from the position designated, must necessarily have been some-where in Apalachee Bay. We cannot therefore err much in placing Anhayca in the vicinity of the Ockockona river. East, and not far from it, the names of Uzachil and Anille [Axille] are mentioned, and there is a river precisely in the same position, which to this day is called Oscilla. But I have not been able to ascertain whether this is either an Uchee or Muskhogee name, or whether it may not have been subsequently given to the river by the Spaniards in commemoration of De Soto's expedition. I have been equally unfortunate in my inquiries respecting the etymology of the name Apalachee; whether it belongs to the language of any of the existing nations, or whether it has been perpetuated from De Soto's time. It is certain that the river Appalachicola is known to the Muskhogees by no other name than that of Chatta Hatchee, or Rock River. The only name mentioned in that vicinity, having any known affinity with an Indian language, is that of a village near the sea-port, which in the Spanish relation is called Aute. In the Muskhogee language, *autti* or *oty*, means an island.

" De Soto's officers discovered in the course of the

g

winter another and better port, sixty computed leagues west of Aute. This was called Ochus, and must have been either Pensacola, or the entrance of the Mobile. Instead, however, of proceeding in that direction, De Soto, on the information of an Indian boy, determined to march northwardly in search of a gold region."

Upon the same subject, Mr. M'Culloh makes the following remarks :—" The Apalachy Indians, at the time the French settled in Louisiana, lived around and above the junction of Flint and Cattahouchie rivers, and, most probably, had lived there since the time of Soto. The town of Anhayca I have placed north of the river Uche, from the following incident in Soto's history:—After Calderona, who was marching to join him at Anhayca, had passed the marsh of Apalache, which I cannot make out to be other than the Oha-hichee swamp, he entered on a large plain, over which he marched about five leagues to a deep stream,—the Uche river, I presume,—where they fought a battle with the Indians. Now near this place must have been the town of Anhayca, for Garcilazo says, that the Spaniards encamped there ought to have heard the noise of the engagement. We cannot be far wrong in thus locating Apa-lache; for the seaport of Aute, which undoubtedly was at the head of the bay of St. Mark's, was about thirty leagues distant."

Dr. Monette's observations place this town some-what more northerly, but yet in a position suffici-ently approximating to the other two, allowance

being made for the almost inevitable want of precision in the original documents. He says:—" That
part of the province in which the town of Anhayca
was situated, is, by general assent, placed from about
one hundred to one hundred and thirty miles north
of the present site of St. Mark's. As to the immediate site of this town, nothing definite can be ascertained; but it was probably in the vicinity of some of
the tributaries of the Suwanee River, or nearer the
Flint. The Spaniards, pursuing their circuitous
marches, considered it nine days' march from the sea,
and near one hundred leagues north from the Bay of
Espiritu Santo. The province was populous, and had
numerous villages and extensive fields. There was
no gold in the country. . . While in winter quarters
at Anhayca, De Soto repeatedly sent out strong de-
tachments through the surrounding country, to the
distance of forty or fifty miles, to explore the country,
and inquire for the gold region. Some of these de-
tachments were out as long as a week or ten days,
and returned and reported the country on the north
fertile, populous, and free from marshes. At length,
one of the most intrepid and persevering captains was
despatched southward, with a strong detachment of
horse and foot, to reach the sea." Mr. Irving places
Anhayca in the neighbourhood of the modern town
of Tallahassee; and Colonel Pickett says, Indian traditions confirm this opinion.

After wintering at Anhayca, they marched northwardly five or six days, and crossing, on the fourth or
fifth, a broad and very rapid river,—probably the

Ochlockony,—they reached Capachiqui. Ten days
from Capachiqui, brings them, on the 21st March, to
Toalli, or 'Otoa, the largest village yet seen, but the
site of which we are unable to conjecture. It is
described, however, as near Achese, on a small river,
which was probably the southern branch of the
Ocmulgee, Ochis being, according to Mr. Gallatin,
the Muskhogee name of that river.

They left Achese—the Chisi of Biedma—on the
1st of April; and on the 4th came to Altamaca, the
Altapaha of Biedma, which name, M'Culloh suggests,
is probably preserved in that of the river Alapapaha,
the midmost branch of the Sawanee river, but which
we presume to be the river Altamaha itself, of which
the Ocmulgee is a branch.

In the middle of April they reached Ocute and
Cofaqui, and on the 28th or 29th of the month came
to Cutifachiqui or Cofachiqui. Dr. Monette places this
province on the head-waters of the Savannah river,
and the chief town probably in the peninsula at the
junction of the Broad and Savannah rivers. On this
point Mr. Gallatin has the following remarks, which
give to the location of Cutifachiqui a tolerable amount
of certainty : " Twelve days' march more, in the same
direction, brought him [De Soto] to Xuala in the mountains; and this was the termination of his travels northwardly. The distance from the vicinity of St. Mark's
to the sources of the French Broad, or of the Hiwas-
see, both tributary streams of the Tennessee, is about
three hundred and fifty miles in a direct line. This
determines the position of Cofachiqui, which was

certainly on a river emptying into the Atlantic, not far south of the thirty-fourth degree of north latitude, on the Oconee, or on the Savannah River. The statement, therefore, that, according to Indian information, it was but two days' journey to the sea, is erroneous. Between Anhayca and Cofachiqui, we find the two names of Achese, on a river which the Spaniards ascended some days, and of Ocute, a fruitful country. Ochis is the Muskhogee name of the Okmulgee river. *Oketa*, in the same language means *woman;* and *Cohwita* in Uchee means *man*, and is the well-known name of a Creek town. These detached names afford but a slight indication of that part of the country having been at that time occupied by the Creeks. But from Cofachiqui to the Mississippi, we have a continued series of names, which seems to leave no doubt respecting the several nations along De Soto's line of march, from the time he left Cofachiqui."

We further quote from a note by Colonel Pickett, which leaves no doubt on our mind as to the real locality of Cofachiqui. The colonel says, " that all Indian tradition places the town of Cofachiqui on the east bank of the Savannah, at the modern Silver Bluff, Barnwell district, South Carolina. About 1735, a young Irishman, George Gilpin, settled upon the ruins of Cofachiqui, and gave it the name of Silver Bluff, owing to the tradition, that De Soto and his troops searched there for silver in the bed of the river, and among the various strata of the Bluff, some of which resembled silver ore."

In seven days' march due north from that place,

De Soto came to Chalaque, probably a tribe of Chero-
kees, some of whom do not pronounce the letter *r*,
and call themselves Chellakees. The next province
reached by the Spaniards was Xualla, from which
their course was westwardly, bending to the south.

It is possible, that the town of Qualatche, which
is situated on the very source of the Catahootche
river, designates the station of Xualla, — Colonel
Pickett says it was probably in Habersham county.
From hence they proceeded, in two days, to Canasagua, a name perhaps retained in the river Connesaugo,
which runs nearly along the 8° of longitude (west
from Washington) from the mountains, and finally
empties into the Coosa river.

Leaving Canasagua, in five days they reached the
town of Chiaha, or Ichiaha, which all agree in placing
on the Etowee branch of the Coosa river; and Dr.
Monette supposes it to have been in that part of
Georgia now designated as Floyd County. Colonel
Pickett places it on the site of the modern town of
Rome. He says, that De Soto had now reached the
confluence of the Oostanaula and Etowah, which
make the Coosa, and that the Spaniards mistook the
peninsula on which the village stood for an island.
Mr. Meek also states, that there is no such island
now in the Coosa, and thinks it probable that the
Spaniards either mistook the peninsula formed by the
junction of the two rivers for an island, or that these
two rivers were originally united so as to form an
island near their present confluence. He adds, that
he has heard this latter supposition asserted by two

persons well acquainted with the country. Crossing this river, they entered the province of Coste or Acoste on the 2nd of July, and thence marched to the province of Coça or Cosa, the principal village of which they reached on the 26th of July. Mr. M'Culloh here says: "From Acoste they marched into the province of Cosa. This province they state to be about one hundred leagues in extent; and that the village of the cacique, which was also called Cosa, was at the other extremity of the province from whence they had entered. It was situated upon the banks of a river. Every part of this description is strictly correct, as applied to that town, which is now called in our maps, 'Old Coosa', in north latitude about 33° 30′, on Coosa river."

They remained at Coça twenty-five days, and left it on the 20th of August; and after passing through several villages, enumerated only by the Portuguese historian, came to Tallise on the 18th of September. This town lay upon a very rapid river, which M'Culloh considers to be the Talisse of the maps, lying at the elbow of Talapoosa river. They crossed this river, and in six days came to Tascaluça. Bossu (*Travels in Louisiana*, 282) says, that above sixty leagues above the junction of the Tombecbe and Alabama rivers, and up this last, is a ford called by the Choctaws Taskaloussas, which signifies *white mountain* or *hill*, where we may suppose the army to have crossed.

A few days afterwards, De Soto proceeded to the south-east, until he arrived at the town of Mauvilla, or Mavilla, on the site of which Mr. Irving gives the following note:—"This town is supposed to have stood on

the north side of the Alabama, and at a place now called
Choctaw Bluff, in the county of Clarke, about twenty-
five miles above the junction of that river with the
Tombecbe, within a hundred miles from Pensacola;
and this opinion is strengthened by the fact, that aged
Indians in the neighbourhood, at the present day,
point it out as the site of the great battle between
De Soto and the Mobilians.   There is little doubt
that it gave the name to the present river and bay of
Mobile.   The letters *v* and *b* are often used indiffer-
ently in Spanish in place of each other, and articu-
lated in nearly the same manner.   Charlevoix, in his
Journal Historique, let. 33, p. 452, says:—' Garcilasso
de la Vega, dans son Histoire de la Floride, parle
d'une Bourgade appellée *Mauvilla*, laquelle a sans
doute donné son nom à la rivière, et à la nation qui
étoit établie sur ses bords.   Ces Mauviliens étoient
alors très-puissans; à peine en reste-t'il aujourd'hui
quelques vestiges.'"

Their onward route from Mauvila has been ela-
borated with such zeal and patient attention by Dr.
Monette, that we feel justified in submitting it to the
reader's favourable acceptance, contenting ourselves
with offering by the way such corrective suggestions
as may arise from our own deductions, or those of
Mr. M'Culloh.   Dr. Monette's remarks run thus:—
" One month after the great disaster of Mauvile, finding that his horses and men were now sufficiently recovered from their wounds to travel, De Soto set out
on his march toward the north, near the last of November.... After five days' march they arrived at ' a deep

and wide river', which was in all probability the
Tombigby, below the mouth of the Black Warrior.
This they crossed after much hard fighting with a
large body of Indians, who disputed the passage for
twelve days, until large boats were constructed to
ferry the army across. This was probably in Marengo
county, Alabama, not far from Chickasâ Creek. After
this they marched on toward the north-west for five
days more, when they came to another river, probably
the Pearl, which was not so large as the first. Here
they met with some opposition from the natives, and
passed on in the province of Chicasâ, within the state
of Mississippi. The first river crossed by De Soto and
his army after leaving Mauvile was ' a deep and wide
river', where they were vigorously opposed by a large
body of Indians, who, stationed for six miles on the
west bank, defeated every attempt to cross for twelve
days, until the Spaniards had completed a very large
scow or ferry-boat. . . . . Some have erroneously supposed this was the Black Warrior itself; but De Soto
directed his general course west of north from Mauvile,
and of course he would not reach the Black Warrior,
which was toward the north-east; besides, the latter
river does not answer to the size and depth of the first
river crossed in their march for Chicasâ. The second
river crossed in this march was probably the main
Pearl river, somewhere in Leake county. Thence the
course was more toward the north; and after eight or
ten days' march in that direction, they came to the
village of Chicasâ, situated in a beautiful plain, fertile
and well-watered, probably in the valley of the Yalobu-

h

sha, and in that portion embraced in Yalobusha county.
The expedition arrived at this village late in December, about one month after its departure from Mauvile. It was composed of about two hundred small
houses or wigwams. . . . . The winter had now set in.
. . . . De Soto determined to remain in the village
until spring. . . . This was supposed by the Spaniards
to have been the chief town of the Chicasâ Indians,
whose territory extended to the first river they crossed
after leaving Mauvile (A.D. 1541). After this disaster
(the battle and conflagration of Chicasâ), the army
soon removed to another village, about three miles
distant, called Chicaçilla, where they fortified themselves, and remained until the last of March . . About
the 1st of April, De Soto broke up his winter-quar-
ters, and set out again toward the north-west. The
first day's march westward brought them to the vicinity of a strongly fortified town called Alibamo, or as
the Portuguese narrator writes it, Alimamu. This is
the town from which the river Alabama takes its
name. It was situated on the east bank of a deep
but narrow river, with high banks, in all probability
the same now known as the Tallahatchy, and probably
not far above the junction of the Yalobusha . . . The
next day this post was regularly attacked and carried
by storm. . . . The Spaniards remained in camp four
days, to recruit their strength and for the recovery of
the wounded.

" Their next march was westward; and crossing
the river at an easy ford they left the province of
Chicasâ. For seven days they traversed an unin-

habited country, abounding in swamps and forests, where they were often compelled to swim their horses in the route. At length they came in sight of a village called Chisca [by Garcilasso de la Vega, and Quizquiz by the Portuguese author and Biedma],—which was seated near a wide river. As this was the largest river they had yet seen, they called it the ' Rio Grande'. It was the same now called the Mississippi. . . . Since their departure from the fortress of Alibamo, the Spaniards had traversed a vast and dense forest, ' intersected by numerous streams'; doubtless the creeks and bayous of the Tallahatchy region. Wearied in the toilsome march, they remained several days in camp at the village of Chisca, near the Great River. ' The river was low and both banks were high.' Incessantly harassed by the hostility of the natives, they resumed the line of march up the eastern bank during four days. Having found an open region, they encamped until boats should be built for crossing to the western side. Twenty days were required to build them in sufficient size and number to transport the army and horses. No sooner were the boats completed, than De Soto began to cross his army to the western shore...He at length succeeded, with the aid of a friendly chief, in obtaining for his whole army a safe passage. ' At this place,' says the Portuguese historian, ' the river was half a league from one shore to the other, so that a man standing still could not be seen from the opposite shore. It was of great depth and of wonderful rapidity. It was very muddy, and was always filled with floating trees and timber, carried down by the force of the current.' Much doubt and uncertainty has obtained as to the precise point at which De Soto reached the Mississippi. It was evidently much below the latitude of Memphis, where he was toiling four days in advancing twelve leagues up the river, and seven days in his westward march through swamps and deep forests from the uplands east of the Tallahatchy. At no point above Helena are the highlands, on the east side of the river, more than ten or fifteen miles distant. The point where De Soto crossed the river was probably within thirty miles of Helena. The changes of the channel in the lapse of three hundred years may have been such as to defy identification now." Mr. Irving says the spot " was probably the lowest Chickasaw Bluff, one of the ancient crossing-places between the thirty-fourth and thirty-fifth parallel of latitude".

We do not venture to trace the route beyond this upon the map, inasmuch as it is so complicated as to have caused the greatest perplexity and difference of opinion to all who have endeavoured to follow it. We shall therefore content ourselves with placing before the reader the respective conclusions of Mr. M'Culloh and of Dr. Monette.

M'CULLOH.	MONETTE.
After having built boats, they crossed the Mississippi, somewhere, I presume, about twenty or thirty miles below the mouth of the Arkansaw river. They call the country where they landed the province of Aquixo, a name	The whole expedition having safely crossed to the west side of the river,... the army prepared to advance north-westward into the interior of what is now the State of Arkansas. After nearly five days' march through a level

M'CULLOH.

we cannot recognize in any Indian words preserved on our maps. As far as can be collected from their account, they marched across the province, crossed a river (the Wachita), and on the fifth day, from a high eminence (probably near the present southern old Cado village), they discovered the town of Casquin, on the banks of a river (Red river) as great as the Guadalquivir at Cordova.

[It is not unlikely that by this name the Kaskaia Indians are intended, but they are now found in the interior of the country. According to Long's *Expedition*, ii, 112, they frequent the country about the sources of the Platte, Arkansaw, and Rio del Norte, and extend their hunting excursions to Red River, and the sources of the Brassos.—*Note.*]

They marched up this river to some little villages where the cacique held his court (probably the northern old Cado villages), and from hence they proceeded to Capaha; in which word we may recognize a town of the Kappas, or Quapaw Indians, who even at this day, have their towns extending across the Wachita from the Red to the Arcansaw river. It is impossible to say where Capaha stood, but if a locality be deemed necessary, we may suppose it to have been about the western Cado village, which on Pike's map is near the 18° of longitude west from Washington. The most embarrassing part of their narration, however, is, that they say there was a canal of water of about three leagues in length from Capaha to the Great river. As the appellation

MONETTE.

wilderness country, intersected in many places with streams, bayous, and lakes, many of which were not fordable, they descried a large Indian village containing about four hundred dwellings. It was situated on the banks of a river, bordered as far as the eye could reach, with luxuriant fields of corn, and fruit trees of different kinds. This town was occupied by the tribe of Casqui or Casquin; and the river upon which it was situated in all probability was White River, about one hundred and fifty miles above its junction with the Mississippi. They remained at this place six days.... They then set out for the chief town or residence of the cacique, which was situated upon the same side of the river, about two days' march above the first town. In this distance they passed through a beautiful rolling country, which was less alluvial than any they had passed since they left the highlands east of the Tallahatchy. It was late in the month of May. Having remained nine or ten days.... De Soto set out toward the north and east. . . . After marching three days through open lands, " they came to a great swamp, rising on the borders, with a lake in the centre too deep to be forded, and which formed a kind of gulf on the Mississippi, into which it emptied itself."

Two days more brought them to some elevated ridges, beyond which they beheld the chief town of the Capahâ tribe. This town, which contained five hundred houses, was situated on an elevated piece of land, nearly sur-

M'CULLOH.

Great river has been but just applied to the Mississippi, I was much perplexed to connect other circumstances with the supposition that Capaha was within three leagues of that river, and not being able to reconcile the future incidents of their route with such a position, I have presumed that the Spaniards have called the river of Casquin (Red river) the Great river in this instance, either from some mistaken idea of its identity with the Mississippi or from its being simply a large river, without any reference to the former. If we admit this misnomer to have existed, there remains no other difficulty to overcome; for the ensuing part of their journey agrees with supposing Capaha to have been on Red river.

At Capaha the Indians informed Soto, that at about forty leagues distant were mountains (Ozark mountains, or Potato hills), at which he could procure salt; and two Spaniards who were despatched for this purpose, returned after an absence of eleven days with a sufficiency of rock salt, "as clear as crystal", and one load of copper. (*Herrera*, v, 339.)

[According to Herrera, this distance is but four leagues, if correctly translated; but in Garcilazo it is as stated in our text. That we are correct in following the latter, is justified by the number of days consumed in the journey. They had probably reached the vicinity of the hot springs of the Washita, near which Major Long's party (*Expedition to Rocky Mountains*, ii, 299) found native copper. In the same region also

MONETTE.

rounded by a deep bayou which communicated with the Mississippi or " Rio Grande", nine miles distant from the town. . . . The town of Capahâ in all probability was situated a few miles south of the present town of Helena in Arkansas, upon the west bank of the Mississippi. The changes in the river channel since that time may have obliterated the ancient landmarks, and have thrown the river several miles further west at this particular point. The numerous old river lakes on the east side of the river are facts which corroborate the inference. The low grounds west of the Mississippi which were traversed by De Soto in this portion of his marches, correspond well with the present region of the White River delta, and its tributary Big Creek. In further confirmation of the inference that De Soto crossed the Mississippi near this point, the reader is referred to the present geography of the country in the vicinity of Helena, which will abundantly satisfy him of its correctness. Helena is on the west side of the river, ten miles by the river below the mouth of the St. Francis river, and twenty miles above the " Horse-shoe Bend", or eighty miles above the mouth of White River. It is situated on alluvial ground, which descends gently back to a low, boggy, cypress bayou, which meanders within a few rods of the town, and near the base of the uplands, which rise fifty or sixty feet above the alluvion. This bayou takes its origin from an old river-lake near the Bluffs, a few miles above Helena, and

M'CULLOH.

is the saline branch of the Wa-shita, near which they probably procured salt.—*Note.*]

Afterwards, Soto returned to Casquin, determining to march to the westward, and after cross-ing the river (Red river) he marched down the stream four or five days, through a fertile country, to Quiguate, a province and town with the same name, fertile and abundant in provi-sions. I cannot detect this name on the map. Lest any of my readers might suppose I had overlooked the apparent resemb-lance of Coshatta in this very neighbourhood to Quiguate, it may be proper to remark, that the Coshattas are a body of Creek Indians who emigrated to that village about thirty or forty years ago. From Quiguate they marched in five days to Colima, still descending the river, which Garcilazo (*Exped. of Soto*, ii, 172) expressly says, ran by Casquin, and which confirms our supposi-tion that Capaha was on Red river; for such a descent along the river side will alone suit that stream. Colima, or Coligoa (for it is spelt both ways) I cannot identify in any Indian name; but the Portuguese gentleman says, they marched seven days from Quiguate under guidance of an Indian, through a marshy country and so wet that they even slept in the water until they came to Coligoa, which lay at the foot of a mountain, and upon a river as large as the Coya in Estrema-dura. This description will apply tolerably well to that hill called Mount Darby, about 32° north latitude, and by which Sibley's river passes.

MONETTE.

winds on about fifteen miles be-low the town, where it unites with the river at "Horse-shoe Bend". Upon this bayou, which is called "Old-town Bayou", about eight miles below Helena, are found the remains of a large Indian town. These remains consist of mounds, embankments, and bricks, of antique appearance and form. They are doubtless the remains of the old Indian town Capahâ. The striking resemb-lance in the general features of the country about the Arkansas, White River, and the St. Francis, compared with that on Red River, the Washita, and the River au Bœuf, or the Tensas, as regards the general description of rivers, swamps, and high rolling lands, has been the cause of much doubt and uncertainty among those who have attempted to trace the route of the Spanish army. Some have supposed that their first sojourn-ing and marches west of the Mississippi were principally in the vicinity of New Madrid; some that it was near the Arkansas; and others that it must have been as low down as Red River. This latter opinion is maintained by Judge Martin in his *History of Louisiana.* In this he is most probably in error. While in the territory of Capahâ, De Soto hav-ing heard of a region to the north, where salt abounded, and where probably gold might be found, sent two Spaniards with Indian guides to ascertain the prospects. After eleven days they returned, having been about one hundred leagues north-west, through a barren and hilly region, abound-ing in buffaloes. They brought a supply of rock salt and some

M'CULLOH.

From Coligoa, after five days' march, they arrived at Palisema; but they do not state in what direction they went. As they say, however, the face of the country was rough, we may presume they had left Red river, and marched westwardly across the hills between Red and Sabine rivers, and from thence they advanced to Tafalicoya, in the province of Cayas,— the Keyes Indians, who live on the east bank of Trinity river at present, but formerly resided on the head waters of the Sabine. Thence they marched to Tanico(Tankaways?), [The Tankaways have no particular place of abode, but are always moving, alternately occupying the country watered by the Trinity, Brassos de Dios, and Colorado rivers.—*Note.*], on a river side (Brassos de Dios), and then in a day and a half more reached Tula. From this town they marched in six days to Vitanque or Autiamque, where they passed the winter of 1541. At this place they say it snowed heavily.

I have not been able to identify any points on their march, or even its general direction after leaving Coligoa; but incline, from their future movements, to suppose that they had ascended the river Brassos de Dios some distance up the valley, through which that stream descends from mountains of St. Saba. I think we may be justified in supposing this to have been their route, as the Portuguese gentleman says, that, in marching from Tula to Autiamque, they were 'five days passing over very rough mountains', which can hardly be applied to any other mountains than those of St. Saba.

MONETTE.

copper, but found no gold. Discouraged by this intelligence, De Soto determined to bear more toward the west. He finally returned to the village of Casqui, probably on White River, and thence, after a few days rest, they advanced down the river, marching through a fertile and populous country for several days, or about one hundred miles, to the principal town of Quigate, where he arrived on the 4th of August. This town must have been on White River, about forty or fifty miles above its mouth.

Mr. Irving says : " From Quigate De Soto shaped his course to the northwest in search of a province called Coligoa, lying at the foot of mountains, beyond which he thought there might be a gold region. After a march of several days through dreary forests and frequent marshes, they came to the village of Coligoa on the margin of a small river." This must have been the Big Meto Creek, about fifty miles south-east of Little Rock.

At Coligoa De Soto learned that the country to the north was thinly inhabited by Indians, but that vast herds of buffaloes ranged the country, and that toward the south there was a populous and fertile country called Cayas. Toward this country his march was next directed. After nine days' march, having passed a large river, he came to a village called Tanico, in the Cayas country. Here he found salt springs. . . He was now probably on the head waters of Saline River, a branch of the Washita.

From Tanico their march was next directed westward, and after several days' march through a

M'CULLOH.

The Portuguese gentleman also says, that the river of Cayas (Red river?) passed by Autiamque, which, to make a position, we shall assume to have been situated on Red river, about the 20° of longitude west from Washington. Autiamque, or Vitangue, it is not unlikely is a corruption of the Yancton Sioux word O-tong-y-a, which signifies a *village*.

While in winter quarters, they made an excursion in quest of slaves into the province of Naguaten or Naguatex (Nacodoche Indians?), which they describe as being very populous.

In the spring of the year 1542, they left Autiamque to return to the great river (Mississippi); for Soto became anxious to make an establishment on its banks, by which he could communicate with the sea. To reach that river they made hasty and long marches by a different route from the one by which they had advanced, but of which scarcely any particulars are stated.

The Portuguese Gentleman relates, that after leaving Autiamque, they proceeded to the province of Ayas (Yawyes or Eyeish Indians), where they found a town upon that river (Red river) which passes by Cayas and Autiamque. To cross the river they had to build a boat, and after three or four days' marching in a very wet country, they came to the town of Tultelpina, where there was a river and a lake which discharged itself impetuously into the river. This is precisely the character of the numerous lakes along the course of Red River. We have no clue given us, to ascertain whether they had got

MONETTE.

wilderness country they reached the chief town of the Tula tribe, situated between two streams, probably the Upper Ouachita and Little Missouri. . . They were obliged to remain here twenty days. . . Having heard of the country of Autiamque or Utiangue toward the north or northwest, the march was next thither. The distance was about two hundred and thirty or forty miles by the route marched over, "five days of their journey was over a rough, mountainous country, closely wooded." At length they reached the chief town of Utiangue. . . The town " contained numerous well built houses, and was situated in a fine plain, watered by a wide running river, the same that passed through the province of Cayas." This " wide running river" was doubtless the Arkansas, the same river crossed by them in their march southward three months before, and the portion of the river upon which this village was situated most likely was not more than fifty miles below Crawford courthouse, in the state of Arkansas. . The winter had already set in with great severity.

The expedition was now on the north side of the Arkansas river, not far from the western boundary of the present State of Arkansas, in latitude about 36° north. . . De Soto determined to take up his winter quarters. . . (A.D. 1542.) As soon . . . as the winter was sufficiently over, he broke up his winter quarters at Utiangue, and marched toward the Mississippi. After several days' march along the river on the south side, they halted ten

M'CULLOH.

entangled between some of the numerous lakes that discharge themselves into Red river, or whether it may not have been some lake on the Wachita river. But they crossed the lake with considerable difficulty on rafts and floats, and then marched in three days' time to Tianto, a frontier town of the province of Nilco or Anilco. *Herrera*, vi, 5, says, from hence they marched thirty leagues through that province to the chief village of the cacique, which stood upon the bank of a river as large as that of Seville. They crossed this river, and marching through a woody desert came into the province of Guachoya, and then to the capital thereof, seated on the hillocks by the side of the Great river.

Of the places last mentioned, Tianto and the river of Nilco, we can find nothing synonymous in the Indian names as laid down in our maps; but taking everything into consideration, both as respects the past events of their journey, and those that presently are to be related, I presume the river of Nilco was the Arkansaw. The Portuguese Gentleman indeed says that it was the same river that ran by Cayas and Autiamque, which we have hitherto considered to have been Red river, and with which Nilco would agree as well as with the Arkansaw, was not the supposition opposed by the length of their voyage down the Mississippi to the ocean. Now, as I think, it will be impossible to reconcile their voyage down that river, with a position near the mouth of Red river, it will follow conclusively, that they debarked above the Arkansaw, for it is impossible

MONETTE.

days at an Indian town until they built boats and crossed the whole army over to the north or east side. This probably he did to reach the Mississippi, near the point where he had left it. Their advance thence was " through a low region and perplexed with swamps". . . . At length, after several days' march, they came to the village of Anilco, situated on " the same river that passed through the provinces of Cayas and Utiangue". There learning that there was a populous and fertile country not far below the junction of these two great rivers, he determined to proceed toward it, in hopes the sea might be at no great distance. He accordingly crossed the river at Anilco to the south side, and after a march of four days over a hilly uninhabited country, arrived at the village of Guachoya, on the Mississippi, about twenty miles below the mouth of the Arkansas. It was situated on two hills, one or two hundred yards from the river, and contained about three hundred houses. . . De Soto . . sent an exploring party down the river to seek tidings of the sea; but after eight days' absence, they returned, having advanced only forty-five miles, " on account of the great windings of the river, and the swamps and torrents with which it was bordered". Thus it seems the river was full, and many sluices were putting out into the swamps and filling the bayous. It was now about the last of May 1542. (*Death of De Soto.*) He expired . . . about the 5th of June. Luis de Moscoso having succeeded to the

M'CULLOH.

that any other river can divide the question of locality with the two we have mentioned.

Garcilazo (*Exped. of Soto*, ii, 221) says, that Guachoya was situated seven leagues from the mouth of Nilco river. That it was above, or north of this river, is evident from *Herrera*, vi, 7, who describes the canoes of a military expedition to have "went down" the great river (Mississippi), and up Nilco river, to the town of that name, a distance in all of about twenty leagues.

At Guachoya, Soto, the commander of these villainous banditti, died, and his body was sunk in the Mississippi, where they say the water was nineteen fathoms deep—if Herrera's Spanish measures be translated correctly, which I very much doubt. I presume the Spanish word used by Herrera, is *vara*, which is but thirty-three inches of our measure.

After Soto's death, his followers made a fruitless attempt to march to Mexico by land. They assert, they went about one hundred and fifty leagues to the westward, and got in sight of vast mountains, but from the desert state of the country, and its unpromising appearance, they again returned to the Great river. Here they commenced building their brigantines, in the province of Aminoya or Minoya, which they state was about seventeen leagues above Guachoya.

We have no means whereby we can ascertain how far west they marched on this expedition. The mountains they mention may have been some of the spurs of the Rocky mountains, though we can hardly think they had reached

MONETTE.

command of the remnant of De Soto's army . . . abandoned the plan of De Soto of descending the river to the sea, and determined to reach Mexico by land. The expedition accordingly set out for the west about the middle of June. They passed near the salines of the Wachita river. . . . Leaving this region, they passed through the country of the Naguatax, now written Natchitoches, and which appears to have been high up Red river, in the south-west corner of the State of Arkansas. At length, after nearly three months, they came upon Red river, in the barrens north of the present country of Texas. . . . Continuing the march south of De Soto's route, they passed through a country abounding in buffaloes ; beyond which, they passed a sterile region, and came in sight of mountains, where the country was almost uninhabited. Here they halted, and sent light exploring parties, who penetrated in every direction nearly ninety miles further, and returned with information that the country grew worse as they advanced. In this region the natives lived in camps. . . . These were evidently the early ancestors of the Pawnees, Camanchees, and other roving tribes of the west. It was now late in October, and they had been nearly five months making their way across from the Mississippi, and had traversed regions which are unknown. . . It was determined at length to return, and retrace their steps to the Mississippi. . . . They returned by forced marches. . . . Before they reached the vicinity of the Arkansas, the that chain. Minoya, or Aminoya, I have been unable to detect in any Indian name in this part of America. There was an Indian nation called Tamaoas, a little above where we have located Aminoya, and it is not impossible the Spaniards may have corrupted that appellation. The Tamaoas, who were of the Illinois stock, lived in the time of the Chevalier Tonti (A.D. 1679), about one hundred and forty years after Soto, on the Mississippi, about ten leagues below the mouth of the Missouri river. This will place them pretty close to where we have supposed Aminoya to have been. (*Tonti in Trans. N. Y Hist. Soc.* ii, 264.) At any rate, Aminoya was, according to Herrera, seventeen leagues above Guachoya. The Portuguese gentleman says, they were two days march distant. That a plausible locality may be assigned for this place, we have ventured to select the neighbourhood of the town of Helena, about thirty-five miles above the mouth of the Arkansas river.

At Aminoya, they built seven brigantines; and having embarked, they descended the Mississippi to the ocean.

The only method by which we can plausibly determine, whether Aminoya was near the mouth of the Arkansas, or Red river, will be to ascertain, as near as possible, the number of days they were actually employed in descending the Mississippi. For as we know the velocity of the current, we may ascertain with tolerable exactness the number of miles per day they would be carried down by the mere force of the stream, and thus learn the

winter had set in. . . At length they reached the Mississippi, not far from the mouth of the Arkansas. . . They determined to winter here, and make preparation to descend the Mississippi to the sea, in order to reach Mexico or some of the West India islands. Here they took possession of an Indian fortified town. . . Moscoso and his companions embarked, and committed themselves to the Mississippi on the 2nd of July 1543. .

At the end of twenty days from their embarkation on the river, they arrived in sight of the open sea; and after coasting westward for fifty days, they arrived at the town of Panuco, on the coast of Mexico. . . . They remained twenty-five days at Panuco. . . . The viceroy sent for them to Mexico, where they were treated with great kindness and attention by the people; yet they became morose, despondent; and as disappointed men do, they entertained much ill will, and mostly entered the armies of Mexico and Peru, hoping there to retrieve their fortunes."

M'CULLOH.

minimum distance they would descend in any certain number of days. We should then, if it be possible, add to the simple force of the stream, an additional velocity from the use of oars and sails; but for this we can have no data, though we must bear the fact in mind.

The Portuguese gentleman says, the voyage lasted seventeen days, and he estimates its length to have been about two hundred and fifty leagues.

Garcilazo relates, the voyage continued during nineteen days and twenty nights, and that they sailed during that time about five hundred leagues.

As the number of leagues stated in either relation was avowedly guess work, no reliance need be given them; and the difference in the number of days may be explained, by considering the Portuguese not to have counted the three days that they stopped to refresh themselves a little above the mouth of the Mississippi before they went to sea, while Garcilazo counts the time to the very ocean. We shall, however, take the account of the Portuguese gentleman, and after ascertaining, as carefully as we can, all the various delays and stoppages that occurred during the voyage, then make a fair estimate of the time during which they actually made progress.

HOURS

They left Aminoya, 2 July, A.D. 1543, but according to the new style to which this time must be reduced, on the 14th July; and descended as far as Guachoya, where they stopped several hours, but did not land: suppose the detention was 6

M'CULLOH.   HOURS

The next day they landed at a wood, but at night they went aboard their vessels: probable stoppage . . . 12

They once more landed at a town, where a party of horse were put on shore, who plundered a village: say . 12

They moreover tarried here a day to embark their plunder 24

After this they embarked and fell down the stream to a town on the river side, where they landed and burnt the village . . .

Their whole force (about 300 men) appear to have been landed and drawn up in battle array: we suppose the detention was . . 24

The next detention appears to have been from a battle on the river with the Indians, during which time they were either at anchor or made very little progress: say 6

They now speak of frequent detentions they had experienced on account of the boats that carried their horses; and to avoid this delay for the future, they landed and killed them, intending to dry their flesh for provisions; but the Indians making a formidable attack at this time, the Spaniards fled to the brigantines. We suppose the whole of the detentions they complain of, as well as this particular landing, may be 48

After this time, no other circumstances are related whereby we could estimate any other detention.

M'CULLOH.

According to our estimate,
they were delayed on their voyage
five days and a half; which, however, we think may be safely
called six entire days; which,
deducted from seventeen, leaves
eleven days for the actual voyage.

The current of the Mississippi
at this time of the year (July)
may be stated at about three miles
per hour.

Having thus settled our data,
we now proceed to observe, that
if Aminoya had been at the
mouth of Red river, their voyage thence to the ocean would
have been about three hundred
and fifty miles, which for eleven
days' progress will average but
about thirty-two miles per day,
or about one and a quarter miles
per hour under the united impe-
tus of sails, oars, and the steady
current of the Mississippi. As
we have every reason to think
a log would be floated down
with twice the velocity, it seems
to follow conclusively, that Aminoya could not have been at the
mouth of Red river.

The Arkansaw falls into the
Mississippi about seven hundred
and twenty miles above its mouth,
which will allow them to have
descended the stream at the rate
of sixty-five miles a day, or about
two and three-quarter miles per
hour during the twenty-four
hours, which is about a fair allowance, as they did not continue
under way during the whole
night, except at particular times.

They also used their oars on
certain occasions with all the
strength they could apply to them,
and their sails, when the wind
served; but we know not how to
estimate the additional velocity
thus acquired. It probably, dur-

M'CULLOH.

ing their voyage, would not com-
pensate for the time they lost,
by stopping for five or six hours
during the nights they were on
the river, when not pursued by
the Indians in their canoes.

But if it be still thought that
they ought to have descended the
Mississippi at a greater rate than
sixty-five miles per day, we can
only support our conjecture by
this supposition, that they either
stopped, or were detained a longer
time than we have allowed, or
that they have omitted other delays in the descriptions they have
given us. But, *cæteris paribus*,
the difficulty will be two-fold, to
reconcile their voyage to have
been from Red river; and thus
being negatively established, it
will follow, that Aminoya must
have been just above the Arkansaw; for I think it impossible
that any other river can be brought
within the bounds of their expedition on the land.

Since writing the above, I feel
satisfied, from the following authority, that their actual progress
down the Mississippi, according
to our estimate, confirms the
position of Aminoya to have been
above the Arkansaw : — " The
general current of the Mississippi
(*Stoddart, Sketches of Louisiana,*
371) is from three and a half to
four miles an hour. In low
water, a boat will float down at
the rate of from forty-five to fifty
miles in twenty-four hours ; in
high water, from ninety to a hundred ; and at a mean height, from
sixty to seventy miles. Between
the Arkansaw and the Delta,
the velocity of the current is
1-3rd less ; and from the Delta to
the outlet, by nearly one-half."

From these accounts, drawn up by two of the most pains-taking investigators of the subject, it will be seen how difficult it is to trace, with any appearance of precision, the route of the expedition west of the Mississippi; but there can be no doubt that the Spaniards must have penetrated to a considerable distance into the interior.

The character of De Soto, as developed in his position of leader of this remarkable expedition, presents us with an amount of hardihood and courageous perseverance under the most fearful trials, unsurpassed perhaps even by Pizarro or Cortes. At the same time we have to deplore, that in his case, as in that of most of the adventurers of the period, his daring was equalled by his cruelty. The couplet of Gay, which is verified we should hope in the majority of instances, that—

> Cowards are cruel, but the brave
> Love mercy and delight to save—

seems here to receive a complete disproval.

Upon the reckless inhumanity of De Soto, and of Moscoso his successor, Bartolome de las Casas, the celebrated "Protector of the Indians", writes in the following emphatic language:—"The fourth tyrant [*i. e.*, Soto] that came last in the yere 1538, cunningly advised, and beeing fully furnished: it is three yeeres since there is no tidinges concerning him. Wee are certaine that incontinent [immediately] after his entrie thither, hee hath behaved himself cruelly, and since hath beene as a man vanished: that if he be alive, hee and his mainies have

k

destroyed these three yeeres a great many mightie
peoples, if hee hath found any in his enquest as hee
hath gone;—for sure he is one of the notoriousest and
best experimented amongest them that have done the
most hurtes, mischieves and destructions in many
realmes with their consorts ("*porq' es de los marcados y
experimentados, & de los que mas daños y males y destruy-
ciones de muchas provincias y reynos con otros sus com-
pañeros a hecho*"): wherefore I beleeve that God hath
given him like end unto the others."

"Three or foure yeeres after the writing of the
above written, there came out of the Florida the head
of the pette tyrants [*i.e.*, Moscoso] which went thither
with this captaine tyrant ("*tirano mayor*") that there
left his bones, of whome wee understood the cruelties
and evilles whiche there during his life-time princi-
pailly, and under his conduct and government, and
since after his cursed death, the unnaturall men have
executed against the Indians innocent, and harmeful
to none, to verifie that which I had prognosticate
before, they being so excessive, that they have the
more confirmed the rule by mee set downe before at
the beginning, that the farther they proceeded to
discover, destroy and to waste countries and lands,
the more cruelties and notorious wickednesses they
woulde doe against God, and against their neighbours. It loatheth mee to recount those actes so
cursed, ghastly and bloodie,—not of men but of
savage beastes," etc. etc. (*The Spanish Colonie, or
briefe chronicle of the acts and gestes of the Spaniardes
in the West-Indies*—[translated from the *Brevissima*

relacion de la destruycion de las Indias, 1552]. 4to., London; 1583.)

The editor, in conclusion, has to acknowledge his obligations to Richard Henry Major, Esq., the zealous and able Secretary of the Hakluyt Society, for much assistance kindly and voluntarily rendered, particularly in that the most difficult part of his task—the route of the Spaniards.

THE
WORTHYE
AND FAMOVS HIS-
TORY OF THE TRAVAILES,

Discouery, & Conquest, of that great
Continent of *Terra Florida*, being liuely
Paraleld, with that of our now Inha-
bited *VIRGINIA.*

As also

The Comodities of the said Country,

With diuers excellent and rich Mynes, of Golde,
Siluer, and other Mettals, &c. which cannot but
giue vs a great and exceeding hope of our
VIRGINIA, being so neere
of one Continent.

Accomplished and effected, by that worthy
Generall and Captaine, *Don Ferdinando
de Soto,* and six hundreth Spaniards
his followers.

LONDON
Printed for Mathew Lownes, *dwelling*
in Paules Church-yard, at the Signe of
the Bishops head. 1611.

THE EPISTLE DEDICATORIE.

TO THE RIGHT HONOURABLE, THE RIGHT
Worshipfull Counsellors, and others the cheerfull
adventurors, for the advancement of that Christian
and noble Plantation in Virginia.

*THIS worke, right honourable, right worshipfull, and the
rest, though small in shew yet great in substance, doth yeeld
much light to our enterprise now on foot; whether you desire
to know the present and future commodities of our countrie;
or the qualities and conditions of the inhabitants, or what
course is best to be taken with them.*

Touching the commodities, besides the generall report of
Cabeça de Vaca[1] *to* Charles *the Emperour (who first travelled
through a great part of the Inland* of Florida, *next adjoining
upon our* Virginia) That *Florida* was the richest countrie of
the world; and, that after hee had found clothes made of
cotton wooll, he saw gold and silver, and stones of great
value: *I referre you first to the rich mines of gold reported* Chap. 35.
to be in the province of Yupaha, *and described in the twelfth
chapter of this Treatise to come within our limits. And
againe, to the copper hatchets found in* Cutifachiqui, *standing
upon the River of* Santa Helena, *which were said to have a
mixture of gold. It seemeth also that the last chronicler of*

[1] See also chap. ii.

B

the West Indies, Antonio de Herrera, *speaking of the foresaid River of* Santa Helena, *which standeth in 32 degrees and an halfe, alludeth to the province of* Yupaha, *in these words :*

Decad. 3, lib. 8, chap. 8. Yel oro, y plata, que hallaron, no era de aquella tierra, sino de 60 leguas, a dentro al norte, de los pueblos dichos *Otapales* y *Olagatanos,* adonde se intiende, que ay minas de oro, plata, y cobre. *That is to say, that the gold and silver which they found, was not of that countrie (of* Santa Helena*), but* 60 *leagues distant towards the north, of the townes called* Otapales *and* Olagatanos, *where we understand that there are mines of gold, silver, and copper. By which reckoning these rich mines are in the latitude of* 35 *degrees and an halfe. I desire you likewise to take knowledge of the famous* Chap. 15. *golden province of* Chisca, *stretching further to the north, whereof the cacique of* Coste *gave notice to* Ferdinando de Soto, *in the towne of* Chiaha, *affirming, that there were mines of copper, and of another mettall of the same colour, save that it was finer, and of a farre more perfect lustre, and farre better in sight, and that they used it not so much, because it was softer. And the selfe same thing was before told the governour in* Cutifachiqui : *who sent two Christians from* Chiaha, *with certaine Indians which knew the countrie of* Chisca, *and the language thereof, to view it, and to make* Chap. 23. *report of that which they should finde. We likewise reade not long after, that the governour set forward to seeke a province called* Pacaha, *which hee was informed to be neere unto* Chisca, *where the Indians told him that there was gold.* Chap. 24. *And in another place hee saith : That from* Pacaha *hee sent thirtie horsemen and fiftie footmen to the province of* Caluça, *to see if from thence he might travell to* Chisca, *where the Indians said, there was a worke of gold and copper. So that here is foure times mention, and that in sundrie places, of the rich and famous golde mines of* Chisca, *and that they lie beyond the mountaines towards the north, over which they were not able to travell for the roughness thereof. But what*

neede I to stand upon forren testimonies, since Master Thomas
Heriot,[1] *a man of much judgement in these causes, signified
unto you all, at your late solemne meeting at the house of the
right honourable the Earle of Exeter,*[2] *how to the southwest
of our old fort in* Virginia, *the Indians often informed him,
that there was a great melting of red mettall, reporting the
manner in working of the same. Besides, our owne Indians*

[1] Thomas Hariot, or Harriot, the eminent mathematician and astro-
nomer; born 1560, died 1621. He was mathematical tutor to Sir
Walter Raleigh; and in 1585 accompanied the first party of colonists to Virginia. Here he was "imployed in the discovery and sur-
veying thereof, and in making what knowledge he could of the commodities it yielded, and concerning the inhabitants, and their manners and
customs." Three years later, he published the result of his labours in a
small quarto volume, bearing the following title : "A briefe and true
Report of the new found land of Virginia . discovered by the English
colony there seated by Sir Richard Greinuile, knight, in the yeere 1585,
which remained under the government of Rafe Lane, Esquier, one of her
maiesties equieres, during the space of twelve monethes, at the speciall
charge and direction of the Honourable Sir Walter Raleigh. By Thomas
Hariot, servant to the above named Sir Walter, a member of the colony,
and there imployed in discovering." This account was republished in
1590, in folio, by the celebrated Frankfort engraver, Theodor de Bry,
who added, as he says in his Dedication to Sir Walter, "figures, cott in
copper, which doe leuelye represent the forme and maner of the inhabitants of the same countrye, with theirs ceremonies, sollemne feastes,
and the manner and situation of their townes or villages." Hakluyt, it
seems, was the first to encourage him to publish the work, and he
also supplied him with the descriptions to accompany his plates. In
his preface to the "gentle reader", De Bry says : "consideringe therefore
that yt was a thinge worthie of admiration, I was verye willinge to offer
vnto you the true pictures of those people wich by the helf of Maister
Richard Hakluyt of Oxford, minister of God's word, who first incouraged
me to publish the worke, I creaued out of the verye original of Maister
Jhon White, an Englisch paynter, who was sent into the contrye by the
queenes maiestye, onlye to draw the description of the place, lyuelye to
describe the shapes of the inhabitants, their apparell, manners of liuinge and
fashions, att the speciall charges of the worthy knight Sir Walter Ralegh,
who bestowed no small sume of monnye in the serche and discouerye of
that countrye from te yeers 1584 to the ende of the years 1588."

[2] Thomas Cecil, second Lord Burleigh, created Earl of Exeter in
1605 ; died in 1622.

have lately revealed either this or another rich mine of copper or gold, in a towne called Ritanoe, *neere certaine mountaines lying west of* Roanoac.

Another very gainfull commoditie is, the huge quantitie of excellent perles, and little babies and birds made of them, that were found in Cutifachiqui. *The abundance whereof is reported to be such, that if they would have searched divers* graves in townes thereabout, they might have laded many of their horses. *Neither are the Turkie stones and cotton wooll found at* Guasco[1] *to be forgotten, nor passed over in silence.*

Chap. 14.

But that, which I make no small account of, is, the multitude of oxen, which, from the beginning of the 16 *to the end of the* 26 *chapter, are nine several times made mention of; and that along from* Chiaha, Coste, Pacaha, Coligoa, *and* Tulla, *still toward the north, to wit, toward us, there was such store of them, that they could keepe no corne for them; and that the Indians lived upon their flesh.* The haire of *these oxen is likewise said to be like a soft wooll, betweene the coarse and fine wooll of sheepe; and that they use them for coverlets, because they are very soft and woolled like sheep; and not so onely, but they make bootes, shooes, targets, and other things necessarie of the same.* Besides the former *benefits, their young ones may be framed to the yoke, for carting and tillage of our ground.* And I am in good hope, *that ere it be long we shall have notice of their being neerer us, by that which I reade in the Italian relation of* Cabeça de Vaca,[2] *the first finder of them; which writeth,* That they spread themselves within the countrie above foure hundred leagues. *Moreover,* Vasques de Coronado, *and long after him,* Antonio de Espejo *(whose voiages are at large in my third volume[3]), travelled many leagues among these heards of*

[1] See chap. xxxiv and xxxv.

[2] See Ramusio *Navigationi*, tom. iii.

[3] The titles of the works referred to by Hakluyt are as follows:—1. "The Relation of Francis Vasquez de Coronado, captaine generall of the people

òxen, and found them from 33 degrees ranging very farre to the north and northeast.

A fourth chiefe commoditie wee may account to be the great number of mulberrie trees, apt to feede silke-wormes to make silke : whereof there was such plentie in many places, that, though they found some hempe in the countrie, the Spaniards made ropes of the barks of them for their brigandines, when they were to put to sea for Nova Hispania.[1]

A fifth is the excellent and perfect colours, as black, white, greene, yellow, and red, and the materials to dye withall, so often spoken of in this discourse : among which, I have some hope to bring you to the knowledge of the rich graine of Cochonillio, so much esteemed, and of so great price. I speake nothing of the severall sorts of passing good grapes for wine and raisons.

Neither is it the least benefit, that they found salt made by the Indians at Cayas, *and in two places of the province of* Aguacay : *the manner also how the inhabitants make it, is very well worth the observation.* Chap. 31 & 32°

One of the chiefest of all the rest may be the notice of the South Sea, leading us to Japan *and* China, *which I finde* Chap. 31 & 32

which were sent in the name of the emperours majestie to the countrey of Cibola, newly discovered, which he sent to Don Antonio de Mendoça, viceroy of Mexico, of such things as happened in his voyage from the 22 of Aprill in the yeere 1540, which departed from Culiacan forward ; and of such things as hee found in the countrey which he passed." (Vol. iii, p. 373.)

2. "A briefe relation of two notable voyages ; the first, made by frier Augustin Ruys, a Franciscan, in the yeere 1581 ; the second by Antonio de Espejo in the yeere 1583 ; who, together with his company, discouered a land wherein they found fifteene provinces all full of townes, conteining houses of foure and five stories high, which they named New Mexico ; for that, in many respects, it resembleth the province of old Mexico. This land is situate to the north of Nueva Espanna, and stretcheth from 24 to 34 degrees and better ; by the which, and by other inhabited lands, it is thought that men may travell even to *Terra de Labrador.* Taken out of the history of China, written by Frier Juan Gonzalez de Mendoça, and printed in Madrid, 1586." (Vol. iii, p. 383.)

[1] New Spain or Mexico.

*here twice to be spoken of.   Whereof long since I have
written a discourse, which I thinke not fit to be made over
common.*

*For closing up this point, the distances of places, the
qualities of the soiles, the situations of the regions, the
diversities and goodnesse of the fruits, the severall sorts of
beasts, the varietie of fowles, the difference betweene the inhabitants of the mountaines and the plaines, and the riches of
the inland in comparison of the sea-coast, are judicially set
downe in the conclusion of this booke, whereunto for mine
owne ease I referre you.*

*To come to the second generall head, which in the begin-
ning I proposed, concerning the manners and dispositions of
the inhabitants ; among other things, I finde them here noted
to be very eloquent and well spoken, as the short orations,
interpreted by* John Ortiz, *which lived twelve yeeres among
them, make sufficient proofe.   And the author, which was a
gentleman of* Eluas, *in* Portugal, *emploied in all the action,
whose name is not set downe, speaking of the cacique of*
Tulla, *saith, that as well this cacique, as the others, and all
those which came to the Governour on their behalfe, delivered
their message or speech in so good order, that no oratour
could utter the same more eloquently.   But for all their faire
and cunning speeches, they are not overmuch to be trusted,
for they be the greatest traitors of the world, as their mani-
fold most craftie contrived and bloody treasons, here set
down at large, doe evidently prove.   They be also as uncon-
stant as the wethercock, and most readie to take all occasions
of advantages to doe mischiefe.   They are great liars and
dissemblers ; for which faults oftentimes they had their
deserved paiments.   And many times they gave good testimonie of their great valour and resolution.   To handle them
gently, while gentle courses may be found to serve, it will be
without comparison the best ; but if gentle polishing will not
serve, then we shall not want hammerours and rough masons*

enow, I meane our old soldiours trained up in the Nether-lands, to square and prepare them to our Preachers hands. To conclude, I trust by your Honours and Worships wise instructions to the noble governour, the worthy experimented Lieutenant and Admirall, and other chiefe managers of the businesse, all things shall be so prudently carried, that the painfull Preachers shall be reverenced and cherished, the valiant and forward soldiour respected, the diligent rewarded, the coward emboldened, the weake and sick relieved, the mutinous suppressed, the reputation of the Christians among the salvages preserved, our most holy faith exalted, all pagan-isme and idolatrie by little and little utterly extinguished. And here reposing and resting myselfe upon this sweete hope, I cease, beseeching the Almightie to blesse this good work in your hands to the honour and glorie of his most holy name, to the inlargement of the dominions of his sacred Maiestie, and to the generall good of all the worthie adven-turers and undertakers. From my lodging in the Colledge of Westminster, this 15 of Aprill, 1609.

By one publicly and anciently devoted to God's service, and all yours in this so good action,

RICHARD HAKLUYT.

A RELATION OF SUCH THINGS AS DON FER-

dinando de Soto,[1] the Adelantado[2] of *Florida,* passed in
seeking to conquer the said countrey, wherein is declared
who he was, and what some of them were that went with
him : and some particulars and diversities of the
countrie, and whatsoever they saw and
happened unto them in the same.

CHAPTER I.

*Which declareth who Don Ferdinando de Soto was, and how he got the
government of Florida.*

Captaine Soto was the son of a squire of Xerez of Badajos.
He went into the Spanish Indies, when Peter Arias[3] of Avila
was governor of the West Indies. And there he was without
any thing else of his owne, save his sword and target: and
for his good qualities and valour, Peter Arias made him
captaine of a troope of horsemen, and by his commandement
hee went with Fernando Pizarro to the conquest of Peru;
where (as many persons of credit reported, which were there

---

[1] The Portuguese form of this name is Souto.

[2] Bartolomé de las Casas, Bishop of Chiapa, whose benevolent exertions
in behalf of the natives of America led to his being honoured with the
distinction of " Protector General of the Indians", gives a caustic etymology of the title of *Adelantado,* so often granted to the Spanish dis-
coverers—" Adelantados porque se adelantaron en hazer males y daños
tan gravisimos á gentes pacificas."—Prescott, *Conq. of Mexico,* i, 213.

[3] Or Pedarias Davila, by which name he is better known. He was
sent by King Ferdinand to supersede Balboa, the discoverer of the
Pacific, in the government of Darien. This great man at length fell a
victim to the jealousy and implacable enmity of the cruel Pedrarias, by
whose orders he was put to death in 1517.—*Herrera,* dec. ii, lib. ii.

present), as well at the taking of Atabalipa, Lord of Peru, as at the assault of the citie of Cusco, and in all other places where they found resistance, wheresover hee was present, hee passed all other captaines and principall persons.[1] For which cause, besides his part of the treasure of Atabalipa, he had a good share; whereby in time he gathered an hundred and fourescore thousand duckets together, with that which fell to his part, which he brought into Spaine; whereof the Emperour borrowed a certaine part, which he repaied againe with 60,000 rials of plate in the rent of the silkes of Granada, and all the rest was delivered him in the contractation house of Sivil.[2] He tooke servants, to wit, a steward, a gentleman usher, pages, a gentleman of the horse, a chamberlaine, lakies, and al other officers that the house of a nobleman requireth. From Sivil hee went to the court, and in the court there accompanied him John Danusco of Sivil,[3] and Lewis Moscoso d'Alvarado, Nunno de Touar, and John Rodriguez Lobillo. Except John Danusco, all the rest came with him from Peru: and every one of them brought fourteene or fifteene thousand duckets; all of them went well and costly apparrelled. And although Soto of his owne nature was not liberall, yet because that was the first time that hee was to shew himselfe in the court, he spent frankly, and went accompanied with those which I have named, and with his servants, and many other which resorted unto him. Hee married with Donna Isabella de Bovadilla, daughter of Peter Arias Avila, Earle of Punno en Rostro. The Emperour made him the Governor of the Isle of Cuba, and Adelantado or President of Florida, with a title of Marques of certaine part of the lands that he should conquer.

[1] The reader is referred to Mr. Prescott's delightful work, "The history of the Conquest of Peru", for a particular account of Soto's Peruvian exploits.

[2] The *Casa de Contratacion*, "House of Trade", or India House, established at Seville in 1503.

[3] Juan de Añasco.

CHAPTER II.

How Cabeça de Vaca came to the court and gave relation of the countrie of Florida : and of the companie that was assembled in Sivil to goe with Don Ferdinando de Soto.

When Don Ferdinando had obtained the government, there came a gentleman from the Indies to the court, named Cabeça de Vaca,[1] which had been with the governor Pamphilo de Narvaez, which died in Florida, who reported that Narvaez was cast away at sea, with all the companie that went with him. And how he with foure more escaped and arrived in Nueva Espanna;[2] and he brought a relation in writing of that which hee had seene in Florida, which said in some places : In such a place I have seene this ; and the rest which here I saw, I leave to conferre of betweene his Maiestic and myselfe. Generally he reported the miserie of the countrie, and the troubles which hee passed : and he told some of his kinsfolke, which were desirous to goe into the Indies, and urged him very much to tell them whether he had seene any rich country in Florida, that he might not tell them, because hee and another, whose name was Orantes[3] (who remained in Nueva Espanna, with purpose to returne

---

[1] Alvar Nuñez Cabeça de Vaca was treasurer to the adventurous but ill-fated expedition into Florida, undertaken by Pamphilo de Narvaez in 1528. Of three hundred men who engaged in the enterprise, five only returned : their daring leader—the same Narvaez who eight years before had made a vain attempt to arrest Cortes in Mexico—perished in a storm near the mouths of the Mississippi. Cabeça de Vaca, one of the survivors, wrote a narrative of his ten years' wanderings and sufferings, which was published in 1555 under the title of " Naufragios de Alvar Nuñez de Cabeça de Vaca." " The story," says Bancroft, " of which the truth was affirmed on oath before a magistrate, is disfigured by bold exaggerations and the wildest fictions"; on the other hand M. Ternaux-Compans, and others, vindicate its credibility and general accuracy. An abridged English version, from the Italian in Ramusio's collection, is in Purchas, vol. iv, pp. 1499-1528.

[2] New Spain or Mexico.   [3] Dorantes.

into Florida; for which intent hee came into Spaine to beg the government thereof of the emperour), had sworne not to discover some of those things which they had seene, because no man should prevent them in begging the same. And hee informed them, *That it was the richest countrie of the world.* Don Ferdinando de Soto was very desirous to have him with him, and made him a favourable offer: and after they were agreed, because Soto gave him not a summe of money which he demanded to buy a ship, they broke off againe. Baltasar de Gallegos, and Christopher de Spindola,[1] the kinsmen of Cabeça de Vaca, told him, that for that which hee had imparted to them, they were resolved to passe with Soto into Florida, and therefore they prayed him to advise them what they were best to doe. Cabeça de Vaca told them, that the cause why he went not with Soto was, because hee hoped to beg another government, and that hee was loth to go under the command of another; and that hee came to beg the conquest of Florida: but seeing Don Ferdinando de Soto had gotten it alreadie, for his othes sake hee might tell them nothing of that which they would know; but he counselled them to sell their goods and goe with him, and that in so doing they should doe well. As soone as he had opportunitie hee spake with the emperour, and related unto him whatsoever hee had passed and seene, and come to understand. Of this relation, made by word of mouth to the emperour, the Marques of Astorga[2] had notice, and forthwith determined to send with Don Ferdinando de Soto his brother Don Antonio Osorio; and with him two kinsmen of his prepared themselves, to wit, Francis Osorio, and Garcia Osorio. Don Antonio dispossessed himselfe of 60,000 rials of rent, which hee held by the Church; and Francis Osorio of a town of Vassals, which he had in the countrie de Campos. And they made their rendezvous with the Adelantado in Sivil. The

[1] Spinola, a Genoese.
[2] Pedro Alvarez Osorio, fourth Marquis of Astorga.

like did Nunnez de Touar, and Lewis de Moscoso, and John Rodriguez Lobillo, each of whom had brought from Peru fourteene or fifteene thousand duckets. Lewis de Moscoso carried with him two brethren : there went also Don Carlos, which had married the Governour's niece, and tooke her with him. From Badajoz there went Peter Calderan, and three kinsmen of the Adelantado, to wit, Arias Tinoco, Alfonso Romo, and Diego Tinoco. And as Lewis de Moscoso passed through Elvas,* Andrew de Vasconcelos spake with him, and requested him to speake to Don Ferdinando de Soto concerning him, and delivered him certaine warrants which he had received from the Marques of Villareal, wherein he gave him the captaineship of Ceuta in Barbarie, that he might shew them unto him. And the Adelantado saw them, and was informed who hee was, and wrote unto him, that hee would favour him in all things, and by al meanes, and would give him a charge of men in Florida. And from Elvas went Andrew de Vasconcelos, and Fernan Pegado, Antonio Martinez Segurado, Men Roiz Pereira, John Cordero, Stephen Pegado, Benedict Fernandez, and Alvaro Fernandez. And out of Salamanca, and Jaen, and Valencia, and Albuquerque, and from other partes of Spaine, many people of noble birth assembled at Sivil : insomuch that in Saint Lucar many men of good account which had sold their goods remained behind for want of shipping, wheras for other known and rich countries they are wont to want men ; and this fell out by occasion of that which Cabeça de Vaca told the emperour, and informed such persons as hee had conference withall touching the state of that countrie. Soto made him great offers ; and being agreed to goe with him (as I have said before), because he would not give him monie to pay for a ship, which he had bought, they broke off, and he went for Governour to the river of Plate. His kinsmen Christopher de Spindola, and Baltasar de Gallegos, went with Soto. Baltasar de Gallegos sold houses and vineyards, and rent corne, and ninetie rankes

*Elvas is a citie in Portugal.

Cabeça de Vaca was the Governour of the River of Plate.

of olive trees in the Xarafe of Sivil.[1]   Hee had the office of
Alcalde Mayor, and tooke his wife with him.   And there
went also many other persons of account with the president,
and had the offices following by great friendship, because
they were offices desired of many ; to wit, Antonio de Biedma[2]
was factor, John Danusco was auditor, and John Gaytan,
nephew to the Cardinall of Ciguenza, had the office of
treasurer.

CHAPTER III.

*How the Portugales went to Sivil, and from thence to S. Lucar : he
appointed captaines over the ships, and distributed the people which
were to goe in them.*

The Portugales departed from Elvas the 15 of Januarie,
and came to Sivil the 19 of the same moneth, and went to

[1] The olive districts in the vicinity of Seville. *Aljarafe* or *Ajarafe*,
or more correctly *Al-Sharaf*, is an Arabic word, signifying a hilly or
elevated country.   Zuñiga (*Annales de Sevilla*, p. 4) describes it as
" Aquella fertilissima porcion de tierra, que los antiguos llamaron Guerta
de Hercules, que desde las riberas de Guadalquivir, interpuesta vega de
media legua de ancho, se và elevando, de que le provino el nombre
Alxarafe, que significa tierra alta ò superior."   Mr. Ford says, " This
fertile district was called the garden of Hercules.   It produced the finest
Bœtican olives of antiquity : under the Moors it was a paradise, but
now all is ruin and desolation.   There is not only excellent lodging for
owls in ruined buildings, but first-rate cover for game of every kind,
which thrive in these wastes, where nature and her *feræ* are left in
undisputed possession."—(*Hand-Book of Spain*, i, 241.)

[2] Among the *Recueil de pièces sur la Floride*, published by Ternaux-
Compans in 1841, is one entitled : " Relation de ce qui arriva pendant
le voyage du capitaine Soto, et détails sur la nature du pays qu'il par-
courut.   Par Luis Hernandez de Biedma."   A note by Muñoz states
that Biedma accompanied Soto in quality of Factor to His Majesty, as
appears by a decision of the Council of the Indies in 1544.   Notwithstanding the discrepancy in the Christian name of the author, it is evident that Antonio and Luis Hernandez are one and the same person.   A
translation of this document is given in the present work.

the lodging of the Governor, and entred into a court, over the which were certaine galleries where hee was, who came downe and received them at the staires, whereby they went up into the galleries: when he was come up, he commanded chaires to be given them to sit on. And Andrew de Vasconcelos told him who hee and the other Portugales were, and how they all were come to accompany him, and serve him in his voiage. He gave him thanks, and made shew of great contentment for his comming and offer. And the table being alreadie laid, he invited them to dinner. And being at dinner, he commanded his steward to seeke a lodging for them near unto his owne, where they might be lodged. The Adelantado departed from Sivil to Saint Lucar with al the people which were to goe with him. And he commanded a muster to be made, at the which the Portugales shewed themselves armed in verie bright armour, and the Castellans very gallant with silke upon silke, with many pinkings and cuts. The Governour, because these braveries in such an action did not like him, commanded that they should muster another day, and every one should come foorth with his armour; at the which the Portugales came as at the first, armed with very good armour. The Governour placed them in order neere unto the standard which the ensigne-bearer carried. The Castellanes for the most part did weare very bad and rustie shirts of maile, and all of them head-peeces and steele cappes, and very bad lances. And some of them sought to come among the Portugales. So those passed and were counted and enroled, which Soto liked and accepted of, and did accompanie him into Florida; which were in all sixe hundred men. He had alreadie bought seven ships, and had all necessarie provision aboord them. He appointed captaines, and delivered to every one his ship, and gave them in a role what people every one should carrie with them.

Sixe hundred men went with Soto into Florida.

CHAPTER IV.

How the Adelantado with his people departed from Spaine, and came to the Canaries, and afterward to the Antiles.

In the yeere of our Lord 1538, in the moneth of Aprill, the Adelantado delivered his shippes to the captaines which were to goe in them; and tooke for himselfe a new ship, and good of saile, and gave another to Andrew de Vasconcelos, in which the Portugales went; hee went over the barre of S. Lucar on Sunday, being S. Lazarus day, in the morning, of the moneth and yeere aforesaid, with great joy, commanding his trumpets to be sounded, and many shots of the ordinance to be discharged. Hee sailed foure daies with a prosperous wind, and suddenly it calmed—the calmes continued eight daies with swelling seas, in such wise, that wee made no way. The 15 day after his departure from S. Lucar, hee came to Gomera, one of the Canaries, on Easter day in the morning. The Earle of that island was apparrelled all in white, cloke, jerkin, hose, shooes, and cappe, so that he seemed a Lord of the Gypses.[1] Hee received the Governour with much joy; hee was well lodged, and all the rest had their lodgings gratis, and gat great store of victuals for their monie, as bread, wine, and flesh; and they tooke what was needful for their ships : and the Sunday following, eight days after their arrivall, they departed from the isle of Gomera. The earle gave to Donna Isabella, the Adelantados wife, a bastard daughter that hee had, to bee her waiting maid.[2]

---

[1] "Ho cõde daquella ylha andaua todo vestido de brãco, capa e pelote e calças e çapatos e carapuça, q' parecia cõde de ciganos."—*Relaçam verdadeira, etc., per hũ fidalgo Deluas.* Evora, 1557.

[2] The name of this lady, "Doña Leonora de Bobadilla", is supplied by Garcilaso de la Vega (*La Florida del Inca*, p. 11), who also adds, that she was seventeen years of age, and extremely beautiful,—"cuya hermosura era estremada".

They arrived at the Antilles, in the isle of Cuba, at the port of the city of Sant Iago, upon Whitsunday. As sone as they came thither, a gentleman of the citie sent to the sea side a very faire roan horse, and well furnished, for the Governour, and a mule for Donna Isabella; and all the horsemen and footemen that were in the towne, came to receive him at the seaside. The Governour was well lodged, visited, and served of all the inhabitants of that citie, and all his companie had their lodgings freely; those which desired to goe into the countrie were divided by foure and foure, and sixe and sixe in the farmes or granges, according to the abilitie of the owners of the farmes, and were furnished by them with all things necessary.

CHAPTER V.

Of the inhabitants which are in the citie of S. Iago, and in the other townes of the island; and of the qualitie of the soile, and fruites that it yeeldeth.

The citie of S. Iago hath fourescore houses, which are great and well contrived. The most part have their walles made of bords, and are covered with thatch; it hath some houses builded with lime and stone, and covered with tiles. It hath great orchards and many trees in them, differing from those of Spaine; there be figge trees, which beare figges as big as ones fist, yellow within, and of small taste; and other trees, which beare a fruit which they call ananes,[1] in making and bignes like to a small pineapple; it is a fruit very sweete in taste; the shel being taken away, the kernel is like

Great figges.

Ananes.

[1] This appears to be an error in spelling; the anana, or pine-apple, not presenting these characteristics. Possibly the anona, or sweet-sop, may be referred to; but the description is too vague to allow us to speak with certainty.

D

a peece of fresh cheese.   In the granges abroad in the

Great pine-apples. countrie there are other great pineapples, which grow on

* Erva babosa.¹ low trees, and are like the *aloe-tree ; they are of a very good smell and exceeding good taste.   Other trees do

Mameis an excellent fruit. beare a fruit which they call mameis,² of the bignes of peaches. This the islanders do hold for the best fruit of the country.

Guayabas. There is another fruit which they call guayabas,³ like filberds, as bigge as figges.   There are other trees as high as a javeline, having one only stocke without any bough, and the leaves as long as a casting dart; and the fruite is of the bignesse and fashion of a cucumber, one bunch beareth 20 or 30, and as they ripen, the tree bendeth downeward with

Plantanos. them: they are called in this countrie plantanos, and are of a good taste, and ripen after they be gathered; but those are the better which ripen upon the tree itselfe ; they beare fruite but once ; and the tree being cut downe, there spring up others out of the but, which beare fruite the next yeere. There is another fruit, whereby many people are sustained,

Batatas, or potatos. and chiefly the slaves, which are called batatas.⁴   These grow now in the isle of Terçera, belonging to the kingdome of Portugal, and they grow within the earth, and are like a fruit called iname ;⁵ they have almost the taste of a chestnut. The bread of this countrie is also made of rootes, which are

The cassavi roote. like the batatas.   And the stocke whereon those rootes doe grow is like an elder-tree; they make their ground in little hillocks, and in each of them they thrust 4 or 5 stakes, and they gather the rootes a yeere and an halfe after they set them.   If any one, thinking it is a batata or potato roote, chance to eate of it never so little, hee is in great danger of death,⁶ which was seene by experience in a souldier, who as

¹ Erba babosa.—The scientific term for the aloe.
² The mammee-apple, well known in the West Indies.
³ Guavas.
⁴ The convolvulus batata, or sweet potato.
⁵ Say Iñame, since corrupted into yam.
⁶ This is only the case with the uncooked cassava root.

sone as hee had eaten a very little of one of those rootes, hee died quicklie. They pare these rootes and stampe them, and squese them in a thing like a presse; the juyce that cometh from them is of an evill smell. The bread is of little taste, and lesse substance. Of the fruites of Spaine, there are figges and oranges, and they beare fruit all the yeere, because the soile is very ranke and fruitfull. In this countrie are many good horses, and there is greene grasse all the yeere. Store of good horses. There be many wild oxen and hogges, whereby the people of the island is well furnished with flesh. Without the townes abroad in the countrie are many fruites. And it happeneth sometimes, that a Christian goeth out of the way and is lost 15 or 20 daies, because of the many paths in the thicke groves that crosse to and fro made by the oxen, and being thus lost, they sustaine themselves with fruites and palmitos,—for there bee many great groves of palme trees through all the island: they yeeld no other fruite that is of any profit. The isle of Cuba is 300 leagues long from the east The length and breadth of Cuba. to the west; and is in some places 30, in others 40, leagues from north to south. It hath 6 townes of Christians; to wit, S. Iago, Baracôa, Bayamo, Puerto de Principes, S. Espirito, and Havana. Every one hath betweene 30 and 40 households, except S. Iago and Havana, which have about 60 or 80 houses. They have churches in each of them, and a chaplen, which confesseth them and saith masse. In S. Iago is a monasterie of Franciscan friers; it hath but few friers, and is well provided of almes, because the countrie is rich. The church of S. Iago hath honest revenew, and there is a curat and prebends and many priests, as the church of that citie, which is the chiefe of all the island. There is in this countrie much gold, and few slaves to get it; for many have made away themselves, because of the Christians evill usage of them in the mines. A steward of Vasques Porcallo, which was an inhabitour in that island, understanding that his A wittie stratagem. slaves would make away themselves, staied for them with a cudgill in his hand at the place where they were to meete, and told them, that they could neither doe nor thinke any thing that hee did not know before ; and that he came thither to kill himselfe with them, to the end, that if he had used them badly in this world, hee might use them worse in the world to come. And this was a meane that they changed their purpose, and turned home againe to doe that which he commanded them.

CHAPTER VI.

How the Governour sent Donna Isabella with the ships to Havana, and he,
with some of his people, went thither by land.

The Governour sent from S. Iago his nephew Don Carlos with the ships, in company of Donna Isabella, to tarrie for him at Havana, which is an haven in the west part, toward the head of the island, 180 leagues from the citie of Saint Iago. The Governour, and those which staied with him, bought horses, and proceeded on their journie. The first *Bayamo.* towne they came unto was Bayamo : they were lodged foure and foure, and sixe and sixe, as they went in company, and where they lodged, they tooke nothing for their diet, for nothing cost them ought save the maiz, or corne for their horses, because the Governor went to visit them from towne to towne, and seased them in the tribute and service of the Indians. Bayamo is 25 leagues from the citie of Saint Iago. Neere unto the towne passeth a great river, which is called Tauto ;[1] it is greater then Guadiana, and in it be very great crocodiles, which sometimes hurt the Indians, or the cattell which passeth the river. In all the countrie are neither wolfe, foxe, beare, lion, nor tiger. There are wild dogges

---

[1] The Rio de Cauto.

which goe from the houses into the woods and feed upon
swine. There be certaine snakes as bigge as a mans thigh,
or bigger: they are very slow, they doe no kind of hurt.
From Bayamo to Puerto dellos principes are 50 leagues. In Puerto dellos Prin-
al the island, from towne to towne, the way is made by cipes.
stubbing up the underwood: and if it bee left but one yeere
undone, the wood groweth so much, that the way cannot be
seene, and the paths of the oxen are so many, that none can
travell without an Indian of the countrie for a guide; for all
the rest is very hie and thicke woods. From Puerto dellos
principes the Governour went to the house of Vasques Porcallo by sea in a bote (for it was neere the sea), to know
there some newes of Donna Isabella, which at that instant
(as afterward was knowne) was in great distresse, in so much
that the ships lost one another; and two of them fell on the
coast of Florida, and all of them endured great want of water
and victuals. When the storme was over, they met together,
without knowing where they were: in the end they descried
the cape of S. Anton, a countrie not inhabited of the island The cape of
S. Antonio.
of Cuba: there they watered; and at the end of 40 daies,
which were passed since their departure from the city of S.
Iago, they arrived at Havana. The Governour was presently
informed thereof, and went to Donna Isabella. And those
which went by land, which were one hundred and fiftie
horsemen, being divided into two parts, because they would
not oppresse the inhabitants, travelled by S. Espirito, which
is 60 leagues from Puerto dellos principes. The food which
they carried with them was caçabe bread, which is that
whereof I made mention before; and it is of such a qualitie,
that if it be wet, it breaketh presently, whereby it happened
to some to eate flesh without bread for many daies. They
carried dogges with them, and a man of the country which
did hunt; and by the way, or where they were to lodge
that night, they killed as many hogges as they needed. In
this journie they were well provided of beefe and porke;

and they were greatly troubled with muskitos, especially in
a lake, which is called the mere of Pia, which they had
much adoe to passe from noone till night; the water might
be some halfe league over, and to be swome about a crossebow shot, the rest came to the waste, and they waded up to
the knees in the mire, and in the bottome were cockle-shels,
which cut their feete very sore; in such sort, that there was
neither boote nor shooe sole that was hole at halfe way.
Their clothes and saddels were passed in baskets of palme
trees. Passing this lake, stripped out of their clothes, there
came many muskitos, upon whose biting there arose a wheale
that smarted very much; they strooke them with their hands,
and with the blowe which they gave they killed so many,
that the blood did runne downe the armes and bodies of the
men. That night they rested very little for them, and other
nights also in the like placces and times. They came to
Santo Espi-
rito. Santo Espirito, which is a towne of thirtie houses; there
passeth by it a little river: it is very pleasant and fruitfull,
having great store of oranges and citrons, and fruites of the
countrie. One halfe of the companie were lodged here, and
the rest passed forward 25 leagues to another towne called
La Trinidad. la Trinidad, of 15 or 20 households. Here is an hospitall
for the poore, and there is none other in all the island. And
they say, that this towne was the greatest in all the countrie;
and that before the Christians came into this land, as a ship
passed along the coast, there came in it a very sicke man,
which desired the captaine to set him on shore; and the
captaine did so, and the ship went her way. The sicke
man remained set on shore in that countrie, which untill
then had not been haunted by Christians; whereupon the
Indians found him, carried him home, and looked unto him
till he was whole; and the lord of that towne maried him
unto a daughter of his, and had warre with all the inhabitants
round about; and by the industrie and valour of the Christian, he subdued and brought under his command all the

people of that island. A great while after, the governour, Diego Velasques, went to conquer it, and from thence discovered New Spaine.[1] And this Christian, which was with the Indians, did pacifie them, and brought them to the obedience and subjection of the governour. From this towne, della Trinidad, unto Havana, are 80 leagues, without any habitation, which they travelled. They came to Havana in Havana. the end of March; where they found the Governor, and the rest of the people which came with him from Spaine. The Governour sent from Havana John Dannusco, with a caravele and two brigantines, with 50 men, to discover the haven of Florida; and from thence hee brought two Indians, which he tooke upon the coast; wherewith (as well because they might be necessarie for guides and for interpretours, as because they said by signes there was much gold in Florida) the Governour and all the companie received much contentment, and longed for the houre of their departure, thinking in himselfe that this was the richest countrie that unto that day had been discovered.

[1] The conquest of Cuba was effected by Diego Velasquez, in 1511. New Spain was discovered, in 1518, by Juan de Grijalva, who set sail from Cuba with four vessels fitted out at the expense of Velasquez, at that time Governor of the island. On receiving intelligence from Grijalva of the important discovery which he had made, the ambitious Velasquez immediately issued orders for the equipment of a fleet for the conquest of the newly-discovered regions, and gave the command of it to Hernando Cortes,—"the man, of all others, best calculated to achieve this great enterprise ; the last man to whom Velasquez, could he have foreseen the results, would have confided it." Prescott, *Conquest of Mexico*, i, 196.

CHAPTER VII.

*How we departed from Havana, and arrived in Florida, and of such things
as happened unto us.*

Before our departure, the Governour deprived Nunno de
Tovar of the office of captaine-generall, and gave it to Porcallo
de Figueroa, an inhabitant of Cuba, which was a meane that
the shippes were well furnished with victuals: for he gave a
great many loads of casabe bread, and manie hogges. The
Governour tooke away this office from Nonno de Tovar, because hee had fallen in love with the daughter of the Earle
of Gomera, Donna Isabella's waighting-maid, who, though his
office were taken from him (to returne againe to the Governours favour), though she were with child by him, yet tooke
her to his wife, and went with Soto into Florida. The
Governour left Donna Isabella in Havana; and with her
remained the wife of Don Carlos, and the wives of Baltasar
de Gallegos, and of Nonno de Tovar. And hee left for his
lieutenant a gentleman of Havana, called John de Roias, for
the government of the island.

May 18, 1539. On Sunday the 18. of May, in the yeere of our Lord
1539, the Adelantado or president departed from Havana in
Cuba with his fleete, which were nine vessels, five great
ships, two caravels, and two brigantines. They sailed seven
daies with a prosperous wind. The 25. day of May, the day
de Pasca de Spirito Santo (which we call Whitson Sonday),
This place was called Baya de Spirito Sancto, being on the west side of Florida, in 29 degrees ½. they saw the land of Florida; and because of the shoalds,
they came to an anchor a league from the shore. On Friday
the 30. of May they landed in Florida, two leagues from a
towne of an Indian lord, called Ucita.[1] They set on land

[1] The reader is referred to the Introduction, for a more particular
notice of the various Indian provinces, towns, and villages, mentioned in
the following pages as falling in Soto's route.

two hundred and thirteene horses, which they brought with them, to unburden the shippes, that they might draw the lesse water. Hee landed all his men, and only the sea men remained in the shippes, which in eight daies, going up with the tide every day a little, brought them up unto the towne. As soone as the people were come on shore, hee pitched his campe on the sea side, hard upon the bay which went up unto the towne. And presently the captaine generall Vasques Porcallo, with other seven horsemen, foraged the countrie halfe a league round about, and found sixe Indians, which resisted him with their arrowes, which are the weapons which they use to fight withall. The horsemen killed two of them, and the other foure escaped; because the countrie is cumbersome with woods and bogs, where the horses stacke fast, and fell with their riders, because they were weake with travelling upon the sea. The same night following, the Governour, with an hundred men in the brigantines, lighted upon a towne, which he found without people, because, that assoone as the Christians had sight of land, they were descried, and saw along the coast many smokes, which the Indians had made to give advice the one to the other. The next day Luys de Moscoso, master of the campe, set the men in order, the horsemen in three squadrons,—the vantgard, the batallion, and the rerewarde : and so they marched that day, and the day following, compassing great creekes which came out of the bay. They came to the towne of Ucita, where the Governour was, on Sunday the first of June, being Trinitie Sunday. The towne was of seven or eight houses. The lordes house stoode neere the shore, upon a very hie mount, made by hand for strength. At another end of the towne stood the church,[1] and on the top of it stood a fowle made of wood, with gilded eies. Heere were found some

---

[1] The original Portuguese word is *mesquita,* which would be more correctly rendered by " temple".

E

pearles of small valew, spoiled with the fire, which the Indians do pierce and string them like beades, and weare them about their neckes and handwrists, and they esteeme them very much. The houses were made of timber, and covered with palme leaves. The Governour lodged himselfe in the lords houses, and with him Vasques Porcallo, and Luys de Moscoso; and in others that were in the middest of the towne, was the chiefe alcalde or justice, Baltasar de Gallegos, lodged; and in the same houses was set in a place by it selfe, al the provision that came in the ships: the other houses and the church were broken down, and every three or foure souldiers made a little cabin wherein they lodged. The countrie round about was very fennie, and encombred with great and hie trees. The Governor commanded to fel the woods a crossebow shot round about the towne, that the horses might runne, and the Christians might have the advantage of the Indians, if by chance they should set upon them by night. In the waies and places convenient, they had their centinelles of footemen by two and two in every stand, which did watch by turnes, and the horsemen did visit them, and were readie to assist them, if there were any alarme. The Governour made foure captaines of the horsemen, and two of the footemen. The captaines of the horsemen were, one of them, Andrew de Vasconcelos, and another, Pedro Calderan de Badajos; and the other two were his kinsemen, to wit, Arias Tinoco and Alfonso Romo, borne likewise in Badajos. The captaines of the footemen, the one was Francisco Maldonado of Salamanca, and the other Juan Rodriguez Lobillo. While wee were in this towne of Ucita, the two Indians which John Danusco had taken on that coast, and the Governor caried along with him for guides and interpretours, through carelessenes of two men which had the charge of them, escaped away one night. For which the Governour and all the rest were very sorie, for they had alreadie made some roades, and no Indians could bee taken, because the countrie was full of marish grounds, and in many places full of very hie and thicke woods.

CHAPTER VIII.

Of some inrodes that were made into the countrie; and how there was a Christian found, which had bin long time in the power of an Indian Lord.

From the towne of Ucita, the Governour sent the alcalde mayor, Baltasar de Gallegos, with 40 horsemen and 80 footemen, into the countrie, to see if they could take any Indians: and the captaine, John Rodriguez Lobillo, another way with 50 footemen; the most of them were swordmen and targettours, and the rest were shot and crossebowmen. They passed through a countrie full of bogges, where horses could not travell. Halfe a league from the campe, they lighted upon certaine cabins of Indians neere a river; the people that were in them leaped into the river; yet they tooke foure Indian women; and twentie Indians charged us, and so distressed us, that wee were forced to retire to our campe, being, as they are, exceeding readie with their weapons. It is a people so warlike and so nimble, that they care not a whit for any footemen. For if their enemies charge them, they runne away, and if they turne their backs, they are presently upon them. And the thing that they most flee, is the shot of an arrow. They never stand still, but are alwaies running and traversing from one place to another; by reason whereof neither crossebow nor arcubuse can aime at them; and before one crossebowman can make one shot, an Indian will discharge three or foure arrowes; and he seldome misseth what

hee shooteth at. An arrow, where it findeth no armour,
pierceth as deepely as a crossebow. Their bowes are very
long, and their arrowes are made of certain canes like reedes,
very heavie, and so strong, that a sharpe cane passeth thorow
a target; some they arme in the point with a sharpe bone of
a fish like a chisel, and in others they fasten certaine stones
like points of diamants. For the most part, when they light
upon an armour, they breake in the place where they are
bound together. Those of cane do split and pierce a coate
of maile, and are more hurtfull then the other. John Rodriguez Lobillo returned to the campe with sixe men wounded,
whereof one died, and brought the foure Indian women,
which Baltasar Gallegos had taken in the cabins or cotages.
Two leagues from the towne, comming into the plaine field,
he espied ten or eleven Indians, among whom was a Christian, which was naked, and scorched with the sunne, and had
his armes razed after the manner of the Indians, and differed
nothing at all from them. And as soone as the horsemen saw
them, they ran toward them. The Indians fled, and some
of them hid themselves in a wood, and they overtooke two
or three of them, which were wounded; and the Christian,
seeing an horseman runne upon him with his lance, began
to crie out, Sirs, I am a Christian, slay me not, nor these
Indians, for they have saved my life. And straightway he
called them, and put them out of feare, and they came
foorth of the wood unto them. The horsemen tooke both
the Christian and the Indians up behind them; and toward
night came into the campe with much joy; which thing
being knowne by the Governour, and them that remained in
the campe, they were received with the like.

CHAPTER IX.

How this Christian came to the land of Florida, and who he was ; and
what conference he had with the Governour.

This Christian's name was John Ortiz, and he was borne John Ortiz lived 12 yeeres among the Floridians of Ucita and Mocoço.
in Sivil, in worshipful parentage.   He was twelve yeeres in
the hands of the Indians.   He came into this countrie with
Pamphilo de Narvaez, and returned in the ships to the
Island of Cuba, where the wife of the Governour, Pamphilo
de Narvaez, was : and by his commandement, with twenty or
thirty other, in a brigandine, returned backe againe to Florida ;
and comming to the port in the sight of the towne, on the
shore they saw a cane sticking in the ground, and riven at
the top, and a letter in it : and they beleeved that the
Governour had left it there to give advertisement of himselfe,
when he resolved to goe up into the land ; and they demanded it of foure or five Indians, which walked along the
sea shore ; and they bad them, by signes, to come on shore
for it, which, against the will of the rest, John Ortiz and
another did.   And as soone as they were on land, from the
houses of the towne issued a great number of Indians, which
compassed them about, and tooke them in a place where
they could not flee ; and the other, which sought to defend
himselfe, they presentlie killed upon the place, and tooke
John Ortiz alive, and carried him to Ucita their lord.   And
those of the brigandine sought not to land, but put themselves to sea, and returned to the island of Cuba.   Ucita
commanded to bind John Ortiz hand and foote upon foure
stakes aloft upon a raft, and to make a fire under him, that
there he might bee burned.   But a daughter of his desired
him that he would not put him to death, alleaging that one
only Christian could do him neither hurt nor good, telling
him, that it was more for his honour to keepe him as a cap-

tive. And Ucita granted her request, and commanded him
to be cured of his wounds; and as soone as he was whole,
he gave him the charge of the keeping of the temple, because
that by night the wolves did cary away the dead corpses out
of the same; who commended himselfe to God, and tooke
upon him the charge of his temple. One night the wolves
gate from him the corpes of a little child, the sonne of a
principal Indian; and going after them, he threw a darte at
one of the wolves, and strooke him that carried away the
corps, who, feeling himselfe wounded, left it, and fell downe
dead neere the place; and hee not woting what he had done,
because it was night, went backe againe to the temple; the
morning being come, and finding not the bodie of the child,
he was very sad. As soone as Ucita knew thereof, he
resolved to put him to death; and sent by the tract, which
he said the wolves went, and found the bodie of the child,
and the wolfe dead a little beyond: whereat Ucita was much
contented with the Christian, and with the watch which hee
kept in the temple, and from thence forward esteemed him
much. Three yeeres after hee fell into his hands, there
came another lord, called Mocoço, who dwelleth two daies
journy from the port, and burned his towne. Ucita fled to
another towne that he had in another sea port. Thus John
Ortiz lost his office and favour that he had with him. These
people being worshippers of the divell, are wont to offer up
unto him the lives and blood of their Indians, or of any
other people they can come by; and they report, that when
he will have them doe that sacrifice unto him, he speaketh
with them, and telleth them that he is athirst, and willeth
them to sacrifice unto him. John Ortiz had notice by the
damsell that had delivered him from the fire, how her father
was determined to sacrifice him the day following, who willed
him to flee to Mocoço, for shee knew that he would use him
well; for she heard say, that he had asked for him, and said
he would be glad to see him; and because he knew not the

Mocoço dwelleth two daies journie from Ucita.

way, she went with him halfe a league out of the towne by
night, and set him in the way, and returned, because she
would not be discovered.   John Ortiz travailed all that
night, and by the morning came unto a river, which is in A river.
the territorie of Mocoço; and there he saw two Indians fishing; and because they were in war with the people of Ucita,
and their languages were different, and hee knew not the
language of Mocoço, he was afraid (because he could not tell
them who hee was, nor how hee came thither, nor was able
to answer any thing for himselfe) that they would kill him,
taking him for one of the Indians of Ucita; and before they
espied him, he came to the place where they had laid their
weapons; and as soone as they saw him, they fled toward
the towne; and although he willed them to stay, because he
meant to do them no hurt, yet they understood him not, and
ran away as fast as ever they could.   And as soone as they
came to the towne with great outcries, many Indians came
forth against him, and began to compasse him to shoote at
him: John Ortiz seeing himselfe in so great danger, shielded
himselfe with certaine trees, and began to shreeke out, and
crie very loud, and to tell them that he was a Christian, and
that he was fled from Ucita, and was come to see and serve
Mocoço his lord.   It pleased God, that at that very instant
there came thither an Indian that could speake the language
and understood him, and pacified the rest, who told them
what hee said.   Then ran from thence three or foure Indians
to beare the newes to their lord, who came foorth a quarter
of a league from the towne to receive him, and was very
glad of him.   He caused him presently to sweare according
to the custome of the Christians, that he would not run away
from him to any other lord, and promised him to entreate
him very well; and that if at any time there came any
Christians into that countrie, he would freely let him goe,
and give him leave to goe to them; and likewise tooke his
oth to performe the same, according to the Indian custome.

About three yeares after, certaine Indians, which were
fishing at sea two leagues from the towne, brought newes to
Mocoço his
towne, two
leagues of
the sea. Mocoço that they had seene ships; and hee called John Ortiz,
and gave him leave to go his way; who, taking his leave of
him, with all the haste he could, came to the sea, and finding
no ships, he thought it to be some deceit, and that the
cacique had done the same to learne his mind; so he dwelt
with Mocoço nine yeeres, with small hope of seeing any
Christians. As soone as our Governor arrived in Florida, it
was knowne to Mocoço, and straightway he signified to John
Ortiz that Christians were lodged in the towne of Ucita:
and he thought he had jested with him, as hee had done
before, and told him, that by this time he had forgotten the
Christians, and thought of nothing else but to serve him.
But he assured him that it was so, and gave him licence to
goe unto them; saying unto him, that if hee would not doe
it, and if the Christians should goe their way, he should not
blame him, for he had fulfilled that which hee had promised
him. The joy of John Ortiz was so great, that hee could
not beleeve that it was true; notwithstanding, he gave him
thankes, and tooke his leave of him; and Mocoço gave him
tenne or eleven principall Indians to beare him companie;
and as they went to the port where the Governour was, they
met with Baltasar de Gallêgos, as I have declared before.

As soone as he was come to the campe, the Governour
commanded to give him a sute of apparrell, and very good
armour, and a faire horse, and enquired of him, whether hee
had notice of any countrie, where there was any gold or
silver? He answered, No, because he never went ten leagues
compasse from the place where he dwelt; but that thirty
Paracossi 30
leagues from
Puerto de
Spirito
Santo. leagues from thence dwelt an Indian lord, which was called
Parocossi, to whom Mocoço and Ucita, with al the rest of that
coast, paied tribute, and that hee peradventure might have
notice of some good countrie; and that his land was better
then that of the sea coast, and more fruitfull and plentifull

of maiz; whereof the Governour received great contentment; and said, that he desired no more then to finde victuals, that hee might goe into the maine land, for the land of Florida was so large that in one place or other there could not chuse but bee some rich countrie. The cacique Mocoço came to the port to visit the Governor, and made this speech following:

Right hie and mightie Lord, I being lesser in mine owne conceit for to obey you, then any of those which you have under your command ; and greater in desire to doe you greater services, doe appeare before your Lordship with so much confidence of receiving favour, as if in effect this my good will were manifested unto you in workes : not for the small service I did unto you, touching the Christian which I had in my power, in giving him freely his libertie (for I was bound to doe it to preserve mine honour, and that which I had promised him), but because it is the part of great men to use great magnificences : and I am perswaded, that as in bodily perfections, and commanding of good people, you doe exceede all men in the world, so likewise you doe in the parts of the minde, in which you may boast of the bountie of nature. The favour which I hope for of your Lordship is, that you would hold mee for yours, and bethinke your selfe to command me any thing, wherein I may doe you service.

The Governour answered him, that although in freeing and sending him the Christian, he had preserved his honour and promise, yet he thanked him, and held it in such esteeme, as it had no comparison ; and that hee would alwaies hold him as his brother, and would favour him in all things to the utmost of his power. Then he commanded a shirt to be given him, and other things, wherewith the cacique being verie well contented, tooke his leave of him, and departed to his owne towne.

F

CHAPTER X.

How the Governour sent the ships to Cuba, and left an hundred men at
the haven de Spirito Santo, and himself with the rest of his people
went into the maine land.

From the port de Spirito Santo, where the Governour lay,
he sent the alcalde mayor, Baltasar de Gallegos, with fifty
horsemen, and thirty or forty footemen, to the province of
Paracossi, to view the disposition of the countrie, and enforme
himselfe of the land farther inward, and to send him word of
such things as he found. Likewise he sent his shippes backe
to the island of Cuba, that they might returne within a certaine time with victuals. Vasques Porcallo de Figueroa,
which went with the Governour as captaine generall (whose
principall intent was to send slaves from Florida to the
island of Cuba, where he had his goods and mines), having
made some inrodes, and seeing no Indians were to be got,
because of the great bogs and thicke woods that were in the
countrie, considering the disposition of the same, determined
to returne to Cuba. And though there was some difference
between him and the Governour, whereupon they neither
dealt nor conversed together with good countenance, yet
notwithstanding with loving words he asked him leave and
Paracossi. departed from him. Baltasar de Gallegos came to the Paracossi. There came to him thirty Indians from the cacique,
which was absent from his towne, and one of them made this
speech.

Paracossi, the Lord of this province, whose vassals we are,
sendeth us unto your worship, to know what it is that you
seeke in this his countrie, and wherein he may doe you service.

Baltasar de Gallegos said unto him, that hee thanked them
very much for their offer, willing them to warne their lord
to come to his towne, and that there they would talke and

confirme their peace and friendship, which he much desired. The Indians went their way, and returned the next day, and said, that their lord was ill at ease, and therefore could not come, but that they came on his behalfe to see what he demanded. He asked them if they knew or had notice of any rich countrie where there was gold or silver. They told them they did: and that towards the west, there was a province which was called Cale; and that others that inhabited other countries had warre with the people of that countrie, where the most part of the yeere was sommer, and that there was much gold: and that when those their enemies came to make warre with them of Cale, these inhabitants of Cale did weare hats of gold, in manner of head peeces. Baltasar de Gallegos, seeing that the cacique came not, thinking all that they said was fained, with intent that in the meane time they might set themselves in safetie, fearing, that if he did let them goe, they would returne no more, commanded the thirty Indians to be chained, and sent word to the Governour, by eight horsemen, what had passed: whereof the Governour with al that were with him, at the port de Spirito Santo, received great comfort, supposing that that which the Indians reported might be true. Hee left Captaine Calderan at the port, with thirtie horsemen, and seventie footemen, with provision for two yeeres, and himselfe with all the rest marched into the maine land, and came to the Paracossi, at whose Paracossi. towne Baltasar de Gallegos was: and from thence with all his men tooke the way to Cale. He passed by a little towne, called Acela, and came to another, called Tocaste: and from Acela. thence he went before with thirtie horsemen, and fiftie footemen toward Cale. And passing by a towne, whence the Another people were fled, they saw Indians a little from thence in a lake; to whom the interpretour spake. They came unto A lake. them and gave them an Indian for a guide: and hee came to a river with a great current, and upon a tree, which was in A swift the midst of it, was made a bridge, whereon the men passed: river.

the horses swam over by a hawser that they were pulled by
from the other side: for one, which they drove in at the first
without it, was drowned.   From thence the Governour sent
two horsemen to his people that were behind, to make haste
after him; because the way grew long, and their victuals
short.   Hee came to Cale, and found the towne without
people.   He tooke three Indians which were spies, and tarried there for his people that came after, which were sore
vexed with hunger and evill waies, because the countrie was
very barren of maiz, low, and full of water, bogs, and thicke
woods; and the victuals which they brought with them from
the port de Spirito Santo, were spent.   Wheresoever any
towne was founde, there were some beetes,[1] and hee that came
first gathered them, and sodden with water and salt, did eate
them without any other thing: and such as could not get
them, gathered the stalkes of maiz and eate them; which, because they were young, had no maiz in them.   When they
came to the river which the Governour had passed, they
found palmitos upon low palme trees, like those of Andaluzia.
There they met with the two horsemen which the Governour
sent unto them, and they brought newes that in Cale there
was plentie of maiz; at which newes they all rejoyced.   As
soone as they came to Cale, the Governour commanded
them to gather all the maiz that was ripe in the field, which
was sufficient for three moneths.   At the gathering of it the
Indians killed three Christians, and one of them which were
taken told the Governour, that within seven daies journie,
there was a very great province, and plentifull of maize,
which was called Apalache.   And presently hee departed
from Cale with fifty horsemen, and sixty footemen.   He left
the master of the campe, Luys de Moscoso, with all the rest
of the people there, with charge that hee should not depart
thence untill he had word from him.   And because hitherto
none had gotten any slaves, the bread that every one was to

[1] Probably related to the beetroot, and used as a salad.

eate, he was faine himselfe to beate in a morter made in a peece of timber, with a pestle, and some of them did sift the flower through their shirts of maile. They baked their bread upon certaine tileshares which they set over the fire, in such sort as heretofore I have said they use to doe in Cuba. It is so troublesome to grind their maiz, that there were many that would rather not eate it, then grind it : and did eate the maiz parched and sodden.

CHAPTER XI.

How the Governour came to Caliquen, and carrying from thence the cacique with him went to Napetuca, where the Indians sought to have taken him from him, and in an assault many of them were slaine, and taken prisoners.

The 11 day of August 1539, the Governour departed from Cale ; hee lodged in a little town called Ytara, and the next day in another called Potano, and the third day at Utinama, and came to another towne, which they named the towne of Evill Peace ; because an Indian came in peace, saying, that he was the cacique, and that he with his people would serve the Governour, and that if he would set free twenty-eight persons, men and women, which his men had taken the night before, he would command provision to be brought him, and would give him a guide to instruct him in his way. The Governour commanded them to be set at libertie, and to keepe him in safegard. The next day in the morning there came many Indians, and set themselves round about the towne neere to a wood. The Indian wished them to carrie him neere them ; and that he would speake unto them, and assure them, and that they would doe whatsoever hee commanded them. And when he saw himselfe neere unto them he brake from them, and ran away so swiftly from the Christians, that there was none that could overtake him, and all

(margin notes) Ytara. Potano. Utinama. The towne of Evill Peace.

of them fled into the woods. The Governour commanded
to loose a grayhound, which was alreadie fleshed on them,
which passing by many other Indians, caught the counterfait
cacique, which had escaped from the Christians, and held
him till they came to take him. From thence the Governour
Cholupaha. lodged at a towne called Cholupaha: and because it had
store of maiz in it, they named it Villa farta. Beyond the
A river. same there was a river, on which he made a bridge of
timber, and travelled two daies through a desert. The 17 of
Caliquen. August, he came to Caliquen, where he was informed of the
province of Apalache. They told him that Pamphilo de
Narvaez had bin there, and that there hee tooke shipping,
because hee could find no way to goe forward: that there
was none other towne at al; but that on both sides was all
water. The whole companie were very sad for these newes;
and counselled the Governour to goe backe to the port de
Spirito Santo, and to abandon the countrie of Florida, lest
hee should perish as Narvaez had done: declaring, that if
he went forward, he could not returne backe when he would,
and that the Indians would gather up that small quantitie of
maiz which was left. Whereunto the Governour answered,
that he would not go backe, till he had seen with his eies
that which they reported; saying, that hee could not beleeve
it, and that wee should be put out of doubt before it were
long. And he sent to Luys de Moscoso to come presently
from Cale, and that he tarried for him here. Luys de
Moscoso and many others thought, that from Apalache they
should returne backe; and in Cale they buried their yron
tooles, and divers other things. They came to Caliquen with
great trouble; because the countrie, which the Governour
had passed by, was spoiled and destitute of maiz. After all
the people were come together, hee commanded a bridge to
A river. be made over a river that passed neere the towne.

Hee departed from Caliquen the 10 of September, and carried the cacique with him. After hee had travelled three daies,

there came Indians peaceably, to visit their lord, and every
day met us on the way playing upon flutes: which is a token
that they use, that men may know that they come in peace.
They said, that in our way before there was a cacique, whose
name was Uzachil, a kinseman of the cacique of Caliquen
their lord, waiting for him with many presents, and they
desired the Governor that he would loose the cacique. But
he would not, fearing that they would rise, and would not
give him any guides, and sent them away from day to day
with good words. He travelled five daies, he passed by
some small townes, he came to a towne called Napetuca, the ^{Some small townes. Napetuca.}
15 day of September. Thither came fourteen or fifteen
Indians, and besought the governor to let loose the cacique
of Caliquen their lord. He answered them that he held him
not in prison, but that hee would have him to accompanie
him to Uzachil. The Governour had notice by John Ortiz,
that an Indian told him how they determined to gather themselves together, and come upon him, and give him battell,
and take away the cacique from him. The day that it was
agreed upon, the Governour commanded his men to bee in a
readines, and that the horsemen should bee readie armed and
on horsebacke every one in his lodging, because the Indians
might not see them, and so more confidently come to the
towne. There came foure hundred Indians in sight of the
campe with their bowes and arrowes, and placed themselves
in a wood, and sent two Indians to bid the Governour to
deliver them the cacique. The Governour, with six footemen leading the cacique by the hand, and talking with him,
to secure the Indians, went toward the place where they
were: and seeing a fit time, commanded to sound a trumpet:
and presently those that were in the towne in the houses,
both horse and foot, set upon the Indians, which were so
suddenly assaulted that the greatest care they had was
which way they should flee. They killed two horses; one
was the Governour's, and he was presently horsed againe

upon another. There were thirty or forty Indians slaine.

The rest fled to two very great lakes, that were somewhat distant the one from the other : there they were swimming, and the Christians round about them. The calievermen and crossebowmen shot at them from the banke ; but the distance being great, and shooting afarre off, they did them no hurt. The Governour commanded that the same night they should compasse one of the lakes, because they were so great, that there were not men enow to compasse them both. Being beset as soone as night shut in, the Indians, with determination to runne away, came swimming very softly to the banke; and to hide themselves, they put a water-lillie leafe on their heads. The horsemen, as soone as they perceived it to stirre, ran into the water to the horses breasts, and the Indians fled againe into the lake. So this night passed without any rest on both sides. John Ortiz persuaded them, that seeing they could not escape, they should yeeld themselves to the Governour: which they did, enforced thereunto by the coldness of the water ; and one by one, hee first whom the cold did first overcome, cried to John Ortiz, desiring that they would not kill him, for he came to put himselfe into the hands of the Governour. By the morning watch they made an end of yeelding themselves : only twelve principall men, being more honorable and valorous then the rest, resolved rather to die then to come into his hands. And the Indians of Paracossi, which were now loosed out of chaines, went swimming to them, and pulled them out by the haire of their heads, and they were all put in chaines ; and the next day were divided among the Christians for their service.

Being thus in captivitie, they determined to rebell; and gave in charge to an Indian, which was interpretour, and held to be valiant, that as soone as the Governour did come to speake with him, he should cast his hands about his necke, and choke him: who, when he saw opportunitie, laid hands on the Governour, and before he cast his hands about his neck, he gave him such a blow on the nostrils, that hee made them gush out with blood, and presently all the rest did rise. He that could get any weapons at hand, or the handle where- with he did grind the maiz, sought to kill his master, or the first hee met before him : and hee that could get a lance or sword at hand, bestirred himselfe in such sort with it, as though he had used it all his life time. One Indian in the market-place, enclosed betweene fifteen or twenty footemen, made away like a bull, with a sword in his hand, till cer- taine halbardiers of the Governour came, which killed him : another got up with a lance to a loft made of canes, which they build to keepe their maiz in, which they call a barbacoa, and there hee made such a noise, as though tenne men had been there defending the doore ; they slew him with a parti- san. The Indians were in all about two hundred men. _{Two hun-} They were all subdued. And some of the youngest the _{dred Indians taken.} Governour gave to them which had good chaines, and were carefull to looke to them that they gat not away. Al the rest he commanded to be put to death, being tied to a stake in the midst of the market-place ; and the Indians of the Paracossi did shoote them to death.

CHAPTER XII.

How the Governour came to Apalache, and was informed, that within the land there was much Gold.

The Governour departed from Napetuca the 23 of Sep- tember ; he lodged by a river, where two Indians brought _{A river.} him a buck from the cacique of Uzachil. The next day he passed by a great towne called Hapaluya, and lodged at _{Hapaluya, a great towne} Uzachil, and found no people in it, because they durst not _{Uzachil.}

tarrie, for the notice the Indians had of the slaughter of
Napetuca.   He found in that towne great store of maiz,
Abobaras. french beanes, and pompions, which is their foode, and
that wherewith the Christians there sustained themselves;
the maiz is like coarse millet, and the pompions are better and more savorie then those of Spaine.   From thence
the Governour sent two captaines, each a sundry way, to
seeke the Indians.   They tooke an hundred men and
women; of which, aswel there as in other places where they
made any inrodes, the captaine chose one or two for the
Governour, and divided the rest to himselfe, and those that
went with him.   They led these Indians in chaines with
yron collars about their neckes; and they served to carrie
their stuffe, and to grind their maiz, and for other services
that such captives could doe.   Sometimes it happened, that
going for wood or maiz with them, they killed the Christian
that led them, and ran away with the chaine; others filed
their chaines by night with a peece of stone, wherewith they
cut them, and use instead of yron.   Those that were perceived paid for themselves, and for the rest, because they
should not dare to doe the like another time.   The women
and young boyes, when they were once an hundred leagues
from their countrie, and had forgotten things, they let goe
loose, and so they served; and in a very short space they
understood the language of the Christians.   From Uzachil
the Governour departed toward Apalache, and in two daies
Axille.   journie hee came to a towne called Axille, and from thence
forward the Indians were carelesse, because they had as yet
no notice of the Christians.

The next day in the morning, the first of October, he
departed from thence, and commanded a bridge to bee made
A river.   over a river, which hee was to passe.   The deepe of the
river where the bridge was made, was a stones cast, and
forward a crossebow shot, the water came to the waste; and
the wood, whereby the Indians came to see if they could

defend the passage, and disturbe those which made the bridge, was very hie and thicke. The crossebow men so bestirred themselves, that they made them give back; and certain plancks were cast into the river, whereon the men passed, which made good the passage. The Governor passed upon Wednesday, which was S. Francis his day, and lodged at a towne which was called Vitachuco, subject to Apalache; Vitachuco. he found it burning, for the Indians had set it on fire. From thence forward the countrie was much inhabited, and had great store of maiz. Hee passed by many granges, like hamlets. On Sunday the 25 of October, he came to a towne, October 25. which is called Uzela, and upon Tuesday to Anaica Apalache, Uzela.
Anaica
Apalache. where the lord of all that countrie and province was resident; in which towne the campe master, whose office it is to quarter out and lodge men, did lodge all the companie round about within a league and halfe a league of it. There were other townes, where was great store of maiz, pompions, french beanes, and plummes of the countrie, which are better then those of Spaine, and they grow in the fields without planting. The victuals that were thought necessarie to passe the winter, were gathered from these townes to Anaica Apalache. Apalache
within ten
leagues of
the sea. The Governour was informed that the sea was ten leagues from thence. Hee presently sent a captaine thither with horsemen and footemen; and sixe leagues on the way he found a towne, which was named Ochete, and so came to the Ochete. sea, and found a great tree felled, and cut into peeces, with The sea. stakes set up like mangers, and saw the skulles of horses. Hee returned with this newes. And that was held for certaine, which was reported of Pamphilo de Narvaez, that there hee had builded the barkes wherewith he went out of the land of Florida, and was cast away at sea. Presently the Governour sent John Danusco, with thirty horsemen, to the port de Spiritu Santo, where Calderan was, with order that they should abandon the port, and all of them come to Apalache. He departed on Saturday, the 17 of November.

In Uzachil and other townes that stood in the way he found
great store of people alreadie carelesse. Hee would take
none of the Indians, for not hindring himselfe, because it
behooved him to give them no leasure to gather themselves
together. He passed through the townes by night, and
rested without the townes three or foure houres. In tenne
The Port de
SpirituSanto daies he came to the port de Spirito Santo. He carried with
tenne daies
journie from
Apalache. him twenty Indian women, which he tooke in Ytara, and
Potano, neere unto Cale, and sent them to Donna Isabella
in the two caravels which hee sent from the port de Spirito
Santo to Cuba. And he carried all the footemen in the
brigandines, and coasting along the shore, came to Apalache.
And Calderan with the horsemen, and some crossebowmen
on foote, went by land; and in some places the Indians set
upon him and wounded some of his men. As soone as he
came to Apalache, presently the Governour sent sawed
plankes and spikes to the sea-side, wherewith was made a
piragua or barke, wherein were embarked thirty men well
armed, which went out of the bay to the sea, looking for
the brigandines. Sometimes they fought with the Indians,
which passed along the harbour in their canoes. Upon
Novem. 29. Saturday, the 29th of November, there came an Indian
through the watch undiscovered, and set the towne on fire,
and with the great wind that blew, two parts of it were con-
Decem. 28. sumed in a short time. On Sonday, the 28 of December,
came John Danusco with the brigandines. The Governour
sent Francisco Maldonado, a captaine of footemen, with fifty
men to discover the coast westward, and to seeke some port,
because he had determined to go by land, and discover that
part. That day there went out eight horsemen by commandement of the Governor into the field, two leagues about
the towne, to seeke Indians; for they were now so emboldened, that within two crossebow shot of the camp, they came
and slew men. They found two men and a woman gathering
french beanes; the men, though they might have fled, yet

because they would not leave the woman, which was one of
their wives, they resolved to die fighting; and before they
were slaine, they wounded three horses, whereof one died
within a few daies after. Calderan going with his men by
the sea coast, from a wood that was neere the place, the
Indians set upon him, and made him forsake his way, and
many of them that went with him forsooke some necessarie
victuals, which they carried with them.

Three or foure daies after the limited time given by the
Governour to Maldonado for his going and comming, being
alreadie determined and resolved, if within eight daies he
did not come, to tarrie no longer for him; he came, and
brought an Indian, from a province which was called Ochus, Ochus sixty
leagues west
sixtie leagues westward from Apalache, where he had found of Apalache.
a good port, of good depth and defense against weather.
And because the Governor hoped to find a good countrie
forward, he was very well contented. And he sent Maldonado for victuals to Havana, with order that he should
tarrie for him at the port of Ochus, which hee had discovered, for hee would goe seeke it by land; and if he should
chance to stay and not come thither that summer, that then
hee should returne to Havana, and should come againe the
next summer after, and tarrie for him at that port; for hee
said hee would doe none other thing but goe to seeke
Ochus. Francisco Maldonado departed, and in his place
for captaine of the footemen remained John de Guzman.

Of those Indians which were taken in Napetuca, the Chap. II.
treasurer, John Gaytan, had a young man, which said that he
was not of that countrie, but of another farre off toward the
sunrising, and that it was long since he had travelled to see
countries; and that his countrie was called Yupaha, and
that a woman did governe it; and that the towne where she
was resident was of a wonderfull bignesse, and that many
lords round about were tributaries to her; and some gave
her clothes, and others gold in abundance; and hee told how Abundance
of gold.

it was taken out of the mines, and was moulten and refined,
as if hee had seene it done, or the divel had taught it him.
So that all those which knew any thing concerning the same,
said that it was impossible to give so good a relation without having seene it ; and all of them, as if they had seene it,
by the signes that he gave, beleeved all that he said to be
true.

CHAPTER XIII.

*How the Governour departed from Apalache to seeke Yupaha, and of that
which happened unto him.*

March the 3, 1540.

On Wednesday the third of March, of the yeere 1540, the
Governor departed from Anaica Apalache to seeke Yupaha.
He commanded his men to goe provided with maiz for sixtie
leagues of desert.   The horsemen carried their maiz on their
horses, and the footemen at their sides : because the Indians
that were for service, with their miserable life that they lead
that winter, being naked and in chaines, died for the most

A great river.

part.   Within foure daies journie they came to a great river ;
and they made a piragua or ferrie bote, and because of the
great current, they made a cable with chaines, which they
fastened on both sides of the river ; and the ferrie bote went
along by it ; and the horses swam over, being drawne with
capstans.   Having passed the river, in a day and an halfe they

Capachiqui.

came to a towne called Capachiqui.   Upon Friday, the 11
of March, they found Indians in armes.   The next day five
Christians went to seeke morters, which the Indians have to
beate their maiz, and they went to certaine houses on the
backside of the campe environed with a wood : and within
the wood were many Indians which came to spie us ; of the

which came other five and set upon us. One of the Christians came running away, giving an alarme unto the campe.
Those which were most readie answered the alarme. They
found one Christian dead, and three sore wounded. The
Indians fled unto a lake adjoining neere a very thicke wood,
where the horses could not enter. The Governour departed
from Capachiqui, and passed through a desert. On Wednesday, the 21 of the moneth, he came to a towne called Toalli.
And from thence forward there was a difference in the houses ;
for those which were behind us were thatched with straw,
and those of Toalli were covered with reeds, in manner of Toalli.
tiles. These houses are verie cleanly. Some of them had
walles daubed with clay, which shewed like a mud wall. In
all the cold countrie the Indians have every one a house for
the winter, daubed with clay within and without, and the
doore is very little : they shut it by night, and make fire
within ; so that they are in it as warmé as a stove : and so it
continueth all night that they need not clothes : and besides
these, they have others for summer ; and their kitchins neere
them, where they make fire and bake their bread : and they
have barbacoas wherein they keepe their maiz ; which is an
house set up in the aire upon foure stakes, boorded about
like a chamber, and the floore of it is of cane hurdles. The
difference which lords or principall mens houses have from
the rest, besides they be greater, is, that they have great
galleries in their fronts, and under them seates made of canes
in manner of benches ; and round about them they have
many lofts, wherein they lay up that which the Indians doe
give them for tribute, which is maiz, deeres skins, and
mantles of the countrie, which are like blankets : they make
them of the inner rinde of the barkes of trees, and some of a
kind of grasse like unto nettles, which being beaten, is like A grasse like
unto flaxe. The women cover themselves with these mantles ; flaxe.
they put one about them from the wast downeward ; and
another over their shoulder, with their right arme out, like

unto the Egyptians.[1] The men weare but one mantle upon their shoulders after the same manner: and have their secrets hid with a deeres skins, made like a linen breech, which was wont to be used in Spaine. The skins are well corried, and they give them what colour they list, so perfect, that if it be red, it seemeth a very fine cloth in graine, and the blacke is most fine: and of the same leather they make shooes; and they die their mantles in the same colours. The Governour departed from Toalli the 24 of March: he came on Thursday at evening to a small river, where a bridge was made whereon the people passed, and Benit Fernandez, a Portugall, fell off from it, and was drowned. As soone as the Governour had passed the river, a little distance thence he found a towne called Achese. The Indians had no notice of the Christians: they leaped into a river: some men and women were taken; among which was one that understood the youth which guided the Governour to Yupaha: whereby that which he had reported was more confirmed. For they had passed through countries of divers languages, and some which he understood not. The Governour sent by one of the Indians that were taken to call the cacique, which was on the other side of the river. Hee came and made this speech following:

Right high, right mightie, and excellent lord, those things which seldome happen doe cause admiration. What then may the sight of your lordship and your people doe to mee and mine, whom we never saw? especially being mounted on such fierce beasts as your horses are, entring with such violence and furie into my countrie, without my knowledge of your comming. It was a thing so strange, and caused such feare and terrour in our mindes, that it was not in our power to stay and receive your lordship with the solemnitie due to so high and renowned a prince, as your lordship is. And

marginal notes: Excellent colours. / A small river. / Achese.

[1] *i.e.*, the gipsies.

trusting in your greatnesse and singular vertues, I doe not onely
hope to be freed from blame, but also to receive favours: and
the first which I demand of your lordship is, that you will
use me, my countrie, and subjects as your owne: and the
second, that you will tell me who you are, and whence you
come, and whither you goe, and what you seeke, that I the
better may serve you therein.

The Governour answered him, that hee thanked him as
much for his offer and good will, as if hee had received it,
and as if hee had offered him a great treasure: and told him
that he was the sonne of the sun, and came from those parts
where he dwelt, and travelled through that countrie, and
sought the greatest lord and richest province that was in it.
The cacique told him, that farther forward dwelt a great
lord, and that his dominion was called Ocute. He gave
him a guide, and an interpretour for that province. The
Governour commanded his Indians to bee set free, and tra-
velled through his countrie up a river very well inhabited. _{A river very well inha-bited.}
He departed from his towne the first of Aprill; and left a
very high crosse of wood set up in the middest of the market
place; and because the time gave no more leasure, hee declared to him onely, that that crosse was a memorie of the
same, whereon Christ, which was God and man, and created
the heavens and the earth, suffered for our salvation: therefore he exhorted them that they should reverence it: and
they made shew as though they would doe so. The fourth
of Aprill the Governour passed by a towne called Altamaca, _{Altamaca.}
and the 10 of the moneth he came to Ocute. The cacique _{Ocute.}
sent him two thousand Indians with a present, to wit, many
conies, and partriges, bread of maiz, two hens, and many _{Conies, par-triges, hens, dogges.}
dogs: which among the Christians were esteemed as if they
had been fat wethers, because of the great want of flesh
meate and salt, and hereof in many places and many times
was great need; and they were so scarse, that if a man fell
sicke, there was nothing to cherish him withall; and with a

H

sicknesse, that in another place easilie might have been re-
medied, he consumed away till nothing but skinne and bones
were left : and they died of pure weaknes, some of them
saying, If I had a slice of meate, or a few cornes of salt, I
should not die.   The Indians want no fleshmeat : for they
kill with their arrowes many deere, hennes, conies, and other
wild fowle : for they are very cunning at it : which skill the
Christians had not : and though they had it, they had no
leisure to use it : for the most part of the time they spent in
travell, and durst not presume to straggle aside.   And because they were thus scanted of flesh, when sixe hundred men
that went with Soto, came to any towne, and found thirty or
forty dogs, he that could get one and kill it, thought himselfe
no small man : and he that killed it, and gave not his captaine one quarter, if he knew it, he frowned on him, and
made him feele it, in the watches, or in any other matter of
labour that was offered, wherein hee might doe him a dis-
pleasure.   On Monday the 12 of Aprill, the Governour departed from Ocute : the cacique gave him two hundred
Tamenes, to wit, Indians to carrie burdens : hee passed
through a towne, the lord whereof was named Cofaqui, and
came to a province of an Indian lord, called Patofa, who,
because he was in peace with the lord of Ocute, and with
the other bordering lords, had many daies before notice of
the Governour, and desired to see him : he came to visit him,
and made this speech following.

*Mightie lord, now with good reason I will crave of fortune
to requite this my so great prosperitie with some small adversitie ; and I will count myselfe verie rich, seeing I have obtained that, which in this world I most desired, which is, to
see, and be able to doe your lordship some service.   And
although the tongue bee the image of that which is in the
heart, and that the contentment which I feele in my heart I
cannot dissemble, yet it is not sufficient wholly to manifest
the same.   Where did this your countrie, which I doe*

Cofaqui.
Patofa.

governe, deserve to be visited of so soveraigne and so excel-
lent a prince, whom all the rest of the world ought to obey
and serve ? And those which inhabit it being so base, what
shall be the issue of such happines, if their memorie doe not
represent unto them some adversitie that may betide them,
according to the order of fortune ? If from this day for-
ward we may be capable of this benefit, that your lordship
will hold us for your owne, we cannot faile to be favoured
and maintained in true justice and reason, and to have the
name of men. For such as are void of reason and justice,
may be compared to brute beasts. For mine owne part, from
my very heart with reverence due to such a prince, I offer
my selfe unto your lordship, and beseech you, that in reward
of this my true good will, you will vouchsafe to make use of
mine owne person, my countrie, and subjects.

The Governour answered him, that his offers and good
will declared by the effect, did highly please him, whereof
he would alwaies be mindfull to honour and favour him as
his brother. This countrie, from the first peaceable cacique
unto the province of Patofa, which were fiftie leagues, is a
fat countrie, beautifull, and very fruitfull, and very well *An excellent countrie for 50 leagues.*
watered, and full of good rivers. And from thence to the
port de Spirito Santo, where we first arived in the land of
Florida (which may be three hundred and fifty leagues, little
more or lesse) is a barren land, and the most of it groves of
wild pine trees, low and full of lakes, and in some places
very hie and thicke groves, whither the Indians that were
in armes fled, so that no man could find them, neither could
any horses enter into them. Which was an inconvenience
to the Christians, in regard of the victuals which they found
conveied away; and of the trouble which they had in seeking of Indians to bee their guides.

CHAPTER XIV.

How the Governour departed from the province of Patofa, and went through a desert ; where he and all his men fell into great distresse, and extreme miserie.

In the towne of Patofa, the youth, which the Governour carried with him for an interpretour and a guide, began to fome at the mouth, and tumble on the ground, as one possessed with the divell. They said a gospel over him ; and the fit left him. And he said, that foure daies journie from thence toward the sunne rising, was the province that he spake of. The Indians of Patofa said, that toward that part they knew no habitation ; but that toward the northwest, they knew a province which was called Coça, a verie plentifull countrie, which had very great townes in it. The cacique told the Governour, that if he would go thither, he would give him guides and Indians for burdens ; and if he would goe whither the youth spake of, that he would likewise give him those that he needed : and so, with loving words and offers of courtesie, they tooke their leaves the one of the other. Hee gave him seven hundred Indians to beare burdens. He tooke maiz for foure daies journie. Hee travelled sixe daies by a path, which grew narrow more and more till it was lost altogether. He went where the youth

Two swift rivers. did lead him, and passed two rivers which were waded ; each of them was two crossebow-shot over : the water came to the stirrops, and had so great a current, that it was needfull for the horsemen to stand one before another, that the footemen might passe above them leaning unto them. He

Another great river. came to another river of a greater current and largenes, which was passed with more trouble, because the horses

did swim at the comming out about a lances length. Having
passed this river, the Governor came to a grove of pine-trees,
and threatened the youth, and made as though hee would
have cast him to the dogges, because he had told him a lie,
saying, it was but foure daies journie, and they had travelled
nine, and every day seven or eight leagues ; and the men by Nine daies journie.
this time were growne wearie and weake, and the horses
leane through the great scanting of the maiz. The youth
said, that hee knew not where hee was. It saved him that
he was not cast to the dogges, that there was never another
whom John Ortiz did understand. The Governour with
them two, and with some horsemen and footemen, leaving
the campe in a grove of pine trees, travelled that day five or
six leagues to seek a way, and returned at night very com-
fortlesse, and without finding any signe of way or towne.
The next day there were sundrie opinions delivered, whether
they should goe backe, or what they should doe : and because backward the countrie whereby they had passed was
greatlie spoiled and destitute of maiz, and that which they
brought with them was spent, and the men were very weake,
and the horses likewise, they doubted much whether they
might come to any place where they might helpe themselves.

And besides this, they were of opinion, that going in that
sort out of order, that any Indians would presume to set
upon them, so that with hunger, or with warre, they could
not escape. The Governour determined to send horsemen
from thence every way to seeke habitation ; and the next
day he sent foure captaines, every one a sundrie way with
eight horsemen. At night they came againe, leading their
horses, or driving them with a sticke before ; for they were
so wearie, that they could not lead them ; neither found
they any way nor signe of habitation. The next day, the
Governour sent other foure, with as many horsemen that

could swim, to passe the ose[1] and rivers which they should find, and they had choice horses, the best that were in the campe. The captaines were Baltasar de Gallegos, which went up the river; and John Danusco, downe the river; Alfonso Romo, and John Rodriquez Lobillo went into the inward parts of the land. The Governour brought with him

The great increase of swine.

into Florida thirteene sowes, and had by this time three hundred swine. He commanded every man should have halfe a pound of hog's flesh every day; and this hee did three or foure daies after the maiz was all spent. With this small quantitie of flesh, and some sodden hearbs, with much trouble the people were sustained. The Governour dismissed the Indians of Patofa, because hee had no food to give them; who desiring to accompanie and serve the Christians in their necessitie, making shew that it grieved them very much to returne, untill they had left them in a peopled countrie, returned to their owne home. John Danusco came on Sunday late in the evening, and brought newes that he had found a little towne twelve or thirteen leagues from thence: he brought a woman and a boy that he tooke there; with his comming and with those newes, the Governour and all the rest were so glad, that they seemed at that instant to have returned from death to life.

Aymay.

Upon Monday, the twentie-sixe of Aprill, the Governour departed to go to the towne, which was called Aymay; and the Christians named it the towne of Relief. He left, where the camp had lien, at the foote of a pine tree, a letter buried, and letters carved in the barke of the pine, the contents whereof was this: *Dig here at the foot of this pine, and you shall find a letter.* And this he did, because when the captaines came, which were sent to seeke some habitation, they might see the letter, and know what was become of the Governour, and which way he was gone. There was no

---

[1] *i. e.,* ooze. The Portuguese word is *vasas.*

other way to the towne, but the markes that John Danusco
left made upon the trees. The Governour, with some of
them that had the best horses, came to it on the Monday.
And all the rest inforcing themselves the best they could,
some of them lodged within two leagues of the towne, some
within three and foure, every one as he was able to goe,
and his strength served him. There was found in the towne
a storehouse full of the flowre of parched maiz; and some
maiz, which was distributed by allowance. Here were foure
Indians taken, and none of them would confess any other
thing, but that they knew of none other habitation. The
Governour commanded one of them to be burned; and presently another confessed, that two daies journie from thence,
there was a province that was called Cutifa-Chiqui. Upon
Wednesday came the captaines Baltasar de Gallegos, Alfonso
Romo, and John Rodriquez Lobillo: for they had found
the letter, and followed the way which the Governour had
taken toward the towne. Two men of John Rodriquez companie were lost, because their horses tired: the Governour checked him very sore for leaving them behind, and
sent to seeke them : and as soone as they came, he departed
towards Cutifa-Chiqui. In the way three Indians were
taken, which said, that the Ladie of that countrie had notice
alreadie of the Christians, and staied for them in a towne of
hers. The Governour sent by one of them to offer her his
friendship, and to advertise her how he was comming thither.
The Governour came unto the towne ; and presently there
came foure canoes to him ; in one of them came a sister of
the ladie, and approching to the Governour, she said these
words :

*Excellent lord, my sister sendeth unto you by me to kisse
your lordship's hands, and to signifie unto you, that the
cause why she came not in person is, that she thinketh to do
you greater service staying behind, as she doth, giving order,
that with all speed, al her canoes be readie, that your lord-*

An Indian burned for his false-hood.

Cutifa-Chiqui.

*ship may passe the river, and take your rest, which shall bee
presentlie performed.*

The Governour gave her thankes, and she returned to the
other side of the river. Within a little while the Ladie came
out of the towne in a chaire, whereon certaine of the principall Indians brought her to the river. She entred into a
barge, which had the sterne tilted over, and on the floore
her mat readie laied with two cushions upon it one upon
another, where she sate her downe; and with her came her
principall Indians in other barges, which did wait upon her.
She went to the place where the Governor was, and at her
comming she made this speech following :

*Excellent lord, I wish this comming of your lordship into
these your countries, to be most happie : although my power
be not answerable to my wil, and my services be not according
to my desire, nor such as so high a prince as your lordship
deserveth ; yet since the good will is rather to be accepted
then all the treasures of the world, that without it are offered,
with most unfaileable and manifest affection I offer you my
person, lands, and subjects, and this small service.*

And therewithal she presented unto him great store of
clothes of the countrie, which she brought in other canoes;
to wit, mantles and skinnes ; and tooke from her owne necke

A great
cordon of
perles.

a great cordon of perles, and cast it about the necke of the
Governour, entertaining him with very gracious speeches of
love and courtesie, and commanded canoes to be brought

They passe
the river.

thither, wherein the Governour and his people passed the
river. As soone as hee was lodged in the towne, she sent

Cutifa-
Chiqui.

him another present of many hens. This countrie was verie
pleasant, fat, and hath goodly meadows by the rivers. Their

Walnut
trees. Mul-
berry trees,
for silke.
The sea two
daies jour-
nie off.

woods are thin, and ful of walnut trees and mulberrie trees.
They said the sea was two daies journie from thence. Within
a league, and halfe a league about this towne, were great
townes dispeopled, and overgrowne with grasse ; which
shewed that they had been long without inhabitants. The

Indians said, that two yeere before there was a plague in
that countrie, and that they remooved to other townes.
There was in their storehouses great quantitie of clothes,
mantles of yarne made of the barkes of trees, and others made Mantles of the barkes of trees.
of feathers, white, greene, red, and yellow, very fine after Mantles of feathers.
their use, and profitable for winter. There were also many
deeres skinnes, with many compartiments traced in them;
and some of them made into hose, stockings, and shooes.
And the ladie perceiving that the Christians esteemed the
perles, advised the Governour to send to search certaine
graves that were in that towne, and that hee should find
many; and that if hee would send to the dispeopled townes,
he might load all his horses.

They sought the graves of that towne, and there found
foureteene rooves of perles, and little babies and birds made Three hundred ninetie two pounds of pearles found.
of them. The people were browne, well made, and well
proportioned, and more civill then any others that were
seene in all the countrie of Florida; and all of them went
shod and clothed.

The youth told the Governour that hee began now to
enter into the land which he spake of; and some credit was
given him that it was so, because hee understood the language of the Indians; and hee requested that he might bee
christened, for he said hee desired to become a Christian.
Hee was christened, and named Peter; and the Governour
commanded him to bee loosed from a chaine, in which, untill
that time, he had gone.

This countrie, as the Indians reported, had been much
inhabited, and had the fame of a good countrie. And, as it
seemeth, the youth, which was the Governour's guide, had
heard of it, and that which he knew by heresay, hee affirmed
that hee had seene, and augmented at his pleasure. In this
towne was found a dagger, and beades, that had belonged to This towne was but two daies journie from the haven of Santa Helena.
Christians. The Indians reported, that Christians had been
in the haven, which was two daies' journie from this towne,

many yeeres agoe. Hee that came thither was the governour, the Licenciate Lucas Vasquez de Ayllon, which went
to conquer this countrie; and at his comming to the port hee
died: and there was a division, quarrels, and slaughters
betweene some principall men which went with him, for the
principall government. And without knowing any thing of
the countrie, they returned home to Hispaniola. All the
companie thought it good to inhabit that countrie, because
it was a temperat climate; and that if it were inhabited, al
the shippes of New Spaine, of Peru, Santa Martha, and
Tierra firme, in their returne for Spaine, might well touch
there, because it was in their way, and because it was a good
countrie, and sited fit to raise commoditie. The Governour,
since his intent was to seeke another treasure like that of
Atabalipa, lord of Peru, was not contented with a good
countrie, nor with pearles, though many of them were worth
their weight in gold. And if the countrie had been divided
among the Christians, those which the Indians had fished
for afterward, would have been of more value; for those
which they had, because they burned them in the fire, did
leese their colour.[1] The Governour answered them that
urged him to inhabit, that in all the countrie there were not
victuals to sustaine his men one moneth, and that it was
needfull to resort to the port of Ocus, where Maldonado was
to stay for them; and that if no richer countrie were found,
they might returne againe to that whensoever they would;
and in the meane time the Indians would sow their fields,
and it would be better furnished with maiz.

He inquired of the Indians, whether they had notice of
any great lord farther into the land. They told him, that
twelve daies journie from thence, there was a province called
Chiaha, subject to the lord of Coça. Presently, the Governour determined to seeke that land. And being a sterne

In the yeere 1525.

It is in 32 degrees ½.

Chiaha 12 daies jour-
nie from Santa He-
lena; and Coste 7
daies journie
from Chia-
ha; at which
towne of
Coste they
had an oxe
hide.—
Chap. 16.

[1] Old word for "*lose*", from the Anglo-Saxon "*leosan*".
"No cause nor client fat, will Chevril leese,
But as they come on both sides he takes fees."—*Ben Jonson.*

man, and of few words, though he was glad to sift and know the opinion of all men, yet after hee had delivered his owne, hee would not be contraried, and alwaies did what liked himselfe, and so all men did condescend unto his will. And though it seemed an errour to leave that countrie (for others might have been sought round about, where the people might have been sustained untill the harvest had been readie there, and the maiz gathered), yet there was none that would say any thing against him after they knew his resolution.

CHAPTER XV.

How the Governour departed from Cutifa-Chiqui to seeke the province of Coça; and what happened unto him in the way.

The Governour departed from Cutifa-Chiqui the third day of May. And because the Indians had revolted, and the will of the ladie was perceived, that if she could, she would depart without giving any guides or men for burdens, for the wrongs which the Christians had done to the Indians (for there never want some among many of a base sort, that for a little gaine doe put themselves and others in danger of undoing): the Governour commanded her to be kept in safegard, and carried with him, not with so good usage as she deserved for the good wil she shewed, and good entertainement that she had made him. And he verified that old proverb which saith: " For weldoing I receive evil." And so he carried her on foot, with his bondwomen to look unto her. In all the townes where the Governour passed, the ladie commanded the Indians to come and carrie the burdens from one towne to another. We passed through her countrie an hundred leagues, in which, as we saw, she was much obeyed. For the Indians did all that she commanded them with great efficacie and diligence. Peter, the youth that was our guide, said, that she was not the ladie herselfe, but a

neece of hers, which came to that towne to execute certaine
principal men by commandement of the ladie, which had
withheld her tribute ; which words were not beleeved, because
of the lies which they had found in him before : but they
bare with all things, because of the need which they had of him,
to declare what the Indians said. In seven daies space the
Governour came to a province called Chalaque, the poorest

Chalaque, seven daies journie from Cutifa-Chiqui.

country of maiz that was seene in Florida. The Indians fed
upon rootes and herbes, which they seeke in the fields, and
upon wild beasts, which they kil with their bowes and arrowes : and it is a verie gentle people. All of them goe
naked, and are very leane. There was a lord, which for a
great present, brought the Governour two deeres skins : and
there were in that countrie many wild hennes.[1] In one towne

700 hennes.

they made him a present of seven hundred hennes, and so in
other townes they sent him those which they had or could
get. From this province to another, which is called Xualla,

Xualla five daies off.

he spent five daies : here he found very little maiz; and for this
cause, though the people were wearied, and the horses very
weake, he staied no more but two daies. From Ocute to Cutifa-
Chiqui, may bee some hundred and thirtie leagues, whereof
eighty are wildernesse. From Cutifa-Chiqui to Xualla, two
hundred and fiftie, and it is an hillie countrie. The Governour

Rough and hie hilles.

departed from Xualla toward Guaxule : he passed very rough
and hie hilles. In that journie, the ladie of Cutifa-Chiqui (whom
the Governour carried with him, as is aforesaid, with purpose
to carrie her to Guaxule, because her territorie reached thither) going on a day with the bondwomen which lead her, went
out of the way, and entered into a wood, saying, she went to
ease herselfe, and so she deceived them, and hid herselfe in
the wood ; and though they sought her they could not find
her. She carried away with her a little chest made of canes,
in manner of a coffer, which they call Petaca, full of unbored
perles. Some which could judge of them, said, that they
were of great value. An Indian woman that waited on her

[1] Probably the prairie hen, a species of grouse, is alluded to.

did carrie them. The Governour, not to discontent her altogether, left them with her, making account that in Guaxule
he would ask them of her, when he gave her leave to returne:
which coffer she carried away, and went to Xualla with three
slaves which fled from the campe, and one horseman which
remained behinde, who falling sick of an ague, went out of
the way and was lost. This man, whose name was Alimamos,
dealt with the slaves to change their evill purpose, and returne
with him to the Christians: which two of them did; and
Alimamos and they overtooke the Governour fifty leagues
from thence, in a province called Chiaha; and reported how
the ladie remained in Xualla with a slave of Andrew de
Vasconcellos, which would nòt come backe with them, and
that of a certaintie they lived as man and wife together, and
meant to goe both to Cutifa-Chiqui. Within five daies the
Governour came to Guaxule. The Indians there gave him a Guaxule five
daies off.
present of three hundred dogges, because they saw the Chris-
tians esteeme them, and sought them to feed on them: for
among them they are not eaten. In Guaxule, and all that
way, was very little maiz. The Governour sent from thence
an Indian with a message to the cacique of Chiaha, to desire
him to gather some maiz thither, that he might rest a few
daies in Chiaha. The Governour departed from Guaxule,
and in two daies journie came to a towne called Canasagua. Canasagua
two daies
journie off.
Great store
of mulberrie
trees to make
silke.
There met him on the way twenty Indians, every one loaden
with a basket ful of mulberries: for there be many, and those
very good, from Cutifa-Chiqui thither, and so forward in
other provinces, and also nuts and plummes. And the trees
grow in the fields without planting or dressing them, and are
as big and as rancke as though they grew in gardens digged
and watered. From the time that the Governour departed
from Canasagua, hee journied five daies through a desert;
and two leagues before hee came to Chiaha, there met him
fifteen Indians loaden with maiz, which the cacique had sent;
and they told him on his behalfe, that he waited his comming

with twenty barnes full of it ; and farther, that himselfe, his countrie, and subjects, and all things els, were at his service.

June 5. Chiaha five daies jour- nie off, and fifty leagues from Xualla. On the 5 day of June, the Governor entred into Chiaha: the cacique voided his owne houses, in which he lodged, and received him with much joy, saying these words following:

Mightie and excellent lord, I hold myselfe for so happie a man, in that it hath pleased your lordship to use me, that nothing could have happened unto me of more contentment, nor that I would have esteemed so much. From Guaxule your lordship sent unto me, that I should prepare maiz for you in this towne for two months. Here I have for you twenty barnes full of the choisest that in all the countrie could be found. If your lordship bee not entertained by me in such sort, as is fit for so hie a prince, respect my tender age, which excuseth me from blame, and receive my good will, which with much loyaltie, truth, and sinceritie, I will alwaies shew in anything which shall concerne your lordships service.

The Governor answered him that he thanked him very much for his service and offer, and that he would alwaies account him as his brother. There was in this towne much butter in The fat of beares. gourds, melted like oile : they said it was the fat of beares. Oile of wal- nuts. There was found also great store of oile of walnuts, which was cleare as butter, and of a good taste, and a pot full of Honie of bees. honie of bees, which neither before nor afterward was seene Chiaha seat- ed in an island. in all the countrie. The towne was in an island, betweene two armes of a river, and was seated nigh one of them. The river divideth itselfe into those two branches two crossebow shot above the towne, and meeteth againe a league beneath the same. The plaine betweene both the branches is some- times one crossebow shot, sometimes two crossebow shot over. The branches are very broad, and both of them may be waded over. There were all along them verie good meadows, and manie fields sowne with maiz. And because the Indians staied in their towne, the Governour only lodged in the houses of the cacique, and his people in the fields ; where there was ever a tree, everie one tooke one for himselfe. Thus the camp lay separated one from another, and out of order. The Governour winked at it, because the Indians were in peace, and because it was very hot, and the people should have suffered great extremitie, if it had not bin so. The horses came thither so weake, that for feeblenesse they were not able to carrie their masters : because that from Cutifa-Chiqui, they alwaies travelled with verie little provender, and were hunger-starved and tired ever since they came from the desert of Ocute. And because the most of them were not in case to use in battell, though need should require, they sent them to feed in the night a quarter of a league from the camp. The Christians were there in great danger, because that if at this time the Indians had set upon them, they had been in evill case to have defended themselves. The Governour rested there thirtie daies, in which time, because the countrie was very fruitfull, the horses grew fat. At the time of his departure, by the importunitie of some, which would have more then was reason, hee demanded of the cacique thirty women to make slaves of. Hee answered that he would conferre with his chiefe men. And before hee returned an answere, one night all of them with their wives and children forsooke the towne, and fled away. The next day the Governour purposing to goe to seeke them, the cacique came unto him, and at his comming used these words unto the Governour :

Mightie lord, with shame and feare of your lordship, because my subjects against my will have done amisse in absenting themselves, I went my way without your license ; and knowing the errour which I have committed, like a loyall subject, I come to yeeld myselfe into your power, to dispose of mee at your owne pleasure. For my subjects do not obey mee, nor doe any thing but what an uncle of mine commandeth, which governeth this countrie for me, until I be of a perfect age. If your lordship will pursue them, and execute on them

The desert of Ocute.— Chap. 14.

Thirty daies rest.

that, which for their disobedience they deserve, I will be your
guide, since at this present my fortune will not suffer me to
performe any more.

Presently the Governour, with thirty horsemen, and as
many footemen, went to seeke the Indians, and passing by
some townes of the principall Indians which had absented
themselves, hee cut and destroyed great fields of maiz, and
went up the river, where the Indians were in an island,
where the horsemen could not come at them. There he sent
them word by an Indian to returne to their towne, and feare
nothing, and that they should give him men to carrie burdens, as al those behind had done; for he would have no
Indian women, seeing they were so loth to part with them.
The Indians accepted his request, and came to the Governour to excuse themselves; and so all of them returned to
their towne.

Certaine
townes.

A cacique of a province called Coste, came to this town to
visit the Governour. After hee had offered himselfe, and
passed with him some words of tendring his service and
curtesie, the Governour asking him whether he had notice of
any rich countrie? He said, Yea; to wit, that toward the
north there was a province named Chisca; and that there
was a melting of copper, and of another metall of the same
colour, save that it was finer, and of a farre more perfect
colour, and farre better to the sight, and that they used it
not so much, because it was softer. And the selfe same
thing was told the Governour in Cutifa-Chiqui, where
we saw some little hatchets of copper, which were said
to have a mixture of gold. But in that part the country
was not well peopled; and they said there were mountaines, which the horses could not passe; and for that
cause, the Governour would not goe from Cutifa-Chiqui
directly thither. And he made account, that travelling
through a peopled countrie, when his men and horses should
bee in better plight, and hee were better certified of the truth

Mines of
copper and
gold in Chis-
ca toward
the north.

Hatchets of
copper hold-
ing gold.

Chisca is di-
rectly north
from Cutifa
Chiqui,
which is
within two
daies of
Santa He-
lena.

of the thing, he would returne toward it by mountaines, and a better inhabited countrie, whereby hee might have better passage. He sent two Christians from Chiaha with certaine Indians which knew the countrie of Chisca, and the language thereof, to view it, and to make report of that which they should find ; where he told them that he would tarrie for them.

Two Christians sent from Chiaha to seeke Chisca.

CHAPTER XVI.

How the Governor departed from Chiaha, and at Coste was in danger to have been slaine by the hands of the Indians, and by a stratageme escaped the same; and what more happened unto him in this journie, and how he came to Coça.

When the Governour was determined to depart from Chiaha to Coste, he sent for the cacique to come before him, and with gentle words tooke his leave of him, and gave him certaine things, wherewith he rested much contented. In seven daies hee came to Coste. The second of Julie he commanded his campe to be pitched two crossebow shot from the town, and with eight men of his guard he went where he found the cacique, which to his thinking received him with great love. As hee was talking with him, there went from the campe certaine footemen to the towne to seeke some maiz ; and not contented with it, they ransacked and searched the houses, and tooke what they found. With this despite the Indians began to rise and to take their armes ; and some of them with cudgils in their hands, ran upon five or sixe Christians which had done them wrong, and beat them at their pleasure. The Governour seeing them al in an uprore, and himselfe among them with so few Christians, to escape their hands used a stratagem, farre against his owne disposition, being, as hee was, very francke and open ;

Coste seven daies from Chiaha.— Chap. 14.

A wise stratagem.

K

and though it grieved him very much that any Indian should
be so bold, as with reason, or without reason, to despise the
Christians, he tooke up a cudgel, and tooke their parts against
his owne men, which was a meanes to quiet them. And presently he sent word by a man very secretly to the campe,
that some armed men should come toward the place where
he was; and hee tooke the cacique by the hand, using very
mild words unto him, and with some principall Indians that
did accompanie him he drew them out of the towne into a
plaine way, and unto the sight of the campe, whither by
little and little with good discretion the Christians began to
come and to gather about them. Thus the Governour led
the cacique and his chiefe men untill he entred with them
into the campe; and neere unto his tent hee commanded
them to be put in safe custodie, and told them, that they
should not depart without giving him a guide, and Indians
for burthens, and till certaine sicke Christians were come,
which he had commanded to come downe the river in canoes
from Chiaha, and those also which he had sent to the province of Chisca (for they were not returned, and he feared
that the Indians had slaine the one and the other). Within

Those which
were sent
to seeke
Chisca re-
turne. three daies after, those which were sent to Chisca returned,
and made report, that the Indians had carried them through
a countrie so poore of maiz, and so rough, and over so high

High moun-
taines. mountaines, that it was impossible for the armie to travell
that way; and that seeing the way grew very long, and that

A little poor
towne. they lingered much, they consulted to returne from a little
poore towne, where they saw nothing that was of any profit,

An oxe hide
with haire
like wooll.
Chap. 26,
and Gomara
Histor. Ge-
neral, chap.
215, saith so.
Tali 1 day
from Coste. and brought an oxe hide, which the Indians gave them, as
thinne as a calves skinne, and the haire like a soft wooll,
betweene the course and fine wooll of sheepe.[1] The cacique
gave a guide, and men for burdens, and departed with the

[1] The 215th chapter of Lopez de Gomara's *Historia general de las
Indias*, 1554, referred to in the margin by Hakluyt, describes the *vacas
corcobadas*, *i. e.* hump-backed oxen, which may be clearly identified with
the bison.

Governour's leave. The Governour departed from Coste the ninth of Julie, and lodged at a towne called Tali. The cacique came foorth to receive him on the way, and made this speech :

Excellent lord and prince, worthie to be served and obeyed of all the princes in the world ; howsoever for the most part by the outward physiognomie, the inward vertue may bee judged, and that who you are, and of what strength, was knowne unto mee before now : I will not inferre hereupon how meane I am in your presence, to hope that my poore services will bee gratefull and acceptable, since whereas strength faileth, the will doth not cease to be praised and accepted. And for this cause I presume to request your lordship, that you will be pleased onely to respect the same, and consider wherein you will command my services in this your countrie.

The Governour answered him, that his good will and offer was as acceptable unto him, as if he had offered him all the treasures of the world, and that he would alwaies intreate, favour, and esteeme him, as if he were his owne brother. The cacique commanded provision necessarie for two daies, while the Governour was there, to be brought thither ; and at the time of his departure he gave him foure women and two men, which hee had need of to beare burthens.

The Governour travelled six daies through many townes subject to the cacique of Coça; and as he entred into his countrie, many Indians came unto him every day from the cacique, and met him on the way with messages, one going and another comming. Hee came to Coça upon Friday, the 26 of Julie. The cacique came foorth to receive him two crossebow shot from the towne in a chaire, which his principall men carried on their shoulders, sitting upon a cushion, and covered with a garment of marterns, of the fashion and bignes of a woman's huke[1]; hee had on his head a diadem of feathers, and round about him many Indians playing upon

Many townes of Coça.

Coça, Julie 26.

Marterns.

---

[1] A kind of mantle, or cloak, worn in Spain and the Low Countries. Huque, *Fr.;* huca, low Latin. *Nares' Glossary.*

flutes, and singing. As soone as he came unto the Governour, he did his obeysance, and uttered these words following :

*Excellent and mightie lord, above all them of the earth ;
although I come but now to receive you, yet I have received
you manie daies agoe in my heart, to wit, from the day wherein
I had first notice of your lordship ; with so great desire to
serve you, with so great pleasure and contentment, that this
which I make shew of, is nothing in regard of that which is
in my heart, neither can it have any kind of comparison.
This you may hold for certaine, that to obtaine the dominion
of the whole world, would not have rejoyced me so much, as
your sight, neither would I have held it for so great a felicitie.
Doe not looke for me to offer you that which is your owne,
to wit, my person, my lands, and subjects : onely I will busie
myselfe in commanding my men with all diligence and due
reverence to welcome you from hence to the towne with playing and singing, where your lordship shall be lodged and attended upon by myselfe and them : and all that I possesse,
your lordship shall use as it were your owne. For your lordship shall doe me a verie great favour in so doing.*

The Governour gave him thankes, and with great joy they
both went conferring together, till they came to the towne ;
and he commanded his Indians to void their houses, wherein
the Governor and his men were lodged. There was in the
barnes, and in the fields, great store of maiz and french
beanes. The country was greatly inhabited with many great
townes, and many sowne fields, which reached from the one
to the other. It was pleasant, fat, full of good meadows upon
rivers. There were in the fields many plum trees, as well of
such as grow in Spaine, as of the countrie, and wild tall
vines, that runne up the trees ; and besides these, there were
other low vines, with big and sweet grapes[1]; but for want of

The towne.
Many great townes.
Many plum trees of divers sorts.
Two sorts of grapes.

[1] Theodore Irving, in his Conquest of Florida, quoting Bancroft, says :
" This is supposed to have been the same native grape, called the Isabella,
which has since been cultivated."

digging and dressing, they had great kirnels in them. The
Governour used to set a guard over the caciques, because
they should not absent themselves, and carried them with
him, till he came out of their countries; because that carrying them along with him, he looked to find people in the
townes, and they gave him guides, and men to carrie burdens; and before hee went out of their countries, he gave
them licence to returne to their houses, and to their porters
likewise, as soone as he came to any other lordship, where
they gave him others.

The men of Coça seeing their lord detained, tooke it in
evil part, and revolted, and hid themselves in the woods, as
well those of the towne of the cacique as those of the other
townes of his principall subjects. The Governour sent out
foure captaines, every one his way to seeke them. They
tooke many men and women, which were put into chaines.
They seeing the hurt which they received, and how little
they gained in absenting themselves, came againe, promising
to do whatsoever they were commanded. Of those which
were taken prisoners, some principall men were set at libertie,
whom the cacique demanded; and every one that had any,
carried the rest in chaines like slaves, without letting them
goe to their countrie; neither did any returne, but some
few, whose fortune helped them with the good diligence
which they used to file off their chaines by night, or such as
in their travelling could slippe aside out of the way, seeing
any negligence in them that kept them; some escaped away
with the chaines, and with the burdens, and clothes which
they carried.

CHAPTER XVII.

How the Governour went from Coça to Tascaluca.

The Governour rested in Coça twenty-five daies. He de-
20 of Aug. parted from thence the 20 of August, to seeke a province
called Tascaluca : hee carried with him the cacique of Coça.
Tallimuchase He passed that day by a great towne called Tallimuchase,
a great
towne. the people were fled : he lodged halfe a league further, neere
Ytava. a brooke. The next day he came to a towne called Ytava,
subject to Coça. Hee staied there sixe daies because of a
A great river that passed by it, which at that time was very hie; and
river. as soone as the river suffered him to passe, he set forward,
Ullibahali. and lodged at a towne named Ullibahali. There came to him
on the way, on the caciques behalfe of that province, ten or
twelve principall Indians to offer him his service; all of them
had their plumes of feathers, and bowes and arrowes. The
Governour coming to the towne with twelve horsemen, and
some footemen of his guard, leaving his people a crossebow
shot from the towne, entered into it ; hee found all the Indians with their weapons : and as farre as he could ghesse,
they seemed to have some evill meaning. It was knowne
afterward, that they were determined to take the cacique of
Coça from the Governour, if hee had requested it. The
Governour commanded all his people to enter the towne,
Ullibahali which was walled about, and neere unto it passed a small
walled
about. river. The wall, as well of that, as of others, which after-
The fashion ward we saw, was of great posts thrust deepe into the ground
of their
walles. and very rough, and many long railes as big as ones arme
laid across between them, and the wall was about the height
of a lance, and it was daubed within and without with clay,
and had loope holes. On the other side of the river was a
A towne. towne, where at that present the cacique was. The Govern-

our sent to call him, and hee came presently. After he had
passed with the Governour some words of offering his services, he gave him such men for his cariages as he needed,
and thirtie women for slaves. In that place was a Christian
lost called Mançano, borne in Salamanca, of noble parentage, Great store of good
which went astray to seeke for grapes, whereof there is great
store, and those very good. The day that the Governour grapes.
departed from thence, he lodged at a towne subject to the A towne.
lord of Ullibahali : and the next day hee came to another
towne, called Toasi. The Indians gave the Governour thirtie Toasi.
women, and such men for his cariages as he needed. Hee He travelled ordinarily
travelled ordinarily five or six leagues a day when he travel- five or six leagues a
led through peopled countries: and going through deserts, he day.
marched as fast as he could, to eschew the want of maiz.

From Toasi, passing through some townes subject to a
cacique, which was lord of a province called Tallise, hee travelled five daies. He came to Tallise the 18 of September. Tallise, a great towne.
The towne was great, and situated neere unto a maine river. Sep. 18. A maine
On the other side of the river were other townes, and many river.
fields sowne with maiz. On both sides it was a very plentifull countrie, and had store of maiz : they had voided the
towne. The Governour commanded to call the cacique, who
came, and betweene them passed some words of love and
offer of his services, and hee presented unto him forty Indians. There came to the Governour in this towne a principall Indian in the behalfe of the cacique of Tascaluca, and
made this speech following :

*Mightie, vertuous, and esteemed lord, the great cacique of
Tascaluca, my lord, sendeth by me to kisse your lordships
hands, and to let you understand, that he hath notice, how
you justly ravish with your perfections and power all men on
the earth ; and that everie one by whom your lordship passeth
doth serve and obey you ; which he acknowledgeth to be due
unto you, and desireth as his life, to see, and to serve your
lordship. For which cause by me he offereth himselfe, his*

*lands and subjects, that when your lordship pleaseth to go
through his countrie, you may be received with all peace and
love, served and obeyed; and that in recompense of the desire
he hath to see you, you will doe him the favour to let him
know when you will come : for how much the sooner, so much
the greater favour he shall receive.*

The Governour received and dispatched him graciously,
giving him beades, which among them were not much esteemed, and some other things to carrie to his lord. And he gave
licence to the cacique of Coça to returne home to his owne
countries. The cacique of Tallise gave him such men for burthens as he needed. And after he had rested there twenty daies,
hee departed thence toward Tascaluca. That day when hee
went from Tallise, hee lodged at a great towne called Casiste.
And the next day passed by another, and came to a small
towne of Tascaluca ; and the next day hee camped in a wood
two leagues from the towne where the cacique resided, and
was at that time. And he sent the master of the campe, Luys
de Moscoso, with fifteen horsemen, to let him know how hee
was comming. The cacique was in his lodgings under a
canopie : and without doores, right against his lodgings, in
an high place, they spread a mat for him, and two cushions
one upon another, where he sat him downe, and his Indians
placed themselves round about him, somewhat distant from
him, so that they made a place, and a void roome where he
sate : and his chiefest men were neerest to him, and one with
a shadow of deeres skinne, which kept the sunne from him,
being round, and of the bignes of a target, quartered with
black and white, having a rundell[1] in the middest : a farre off
it seemed to be of taffata, because the colours were very perfect. It was set on a small staffe stretched wide out. This
was the device which hee carried in his warres. Hee was a
man of very tall stature, of great limmes, and spare, and well

(margin) Casiste, a great towne.

(margin) Tascaluca.

[1] A rundle, or circle, from the *Fr.* rondelle, which in Cotgrave is
described as " a buckler, or little target"

proportioned, and was much feared of his neighbours and subjects. He was lord of many territories and much people. In his countenance hee was very grave. After the master of the campe had spoken with him, he and those that went with him coursed their horses, pransing them to and fro, and now and then toward the place where the cacique was, who with much gravitie and dissimulation now and then lifted up his eies, and beheld them as it were with disdaine. At the Governours comming, hee made no offer at all to rise. The Governour tooke him by the hand, and both of them sat downe together on a seate which was under the cloth of estate. The cacique said these words unto him :

Mighty lord, I bid your lordship right hartily welcome. I receive as much pleasure and contentment with your sight, as if you were my brother whom I dearely loved : upon this point it is not needfull to use many reasons ; since it is no discretion to speake that in many wordes which in few may be uttered. How much the greater the will is, so much more giveth it name to the workes, and the workes give testimonie of the truth. Now touching my will, by it you shall know, how certain and manifest it is, and how pure inclination I have to serve you. Concerning the favour which you did me, in the things which you sent me, I make as much account of them as is reason to esteeme them : and chiefly because they were yours. Now see what service you will command me.

The Governour satisfied him with sweet words, and with great brevitie. When hee departed from thence, he determined to carrie him along with him for some causes, and at two daies journie hee came to a towne called Piache, by which *Piache.* there passed a great river. The Governour demanded canoes *A great river.* of the Indians : they said, they had them not, but that they would make rafts of canes and drie timber, on which he might passe well enough. And they made them with all diligence and speed, and they governed them ; and because

L

the water went very slow, the Governour and his people passed very well.

From the port de Spirito Santo to Apalache, which is about an hundred leagues, the Governour went from east to west; and from Apalache to Cutifa-Chiqui, which are four hundred and thirty leagues, from the south-west to the northeast: and from Cutifa-Chiqui to Xualla, which are about two hundred and fiftie leagues, from the south to the north; and from Xualla to Tascaluca, which are two hundred and fiftie leagues more, an hundred and ninetie of them he travelled from east to west, to wit, to the province of Coça: and the other sixty from Coça to Tascaluca, from the north to the south.

Having passed the river of Piache, a Christian went from his companie from thence to seeke a woman slave that was runne away from him, and the Indians either tooke him captive, or slue him. The Governour urged the cacique that he should give account of him, and threatned him, that if he were not found, he would never let him loose. The cacique sent an Indian from thence to Mavilla, whither they were travelling, which was a towne of a principall Indian and his subject, saying, that he sent him to advise them to make readie victuals, and men for carriages. But (as afterward appeared) hee sent him to assemble all the men of warre thither, that hee had in his countrie.

The Governour travelled three daies; and the third day he passed all day through a peopled countrie: and he came to
Mavilla. 18 of October. Mavilla upon Monday the 18 of October. He went before the camp with fifteen horsemen and thirty footemen. And from the towne came a Christian, whom he had sent to the principall man three or foure daies before, because he should not absent himselfe, and also to learne in what sort the Indians were: who told him that hee thought they were in an evill purpose: for while hee was there, there came manie people into the towne, and many weapons, and that they

made great haste to fortifie the wall.   Luys de Moscoço told Mavilla walled.
the Governour, that it would bee good to lodge in the field,
seeing the Indians were of such disposition: and hee answered,
that he would lodge in the towne, for hee was wearie of lodging in the field.   When hee came neere unto the towne, the
cacique came foorth to receive him, with many Indians playing upon flutes and singing : and after hee had offered him-
selfe, hee presented him with three mantles of marterns.   The Three man-tles of mar-terns.
Governour, with both the caciques, and seven or eight men
of his guard, and three or foure horsemen, which alighted to
accompanie him, entred into the towne, and sat him downe
under a cloth of estate.   The cacique of Tascaluca requested
him, that hee would let him remaine in that towne, and trouble him no more with travelling : and seeing he would not
give him leave, in his talke he changed his purpose, and
dissemblinglie fained that he would speake with some principall Indians, and rose up from the place where hee sate
with the Governour, and entred into a house, where many
Indians were with their bowes and arrowes.   The Governour when he saw he returned not, called him, and he answered, that he would not come out from thence, neither
would he goe any farther then that towne, and that if he
would goe his way in peace, hee should presently depart,
and should not seeke to carrie him perforce out of his countrie and territorie.

CHAPTER XVIII.

How the Indians rose against the Governour, and what ensued
thereupon.

The Governour seeing the determination and furious
answere of the cacique, went about to pacifie him with faire
words; to which he gave no answere, but rather with much
pride and disdaine withdrew himselfe where the Governour
might not see him, nor speake with him. As a principall
Indian passed that way, the Governor called him, to send
him word that hee might remaine at his pleasure in his
countrie, and that it would please him to give him a guide,
and men for carriages, to see if hee could pacifie him with
mild words. The Indian answered with great pride, that
hee would not hearken unto him. Baltasar de Gallegos, which
stood by, tooke hold of a gowne of marterns which hee had
on, and hee cast it over his head and left it in his hands;
and because all of them immediately began to stirre, Baltasar
de Gallegos gave him such a wound with his coutilas, that
hee opened him downe the backe, and presently all the Indians
with a great crie came out of the houses shooting their
arrowes. The Governour considering that if hee tarried there,
hee could not escape, and if hee commanded his men to come
in, which were without the towne, the Indians within the
houses might kill their horses, and doe much hurt, ranne out
of the towne; and before hee came out, hee fell twice or
thrice, and those that were with him did helpe him up againe;
and he and those that were with him were sore wounded; and
in a moment there were five Christians slaine in the towne.
The Governour came running out of the towne, crying out,
that every man should stand farther off, because from the
wall they did them much hurt. The Indians seeing that the
Christians retired, and some of them, or the most part, more

then an ordinary pase, shot with great boldnesse at them, and strooke downe such as they could overtake. The Indians which the Christians did lead with them in chaines, had laid downe their burthens neere unto the wall; and as soone as the Governour and his men were retired, the men of Mavilla laid them on the Indians backs againe, and tooke them into the towne, and loosed them presently from their chaines, and gave them bowes and arrowes to fight withall. Thus they possessed themselves of al the clothes and perles, and all that the Christians had, which their slaves carried. And because the Indians had been alwaies peaceable untill wee came to this place, some of our men had their weapons in their fardels[1] and remained unarmed. And from others that had entred the towne with the Governour, they had taken swords and halebards, and fought with them. When the Governour was gotten into the field, hee called for an horse, and with some that accompanied him, hee returned and slew two or three Indians. All the rest retired themselves to the towne, and shot with their bowes from the wall. And those which presumed of their nimblenes, sallied foorth to fight a stones cast from the wall; and when the Christians charged them, they retired themselves at their leasure into the towne. At the time that the broile began, there were in the towne a frier and a priest, and a servant of the Governour, with a woman slave; and they had no time to come out of the towne; and they tooke an house, and so remained in the towne.

The Indians being become masters of the place, they shut the doore with a field gate; and among them was one sword which the Governour's servant had, and with it he set himselfe behind the door, thrusting at the Indians which sought to come into them; and the frier and the priest stood on the other side, each of them with a barre in their hands to beate him downe that first came in. The Indians seeing they could not get in by the doore, began to uncover the house

Al the clothes and perles of the Christians were lost.

---

[1] The bundles, or packs, which each man carried.

top. By this time, all the horsemen and footemen which were
behind, were come to Mavilla. Here there were sundrie
opinions, whether they should charge the Indians, to enter
the towne, or whether they should leave it, because it was
hard to enter: and in the end it was resolved to set upon
them.

CHAPTER XIX.

*How the Governour set his men in order, and entred the towne of
Mavilla.*

As soone as the battell and the rereward were come to
Mavilla, the Governour commanded all those that were best
armed to alight, and make foure squadrons of footmen. The
Indians, seeing how he was setting his men in order, concluded with the cacique, that hee should goe his way, saying unto him, as after it was knowne by certaine women that
were taken there, that he was but one man, and could fight
but for one man, and that they had there among them many
principall Indians verie valiant and expert in feates of armes,
that any one of them was able to order the people there; and
forasmuch as matters of warre were subject to casualtie, and
it was uncertaine which part should overcome, they wished
him to save himselfe, to the end that if it fel out that they
should end their daies there, as they determined, rather then
to be overcome, there might remaine one to governe the
countrie. For all this hee would not have gon away: but
they urged him so much, that with fifteene or twentie Indians
of his owne, hee went out of the towne, and carried away a
skarlat cloke, and other things of the Christians goods; as
much as hee was able to carrie, and seemed best unto him.
The Governour was informed how there went men out of the
towne, and hee commanded the horsemen to beset it, and

*A consulta-
tion of the
Indians to
send away
their caci-
que.*

sent in every squadron of footemen one souldier with a fire-brand to set fire on the houses, that the Indians might have no defense. All his men being set in order, hee commanded an harcubuz to bee shot off. The signe being given, the foure squadrons, every one by itselfe with great furie, gave the onset, and with great hurt on both sides they entred the towne. The frier and the priest, and those that were with them in the house were saved, which cost the lives of two men of account and valiant, which came thither to succour them. The Indians fought with such courage, that many times they drave our men out of the towne. The fight lasted so long, that for wearinesse and great thirst many of the Christians went to a poole that was neere the wal, to drink, which was all stained with blood of the dead, and then came againe to fight. The Governour seeing this, entered among the foote-men into the towne on horseback, with certaine that accom-panied him, and was a meane that the Christians came to set fire on the houses, and brake.and overcame the Indians, who running out of the towne from the footemen, the horsemen without drave in at the gates again, where being without all hope of life, they fought valiantly, and after the Christians came among them to handy blows, seeing themselves in great distresse without any succour, many of them fled into the burning houses, where one upon another they were smo-thered and burnt in the fire.

The whole number of the Indians that died in this towne, were two thousand and five hundred, little more or lesse. Of the Christians there died eighteene ; of which one was Don Carlos, brother-in-law to the Governour, and a nephew of his, and one John de Games, and Men Rodrigues, Portugals, and John Vasquez de Villanova de Barca Rota, all men of honour, and of much valour : the rest were footemen. Besides those that were slaine, there were an hundred and fiftie wounded with 700 wounds of their arrowes : and it pleased God that of very dangerous wounds they were quickly healed.

The death of 2,500 Indians.

Moreover, there were twelve horses slaine, and seventie hurt.
All the clothes which the Christians carried with them to
clothe themselves withall, and the ornaments to say masse,
and the perles, were all burnt there: and the Christians did
set them on fire themselves, because they held for a greater
inconvenience the hurt which the Indians might doe them
from those houses, where they had gathered all those goods
together, then the losse of them. Here the Governour understood that Francisco Maldonado waited for him at the port of
Ochuse, and that it was sixe daies journie from thence; and
he dealt with John Ortiz to keepe it secret, because he had
not accomplished that which he determined to doe, and
because the perles were burnt there, which he meant to have
sent to Cuba for a shew, that the people, hearing the newes,
might be desirous to come to that countrie. He feared also,
that if they should have newes of him without seeing from
Florida neither gold, nor silver, nor anything of value, it
would get such a name, that no man would seeke to goe
thither, when he should have neede of people. And so he
determined to send no newes of himselfe, untill hee had found
some rich countrie.

The port of Ochuse sixe daies jour-
nie from Mavilla.

CHAPTER XX.

*How the Governour departed from Mavilla toward Chicaça, and what
happened unto him.*

From the time that the Governour entred into Florida,
untill his departure from Mavilla, there died an hundred and
two Christians, some of sickenesse, and others which the
Indians slew. Hee staied in Mavilla, because of the wounded
men, eight and twentie daies; all which time he lay in the
field. It was a well inhabited and a fat countrie: there were

some great and walled townes ; and many houses scattered _{Great and walled townes.}
all about the fields, to wit, a crossebow shot or two the one
from the other.   Upon Sonday the 18th of November, when _{18 of November.}
the hurt men were knowne to bee healed, the Governour
departed from Mavilla.   Every one furnished himselfe with
maiz for two daies, and they travelled five daies through a
desert: they came to a province called Pafallaya, unto a
towne, named Taliepatava; and from thence they went to _{Taliepatava.}
another, called Cabusto : neere unto it ran a great river. _{Cabusto.}
The Indians on the other side cried out, threatning the _{A great river.}
Christians to kill them, if they sought to passe it.   The
Governour commanded his men to make a barge within the
towne, because the Indians should not perceive it : it was
finished in foure daies ; and being ended, he commanded it
to be carried one night upon sleds halfe a league up the
river.   In the morning there entred into it thirtie men well
armed.   The Indians perceived what was attempted, and
those which were neerest came to defend the passage.   They
resisted what they could, till the Christians came neere them ;
and seeing that the barge came to the shore, they fled away _{Canavarales.}
into the groves of canes.

The Christians mounted on horseback, and went up the
river to make good the passage, whereby the Governour and
his companie passed the river.   There were along the river
some townes well stored with maiz and french beanes.   From _{Some townes.}
thence to Chicaça the Governour travelled five daies through
a desert.   Hee came to a river, where on the other side were _{A river.}
Indians to defend the passage.   He made another barge in
two daies ; and when it was finished, the Governour sent an
Indian to request the cacique to accept of his friendship, and
peaceably to expect his comming, whom the Indians that were
on the other side the river slew before his face, and presently,
making a great shout, went their way.

Having passed the river, the next day, being the 17th of _{December 17}
December, the Governour came to Chicaça, a small towne of _{Chicaça.}

twentie houses. And after they were come to Chicaça, they were much troubled with cold, because it was now winter and

Snow and much cold.

it snowed, while most of them were lodged in the field, before they had time to make themselves houses. This countrie was very well peopled, and the houses scattered like those of Mavilla, fat and plentifull of maiz, and the most part of it was fielding: they gathered as much as sufficed to passe the winter. Some Indians were taken, among which was one whom the cacique esteemed greatly. The Governour sent an Indian to signifie to the cacique that he desired to see him, and to have his friendship. The cacique came unto him to offer his person, countrie, and subjects, and told him that he would cause two other caciques to come to him in peace; who, within few daies after, came with him, and with their Indians: the one was called Alimamu, the other Nicalasa.

Conies.

They gave a present unto the Governour of an hundred and fiftie conies, and of the countrie garments, to wit, of mantles and skinnes. The cacique of Chicaça came to visit him many times; and sometimes the Governour sent to call him, and sent him an horse to goe and come. He complained unto him, that a subject of his was risen against him, and deprived him of his tribute, requesting his aide against him, for hee meant to seeke him in his countrie, and to punish him accord-

An Indian stratageme.

ing to his desert; which was nothing els but a fained plot. For they determined, as soone as the Governour was gone with him, and the campe was divided into two parts, the one part of them to set upon the Governour, and the other upon them that remained in Chicaça. Hee went to the towne where he used to keep his residence, and brought with him two hundred Indians with their bowes and arrowes. The Governour tooke thirtie horsemen and eightie footemen, and they went to

Saque-chuma. A walled town.

Saquechuma (for so was the province called of that chiefe man, which he said had rebelled): they found a walled town, without any men; and those which went with the cacique set fire on the houses, to dissemble their treason. But by

reason of the great care and heedfulnesse, that was as well
in the Governour's people which hee carried with him, as of
those which remained in Chicaça, they durst not assault them
at that time. The Governour invited the cacique, and certaine principall Indians, and gave them hogges flesh to eate.
And though they did not commonly use it, yet they were so
greedie of it, that every night there came Indians to certaine
houses a crossebow shot from the camp, where the hogges
lay, and killed and carried away as many as they could.
And three Indians were taken in the manner. Two of them
the Governor commanded to be shot to death with arrowes;
and to cut off the hands of the other; and he sent him so
handled to the cacique, who made as though it grieved him
that they had offended the Governour, and that he was glad
that he had executed that punishment on them. He lay in a
plaine countrie halfe a league from the place where the Christians lodged. Foure horsemen went a stragling thither, to
wit, Francisco Osorio, and a servant of the Marques of Astorga,
called Reynoso, and two servants of the Governour, the one
his page, called Ribera, and the other, Fuentes his chamberlaine : and these had taken from the Indians some skinnes,
and some mantles, wherewith they were offended, and forsooke their houses. The Governour knew of it, and commanded them to bee apprehended; and condemned to death
Francisco Osorio and the chamberlaine, as principals; and al
of them to losse of goods. The friers and priests, and other
principall persons, were earnest with him to pardon Francisco
Osorio his life, and to moderate his sentence; which hee
would not grant for any of them. While he was readie to
command them to be drawne to the market-place to cut off
their heads, there came certaine Indians from the cacique to
complaine of them. John Ortiz, at the request of Baltasar
de Gallegos and other persons, changed their words, and told
the Governour, that the cacique said, he had notice how his
lordship held those Christians in prison for his sake, and that

they were in no fault, neither had they done him any wrong, and that if he would do him any favour, he should set them free. And he told the Indians, that the Governour said, he had them in prison, and that he would punish them in such sort, that they should bee an example to others. Hereupon the Governour commanded the prisoners to be loosed. As soone as March was come, hee determined to depart from Chicaça, and demanded of the cacique two hundred men for cariages. He sent him answere, that hee would speake with his principall men.

March 1541.

Upon Twesday the eight of March, the Governour went to the towne where he was, to aske him for the men. Hee told him, he would send them the next day. As soone as the Governour was come to Chicaça, he told Luys de Moscoso, the camp master, that he misliked the Indians, and that he should keepe a strong watch that night, which hee remembred but a little. The Indians came at the second watch in foure squadrons, every one by itselfe; and as soone as they were descried, they sounded a drum, and gave the assault with a great cry, and with so great celeritie, that presently they entred with the scoutes, that were somewhat distant from the campe. And when they were perceived of them which were

Chicaça set on fire by the Indians.

in the towne, halfe the houses were on fire, which they had kindled. That night three horsemen chanced to bee skouts; two of them were of base calling, and the worst men in all the camp, and the other, which was a nephew of the Governour, which untill then was held for a tall man, shewed himselfe there as great a coward as any of them : for all of them ran away. And the Indians without any resistance came and set the towne on fire; and taried without behind the doores for the Christians, which ran out of the houses, not having any leasure to arme themselves; and as they ran hither and thither, amazed with the noise, and blinded with the smoke and flame of the fire, they knew not which way they went, neither could they light upon their weapons, nor saddle their horses,

neither saw they the Indians that shot at them.   Manie of
the horses were burned in the stables, and those which could
breake their halters gat loose.   The disorder and flight was
such, that every man fled which way he could, without leaving any to resist the Indians.   But God (which chastiseth
his according to His pleasure, and in the greatest necessities
and dangers sustaineth them with His hand) so blinded the
Indians, that they saw not what they had done, and thought
that the horses which ran loose were men on horseback,
that gathered themselves together to set upon them.   The
Governour only rod on horsebacke, and with him a soldier
called Tapia, and set upon the Indians ; and striking the first
he met with his lance, the saddle fell with him, which with
haste was evill girded, and so hee fell from his horse.   And
all the people that were on foote were fled to a wood out of
the towne, and there assembled themselves together.   And
because it was night, and that the Indians thought the horses
were men on horsebacke which came to set upon them, as I
said before, they fled ; and one onely remained dead, and
that was he whom the Governour slew with his lance.   The
towne lay all burnt to ashes.   There was a woman burned,
who, after shee and her husband were both gone out of their
house, went in againe for certaine perles, which they had
forgotten ; and when she would have come out, the fire was
so great at the doore that shee could not, neither could her
husband succour her.   Other three Christians came out of
their lodgings so cruelly burned, that one of them died within
three daies, and the other two were carried many daies each
of them upon a couch betweene staves, which the Indians carried on their shoulders, for otherwise they could not travell.
There died in this hurliburlie eleven Christians, and fiftie
horses ; and there remained an hundred hogges, and foure ⟶ The increase
hundred were burned.   If any perchance had saved any ⟵ of hogges.
clothes from the fire of Mavilla, here they were burned, and
many were clad in skinnes, for they had no leasure to take

their coates. They endured much cold in this place, and the
chiefest remedie were great fires. They spent all night in
turnings without sleepe: for if they warmed one side, they
freesed on the other. Some invented the weaving of certaine
mats of drie ivie, and did weare one beneath, and another
above: many laughed at this device, whom afterward necessity inforced to doe the like. The Christians were so spoiled,
and in such want of saddles and weapons which were burned,
that if the Indians had come the second night, they had
overcome them with little labour. They remooved thence to

The towne where the cacique lay. the towne where the cacique was wont to lie, because it was
in a champion[1] countrie. Within eight daies after, there were
Ash trees. many lances and saddles made. There were ash trees in
those parts, whereof they made as good lances as in Biscay.

CHAPTER XXI.

*How the Indians set againe upon the Christians, and how the Governour
went to Alimamu, beyond which towne in warlike sort they
tarried for him in the way.*

Upon Wednesday, the 15 of March 1541, after the Governour had lodged eight daies in a plaine, halfe a league from
the place which he had wintered in, after he had set up
a forge, and tempered the swords which in Chicaça were
burned, and made many targets, saddles, and lances, on
Tuesday night, at the morning watch, many Indians came to
assault the campe in three squadrons, every one by themselves. Those which watched gave the alarme. The Governour with great speed set his men in order in other three
squadrons, and leaving some to defend the campe, went out
to incounter them. The Indians were overcome and put to

---

[1] Champaign.

flight. The ground was champion and fit for the Christians
to take the advantage of them; and it was now breake of
day. But there happened a disorder, whereby there were
not past thirtie or fortie Indians slaine; and this it was, that
a frier cried out in the campe without any just occasion, *To
the campe, To the campe;* whereupon the Governour and
all the rest repaired thither, and the Indians had time to
save themselves. There were some taken, by whom the
Governour informed himselfe of the countrie through which
he was to passe.

The 25 of Aprill he departed from Chicaça, and lodged at ^{25 of April.}
a small towne called Alimamu. They had very little maiz, ^{Alimamu.}
and they were to passe a desert of seven daies journie. The
next day, the Governour sent three captaines, everie one
his way, with horsemen and footemen, to seeke provision to
passe the desert. And John Dannusco, the auditor, went
with fifteene horsemen and forty footemen that way that the
Governour was to goe, and found a strong fort made, where
the Indians staied for him, and many of them walked on the
top of it with their weapons, having their bodies, thighes,
and armes, okered and died with blacke, white, yellow, and ^{Blacke,}
^{white, yel-}
red, striped like unto panes, so that they shewed as though ^{low, and red}
^{colours.}
they went in hose and doublets; and some of them had
plumes, and others had hornes on their heads, and their faces
blacke, and their eies done round about with strakes of red,
to seeme more fierce. As soone as they saw that the Christians approched, with a great crie, sounding two drummes
with great furie, they sallied foorth to receive them. John
Dannusco, and those that were with him, thought good to
avoid them, and to acquaint the Governour therewith. They
retired to a plaine place, a crossebow shot from the fort in
sight of it, the footemen, the crossebowmen, and targetters,
placed themselves before the horsemen, that they might not
hurt the horses. The Indians sallied out by seven and seven,
and eight and eight, to shoote their arrowes, and retired

againe; and in sight of the Christians they made a fire, and
tooke an Indian, some by the feete, and some by the head,
and made as though they went to cast him into the fire, and
gave him first many knocks on the head; signifying, that
they meant so to handle the Christians. John Danusco
sent three horsemen to advertise the Governour hereof. He
came presently; for his intent was to drive them from
thence; saying, that if he did it not, they would be em-
boldned to charge him another time, when they might doe
him more harme. He made the horsemen to alight, and
set his men in foure squadrons; the signe being given, they
set upon the Indians, which made resistance till the Christians came neere the fort, and as soone as they saw they
could not defend themselves, by a place where a brooke
passed neere the fort, they ran away, and from the other side
they shot some arrowes; and because at that instant we knew
no ford for the horses to passe, they had time enough to get
out of our danger. Three Indians were slaine there, and
many Christians were hurt, whereof within few daies there
died fifteene by the way.

All men thought the Governour to bee in fault, because he
sent not to see the disposition of the place on the other side
of the river, and to know the passage before hee set upon
them. For with the hope they had to save themselves by
flight that way, when they saw none other meanes, they
fought till they were broken, and it was an incouragement to
defend themselves untill then, and to offend the Christians
without any danger to themselves.

CHAPTER XXII.

*How the Governour went from Alimamu to Quizquiz, and from thence
to Rio Grande, or the Great River.*

Three daies after they had sought some maiz, whereof
they found but little store, in regard of that which was needfull, and that for this cause, as well for their sakes that were
wounded, it was needfull for them to rest, as for the great
journie they were to march to come where store of maiz was ;
yet the Governour was inforced to depart presentlie toward
Quizquiz. He travelled seven daies through a desert of many ^{A desert of seven daies.}
marishes and thicke woods ; but it might all be travelled on
horseback, except some lakes, which they swamme over.
Hee came to a towne of the province of Quizquiz without ^{A towne of Quizquiz.}
being descried, and tooke all the people in it before they
came out of their houses. The mother of the cacique was
taken there ; and he sent unto him by an Indian, that he
should come to see him, and that he would give him his
mother, and al the people which he had taken there. The
cacique sent him answere againe, that his lordship should
loose and send them to him, and that he would come to visit
and serve him. The Governour, because his people for want
of maiz were somewhat weake and wearie, and the horses
also were leane, determined to accomplish his request, to see
if hee could have peace with him, and so commanded to set
free his mother and all the rest, and with loving words dismissed them, and sent them to him.

The next day, when the Governour expected the cacique,
there came many Indians with their bowes and arrowes, with
a purpose to set upon the Christians. The Governor had
commanded all the horsemen to be armed, and on horsebacke,
and in a readines. When the Indians saw that they were
readie, they staied a crossebow shot from the place where

N

the Governour was, neere a brooke. And after halfe an houre that they had stood there stil, there came to the camp sixe principall Indians, and said, they came to see what

An old prophecie. people they were; and that long agoe they had been informed by their forefathers, that a white people should subdue them; and that therefore they would returne to their cacique, and bid him come presently to obey and serve the Governour: and after they had presented him with sixe or seven skinnes and mantles which they brought, they tooke their leave of him, and returned with the other, which waited for them by the brookes side. The cacique never came againe nor sent other message.

Another towne. And because in the towne where the Governour lodged there was small store of maiz, he remooved to another halfe

Rio Grande, or Rio de Espiritu Sauto.[1] a league from Rio Grande, where they found plentie of maiz. And he went to see the river, and found that neere unto it was great store of timber to make barges, and good situation of ground to incampe in. Presently he remooved himselfe thither. They made houses, and pitched their campe in a plaine field a crossebow shot from the river. And thither was gathered all the maiz of the townes which they had latelie passed. They began presently to cut and hew down timber, and to saw plankes for barges. The Indians came presently down the river; they leaped on shore, and declared to the Governour, that they were subjects of a great lord, whose

Aquixo, a great lord on the west side of Rio Grande. name was Aquixo, who was lord of many townes, and governed many people on the other side of the river, and came to tell him on his behalfe, that the next day he with al his men would come to see what it would please him to command him.

[1] The Mississippi, the great river here referred to, is rightly called by Hakluyt in his marginal note Rio de Espiritu Santo, as is proved by collation with Biedma's account in the appendix to the present work. This name is applied to the Mississippi in Ogilby's map of America, 1671; but in the later Dutch maps was transferred erroneously to the river Apalachicola.

The next day with speed, the cacique came with two hun- Two hundred canoes.

dred canoes full of Indians with their bowes and arrowes, painted, and with great plumes of white feathers, and many other colours, with shields in their hands, wherewith they defended the rowers on both sides, and the men of warre stood from the head to the sterne, with their bowes and arrowes in their hands. The canoe wherein the cacique was, had a tilt[1] over the sterne, and hee sate under the tilt; and so were other canoes of the principall Indians. And from under the tilt where the chiefe man sat, hee governed and commanded the other people. All joyned together, and came within a stones cast of the shore. From thence the cacique said to the Governour, which walked along the rivers side with others that waited on him, that he was come thither to visit, to honour, and to obey him; because he knew he was the greatest and mightiest lord on the earth: therefore he would see what he would command him to doe. The Governour yeelded him thankes, and requested him to come on shore, that they might the better communicate together. And without any answere to that point, hee sent him three canoes, wherein was great store of fish, and loaves made of Loves made of prunes. the substance of prunes,[2] like unto brickes. After he had received al, he thanked him, and prayed him againe to come on shore. And because the caciques purpose was, to see if with dissimulation he might doe some hurt, when they saw that the Governour and his men were in readinesse, they began to goe from the shore; and with a great crie, the crossebowmen which were ready, shot at them, and slue five or sixe of them. They retired with great order; none did leave his oare, though the next to him were slaine; and shielding themselves, they went farther off. Afterward they came many times and landed: and when any of us came toward them, they fled unto their canoes, which were verie Goodly great canoes. pleasant to behold; for they were very great and well made,

---

[1] An awning or canopy.   [2] The persimon—*diospyros Virginiana.*

and had their tilts, plumes, paveses,[1] and flagges, and with the multitude of people that were in them, they seemed to be a faire armie of gallies. In thirtie daies space, while the Governour remained there, they made foure barges : in three of which hee commanded twelve horsemen to enter, in each of them foure ; in a morning, three houres before day, men which hee trusted would land in despight of the Indians, and make sure the passage, or die, and some footemen being crossebowmen went with them, and rowers to set them on the other side. And in the other barge, he commanded John de Guzman to passe with the footemen, which was made captaine instead of Francisco Maldonado. And because the streame was swift, they went a quarter of a league up the river along the bancke, and crossing over, fell downe with the streame, and landed right over against the camp. Two stones-cast before they came to land, the horsemen went out of the barges on horsebacke to a sandie plot of very hard and cleere ground, where all of them landed without any resistance. As soone as those that passed first were on land on the other side, the barges returned to the place where the Governour was : and within two houres after sunne-rising, all the people were over. The river was almost halfe a league broad. If a man stood still on the other side, it could not be discerned whether he were a man or no. The river was of great depth, and of a strong current; the water was alwaies muddie : there came downe the river continually many trees and timber, which the force of the water and streame brought downe. There was great store of fish in it of sundrie sorts, and the most of it differing from the freshwater fish of Spaine, as hereafter shall be shewed.

Foure barges made.

They passe over Rio Grande.

The river here almost halfe a league broad.

---

[1] Waste cloths which hung round about the ship to hinder men from being seen in the fight : literally, shields or bucklers.

CHAPTER XXIII.

*How the Governour departed from Aquixo to Casqui, and from thence to
Pacaha : and how this countrie differeth from that which
we had passed.*

Having passed Rio Grande, the Governour travelled a
league and an halfe, and came to a great towne of Aquixo,
which was dispeopled before hee came thither. They espied
thirtie Indians comming over a plaine, which the cacique sent
to discover the Christians determination : and as soone as
they had sight of them, they tooke themselves to flight. The
horsemen pursued them, and slue tenne, and tooke fifteene.
And because the towne, whither the Governour went, was
neere unto the river, he sent a captaine, with as many men
as he thought sufficient to carrie the barges up the river.
And because in his travelling by land many times he went
farre from the river to compasse the creekes that came from
it, the Indians tooke occasion to set upon them of the barges,
and put them in great danger, because that by reason of the
great current, they durst not leave the shore, and from the
bancke they shot at them.   As soone as the Governour was
come to the towne, hee presently sent crossebow men downe A towne.
the river, which came to rescue them : and upon the comming
of the barges to the towne, hee commanded them to bee
broken, and to save the iron for others, when it should bee
needfull.   Hee lay there one night, and the day following
hee set forward to seeke a province called Pacaha, which Pacaha
hee was informed to bee neere unto Chisca, where the In- Chisca.
dians told him there was gold. He passed through great Great townes.
townes of Aquixo, which were all abandoned for feare of the
Christians.   Hee understood by certaine Indians that were
taken, that three daies journie from thence dwelt a great

cacique, whose name was Casqui. Hee came to a small river, where a bridge was made, by which they passed : that day till sunset they went all in water, which in some places came to the waste, and in some to the knees. When they saw themselves on dry land, they were very glad, because they feared they should wander up and downe as forlorne men al night in the water.

The first
towne of
Casqui. At noone they came to the first towne of Casqui : they found the Indians carelesse, because they had no knowledge of them. There were many men and women taken, and store of goods, as mantles and skinnes, as well in the first towne, Another
towne. as in another, which stood in a field halfe a league from thence in sight of it, whither the horsemen ran. This countrie is higher, drier, and more champion, then any part bordering neere the river, that untill then they had seene. Walnuttrees
with soft
shels. There were in the fields many walnut trees, bearing soft shelled walnuts,[1] in fashion like bullets ; and in the houses they found many of them, which the Indians had laid up in store. The trees differed in nothing else from those of Spaine, nor from those which we had seene before, but onely Many mul-
berrie trees
and plum
trees. that they had a smaller leafe. There were many mulberrie trees and plum trees, which bare red plums like those of Spaine, and other gray, somewhat differing, but farre better. And all the trees are all the yeare so fruitfull, as if they were planted in orchards : and the woods were verie thinne. The Governour travelled two daies through the countrie of Casqui, before hee came to the towne where the cacique was : and the most of the way was alway by champion ground, which Many great
townes. was full of great townes ; so that from one towne, you might see two or three. He sent an Indian to certifie the cacique, that hee was comming to the place where hee was, with intent to procure his friendship, and to hold him as his brother. Whereunto he answered, that he should be welcome, and

[1] The pecan nut—*juglans olivæformis* of Michaux.

that he would receive him with speciall good wil, and accomplish all that his lordship would command him. Hee sent him a present upon the way ; to wit, skinnes, mantles, and fish. And after these compliments, the Governour found all the townes, as he passed, inhabited with people, which peaceablie attended his comming, and offered him skinnes, mantles, and fish. The cacique, accompanied with many Indians, came out of the towne, and staied halfe a league on the way to receive the Governour ; and when hee came to him, he spake these words following :

Right high, right mighty, and renowned lord, your lordship is most hartilie welcome. As soone as I had notice of your lordship, of your power, and your perfections, although you came into my countrie, killing and taking captives the inhabitants thereof and my subjects : yet I determined to conforme my will unto yours, and as your owne to interpret in good part all that your lordship did : beleeving that it was convenient it should be so for some just respect, to prevent some future matter revealed unto your lordship, and concealed from me. For well may a mischiefe be permitted to avoid a greater, and that good may come thereof : which I believe will so fall out. For it is no reason to presume of so excellent a prince, that the noblenesse of his heart and the effect of his will would permit him to suffer any unjust thing. My abilitie is so small to serve you as your lordship deserveth, that if you respect not mine abundant good will, which humblie offereth all kind of service, I deserve but little in your presence. But if it bee reason that this be esteemed, receive the same, my selfe, my countrie, and subjects for yours, and dispose of me and them at your pleasure. For if I were lord of all the world, with the same good will should your lordship by me be received, served, and obeyed.

The Governour answered him to the purpose, and satisfied him in few words. Within a while after, both of them used words of great offers and courtesie the one to the other, and

the cacique requested him to lodge in his houses. The
Governour, to preserve the peace the better, excused himselfe, saying, that hee would lodge in the fields. And because it was very hot, they camped neere certaine trees a
quarter of a league from the towne. The cacique went to
his towne, and came againe with many Indians singing. As
soone as they came to the Governour, all of them prostrated
themselves upon the ground. Among these came two Indians that were blind. The cacique made a speech : to avoid
tediousnesse, I will onely tell in few words the substance of
the matter. Hee said, that seeing the Governour was the
sonne of the sunne, and a great lord, he besought him to doe
him the favour to give sight to those two blind men. The
blind men rose up presently, and very earnestly requested
the same of the Governour. He answered, that in the high
heavens was He that had power to give them health, and
whatsoever they could aske of Him ; whose servant he was.
And that this Lord made the heavens and the earth, and man
after His owne likenesse, and that He suffered upon the
crosse to save mankind, and rose againe the third day ; and
that He died as He was man ; and as touching His divinitie,
He was, and is immortall ; and that He ascended into heaven,
where He standeth with His armes open to receive all such
as turne unto Him. And straightway he commanded him to
make a verie high crosse of wood, which was set up in the
highest place of the towne ; declaring unto him, that the
Christians worshipped the same, in resemblance and memorie
of that whereon Christ suffered. The Governour and his
men kneeled downe before it, and the Indians did the like.
The Governour willed him, that from thenceforth hee should
worship the same, and should aske whatsoever they stoode in
need of, of that Lord that he told him was in heaven. Then
he asked him how far it was from thence to Pacaha. He
said, one daies journie ; and at the end of his countrie, there
was a lake like a brooke, which falleth into Rio Grande, and

The chiefe
towne of the
cacique of
Casqui.

that hee would send men before to make a bridge whereby he might passe.

The same day that the Governour departed thence, he lodged at a towne belonging to Casqui: and the next day hee passed in sight of other townes, and came to the lake, which was halfe a crossebow shot over, of a great depth and current. At the time of his comming, the Indians had made an end of the bridge, which was made of timber, laid one tree after another: and on one side it had a course of stakes higher then the bridge, for them that passed to take hold on. The cacique of Casqui came to the Governour, and brought his people with him. The Governour sent word by an Indian to the cacique of Pacaha, that though hee were enemie to the cacique of Casqui, and though hee were there, yet he would doe him no disgrace nor hurt, if he would attend him peaceablie, and embrace his friendship; but rather would intreate him as a brother. The Indian, which the Governour sent, came againe, and said, that the cacique made none account of that which hee told him, but fled with all his men out at the other side of the towne. Presentlie the Governour entred, and ran before with the horsemen that way by which the Indians fled; and at another towne distant a quarter of a league from thence, they tooke many Indians: and as soone as the horsemen had taken them, they delivered them to the Indians of Casqui, whom, because they were their enemies, with much circumspection and rejoycing they brought to the towne where the Christians were: and the greatest grief they had, was this, that they could not get leave to kill them. There were found in the towne many mantles, and deere skinnes, lions skins,[1] and beares skinnes, and many cats skins. Many came so farre poorely apparrelled, and there they clothed themselves: of the mantles, they made them cotes and cassocks, and some made gownes, and lined them with

Margin notes: A towne belonging to Casqui. Other townes. Another towne. Mantles, deere skins, lions skinnes, beares skins, and cats skinnes.

[1] Most probably puma skins *(felis concolor)*, there being no lions in North America.

cats skins ; and likewise their cassocks. Of the deeres skinnes, some made them also jerkins, shirts, hose, and shooes: and of the beare skinnes, they made them verie good clokes: for no water could pierce them.   There were targets of raw oxe hides found there, with which hides they armed their horses.

Targets of raw oxe hides.

CHAPTER XXIV.

How the cacique of Pacaha came peaceablie to the Governour, and the cacique of Casqui absented himselfe, and came againe to make his excuse ; and how the Governour made them both friends.

Upon Wednesday, the 19 of June, the Governour entred into Pacaha. He lodged in the towne, where the cacique used to reside, which was very great, walled, and beset with towers, and many loopeholes were in the towers and wall. And in the towne was great store of old maiz, and great quantitie of new in the fields.   Within a league and halfe a league were great townes all walled.   Where the Governour was lodged, was a great lake, that came neere unto the wall ; and it entred into a ditch that went round about the towne, wanting but a little to environ it round.   From the lake to the great river was made a weare, by the which the fish came into it, which the cacique kept for his recreation and sport: with nets, that were found in the towne, they tooke as much as they would ; and tooke they never so much, there was no want perceived.   There was also great store of fish in many other lakes that were thereabout, but it was soft, and not so good as that which came from the river, and the most of it was different from the fresh-water fish of Spaine.   There was a fish which they call bagres :[1] the third part of it was head,

Pacaha, a very great towne beset with towers.

Great walled townes.

Nets found.

The divers sorts of excellent fish in Rio Grande.

[1] The cat-fish of the Mississippi—*silurus Mississippiensis.*

and it had on both sides the gilles, and along the sides great pricks like very sharpe aules: those of this kind that were in the lakes were as big as pikes : and in the river, there were some of an hundred, and of an hundred and fiftie pounds weight, and many of them were taken with the hooke. There was another fish like barbilles; and another like breames, headed like a delicate fish, called in Spaine besugo, betweene red and gray. This was there of most esteeme. There was another fish, called a pele fish :[1] it had a snout of a cubit long, and at the end of the upper lip it was made like a peele. There was another fish like a westerne shad : and all of them had scales, except the bagres, and the pele fish. There was another fish, which sometimes the Indians brought us, of the bignes of an hog ; they called it the pereo fish :[2] it had rowes of teeth beneath and above. The cacique of Casqui sent many times great presents of fish, mantles, and skinnes. Hee told the Governour, that he would deliver the cacique of Pacaha into his hands. He went to Casqui, and sent many canoes up the river, and came himselfe by land with many of his people. The Governour with forty horsemen and sixty footemen, tooke him along with him up the river. And his Indians which were in the canoes, discovered where the cacique of Pacaha was in a little island, situated betweene two armes of the river. And five Christians entred into a canoe wherein Don Antonio Osorio went before, to see what people the cacique had with him. There were in the isle five or sixe thousand soules. And as soone as they saw them, supposing

Five or sixe thousand Indians.

[1] The spade or shovel fish—*polyodon spatula*. Flint says (Geography of the Mississippi Valley, i, 129), " We have never remarked this fish in any Museum, although to us the most strange and whimsical-looking fish we have seen." There are several specimens in the British Museum.

[2] The words " pexe pereo", in the original Portuguese, are in all probability a misprint for pexe, or peyxe, *fish*, and porco, *hog*, the two words together meaning a porpoise, which English word indeed is derived from the corresponding Latin words *porcus piscis*. A doubt arising from the misprint, Hakluyt has, perhaps not injudiciously, preserved in his translation the word *pereo* exactly as he found it.

that the Indians which were in the other canoes were also Christians, the cacique, and certaine which were in three canoes, which they had there with them, fled in great haste to the other side of the river. The rest, with great feare and danger, lept into the river, where much people was drowned, especially women and little children.

Presently the Governour, which was on land, not knowing what had happened to Don Antonio, and those that went with him, commanded the Christians with all speed to enter with the Indians of Casqui in the canoes, which were quickly with Don Antonio in the little island, where they tooke many men and women, and much goods. Great store of goods, which the Indians had laid upon hurdles of canes, and rafts of timber, to carrie over to the other side, drave downe the river, wherewith the Indians of Casqui filled their canoes: and for feare lest the Christians would take it from them, the cacique went home with them downe the river, without taking his leave of the Governour; whereupon the Governour was highly offended with him, and presently returning to Pacaha, he overran the countrie of Casqui the space of two leagues, where hee tooke twentie or thirtie of his men. And because his horses were wearie, and he wanted time that day to goe any farther, hee returned to Pacaha, with determination within three or foure daies after to invade Casqui. And presently he let loose one of the Indians of Pacaha, and sent word by him to the cacique, that if hee would have his friendship, he should repaire unto him, and that both of them would make warre upon Casqui. And presently came many Indians that belonged to Pacaha, and brought an Indian, instead of the cacique, which was discovered by the caciques brother which was taken prisoner. The Governour wished the Indians that their master himselfe should come : for hee knew very well that that was not hee ; and told them, that they could doe nothing which he knew not before they thought it.

The next day the cacique came, accompanied with many Indians, and with a present of much fish, skinnes, and mantles. He made a speech that all were glad to heare, and concluded, saying, that though his lordship, without his giving occasion of offence, had done him hurt in his countrie and subjects ; yet he would not therefore refuse to bee his, and that he would alwaies be at his commandement. The Governour commanded his brother to be loosed, and other principall Indians that were taken prisoners. That day came an Indian from the cacique of Casqui, and said, that his lord would come the next day to excuse himselfe of the error which he had committed, in going away without licence of the Governour. The Governour willed the messenger to signifie unto him, that if he came not in his owne person, he would seeke him himselfe, and give him such punishment as he deserved. The next day with all speede came the cacique of Casqui, and brought a present to the Governour of many mantles, skinnes, and fish, and gave him a daughter of his, saying, that he greatly desired to match his blood with the blood of so great a lord as he was, and therefore he brought him his daughter, and desired him to take her to his wife. Hee made a long and discreet oration, giving him great commendations, and concluded, saying, that hee should pardon his going away without licence, for that crosses sake, which he had left with him : protesting, that hee went away for shame of that which his men had done without his consent. The Governour answered him, that hee had chosen a good patrone ; and that if he had not come to excuse himselfe, hee had determined to seeke him, to burne his townes, to kill him and his people, and to destroy his countrie. To which he replied, saying :

My lord, I and mine are yours, and my countrie likewise is yours : therefore if you had done so, you should have destroyed your owne countrie, and have killed your owne people : whatsoever shall come unto me from your hand, I will receive

as from my lord, as well punishment as reward. And know
you, that the favour which you did me in leaving me the crosse,
I do acknowledge the same to be a very great one, and greater
than I have ever deserved. For you shall understand, that
with great droughts, the fields of maiz of my countrie were
withered; and as soone as I and my people kneeled before the
crosse, and prayed for raine, presently our necessitie was re-
lieved.

The Governour made him and the cacique of Pacaha
friends; and set them with him at his table to dine with him:
and the caciques fell at variance about the seates, which of
them should sit on his right hand. The Governour pacified
them; telling them, that among the Christians, all was one to
sit on the one side or on the other, willing them so to behave
themselves, seeing they were with him, that no bodie might
heare them, and that every one should sit in the place that
first hee lighted on. From thence he sent thirtie horsemen,
and fiftie footemen to the province of Caluça, to see if from
thence hee might travell to Chisca, where the Indians said

Gold and copper in Chisca.

there was a worke of gold and copper. They travelled seven
daies journie through a desert, and returned verie wearie,
eating greene plums and stalkes of mais, which they found

A poore towne.

in a poore towne of sixe or seven houses. From thence forward toward the north, the Indians said, that the country was
very ill inhabited, because it was very cold: and that there

Great store of oxen to-ward the north of Pacaha. This is like Quivera.

were such store of oxen, that they could keepe no corne for
them: that the Indians lived upon their flesh. The Governor
seeing that toward that part the countrie was so poore of
maiz, that in it they could not bee sustained, demanded of
the Indians, which way it was most inhabited: and they
said, they had notice of a great province, and a very plentifull countrie, which was called Quigaute, and that it was
toward the south.

CHAPTER XXV.

How the Governour departed from Pacaha to Quigaute, and to Coligoa,
and came to Cayas.

The Governour rested in Pacaha fortie daies.   In all
which time the two caciques served him with great store of
fish, mantles, and skinnes, and strove who should doe him
greatest service.   At the time of his departure, the cacique
of Pacaha gave him two of his sisters, saying, that in signe
of love that he might remember him, he should take them
for his wives : the ones name was Macanoche, and the others
Mochila.   They were well proportioned, tall of bodie, and
well fleshed.   Macanoche was of a good countenance, and
in her shape and physiognomie looked like a ladie ; the other
was strongly made.   The cacique of Casqui commanded the
bridge to be repaired, and the Governour returned through
his countrey, and lodged in the field neere his towne, whither The caciques towne.
hee came with great store of fish and two women, which hee
exchanged with two Christians for two shirts.   He gave us
a guide and men for cariages.   The Governour lodged at a A towne of
Casqui.
towne of his, and the next day at another neere a river,
whither he caused canoes to be brought for him to passe Another
towne.
over, and with his leave returned.   The Governour tooke
his journie toward Quigaute. Quigaute.

The fourth day of August, he came to the towne where The fourth
of August.
the cacique used to keep his residencie : on the way he sent
him a present of many mantles and skinnes, and not daring
to stay for him in the towne, he absented himselfe.   The The greatest
towne seene
towne was the greatest that was seene in Florida.   The in Florida.
Governour and his people lodged in the one halfe of it ; and
within few daies, seeing the Indians became liars, he commanded the other halfe to be burned, because it should not

bee a shelter for them, if they came to assault him by night, nor an hindrance to his horsemen for the resisting of them. There came an Indian, very well accompanied with many Indians, saying, that hee was the cacique. He delivered him over to the men of his guard to look unto him.

There went and came many Indians, and brought mantles and skinnes. The counterfeit cacique, seeing so little opportunity to execute his evill thought, as hee went one day abroad talking with the Governour, he shewed him such a paire of heeles, that there was no Christian that could overtake him, and he leaped into the river, which was a crossebow shot from the towne; and as soone as he was on the other side, many Indians that were thereabout making a great crie, began to shoote. The Governour passed presently over to them with horsemen and footemen, but they durst not tarrie for him. Going forward on his way, hee came to

A towne. a towne where the people were fled, and a little further to a lake, where the horses could not passe, and on the other side were many women. The footemen passed, and tooke many of them, and much spoile. The Governour came to the camp; and that night was a spie of the Indians taken by them of the watch. The Governour asked him, whether he would bring him where the cacique was? he said he would. And he went presently to seeke him with twentie horsemen and fiftie footemen; and after he had sought him a day and an halfe, hee found him in a strong wood; and a souldiour not knowing him, gave him a wound on the head, and he cried out that he should not kill him, saying, that he was the cacique; so he was taken, and an hundred and fortie of his men with him. The Governour came againe to Quigaute, and willed him to cause his men to come to serve the Christians; and staying some daies for their comming, and seeing they came not, he sent two captaines, every one his way, on both sides of the river, with horsemen and footemen. They tooke many men and women. Now seeing the hurt which they sustained

for their rebellion, they came to see what the Governour
would command them, and passed to and fro many times,
and brought presents of cloth and fish.   Cloth.

The cacique and his two wives were in the lodging of the
Governour loose, and the halbardiers of his guard did keepe
them.   The Governour asked them which way the countrie
was most inhabited ?   They said, that toward the south,
downe the river, were great townes and caciques, which
commanded great countries, and much people.   And that
toward the northwest, there was a province neere to certaine
mountaines, that was called Coligoa.   The Governour and   Coligoa,
all the rest thought good to goe first to Coligoa, saying, that   neere to certaine moun-
peradventure the mountaines would make some difference of   taines north-
west.
soile, and that beyond them there might be some gold or
silver.   As for Quigaute, Casqui, and Pacaha, they were
plaine countries, fat grounds, and full of good medowes on
the rivers, where the Indians sowed large fields of maiz.
From Tascaluca to Rio Grande, or the Great River, is about
three hundred leagues; it is a very low countrie, and hath
many lakes.   From Pacaha to Quigaute may be an hundred
leagues.   The Governour left the cacique of Quigaute in his
owne towne; and an Indian, which was his guide, led him
through great woods without any way seven daies journie
through a desert, where, at every lodging, they lodged in
lakes and pooles in verie shold water : there was such store
of fish that they killed them with cudgils; and the Indians,
which they carried in chaines, with the mud troubled the
waters, and the fish being therewith, as it were, astonied,   A new way
to take fish.
came to the top of the water, and they tooke as much as
they listed.

The Indians of Coligoa had no knowledge of the Chris-   Coligoa.
tians; and when they came so neere the towne that the
Indians saw them, they fled up a river, which passed neere
the towne, and some leaped into it, but the Christians went
on both sides of the river and tooke them.   There were

P

many men and women taken, and the cacique with them. And by his commandement, within three daies came many Indians with a present of mantles and deeres skinnes, and

Two oxe hides.

two oxe hides; and they reported, that five or sixe leagues from thence toward the north, there were many of these

Store of oxen to- ward the north.

oxen, and that because the countrie was cold, it was evill inhabited : that the best countrie which they knew, the most plentifull, and most inhabited, was a province called

From Qui- guate to Coligoa are 40 leagues.

Cayas, lying toward the south. From Quiguate to Coligoa may be forty leagues. This town of Coligoa stood at the foote of an hill, on the bank of a meane river, of the bignesse of Cayas, the river that passeth by Estremadura. It was a fat soile, and so plentifull of maiz, that they cast out the old to bring in the new. There was also great plentie of french beanes and pompions. The french beanes were greater and better then those of Spaine, and likewise the pompions, and being rosted, they have almost the taste of chestnuts. The cacique of Coligoa gave a guide to Cayas, and staied behind in his owne towne. Wee travelled five daies, and came to

The pro- vince of Palisema.

the province of Palisema. The house of the cacique was found covered with deeres skinnes of divers colours and works drawne in them, and with the same in manner of car- pets was the ground of the house covered. The cacique left it so, that the Governour might lodge in it, in token that he sought peace and his friendship. But hee durst not tarrie his comming. The Governour, seeing he had absented himselfe, sent a captaine with horsemen and footemen to seeke him. Hee found much people, but by reason of the roughnesse of the countrie, he tooke none save a few women and children. The towne was little and scattering, and had very little maiz ; for which cause the Governour speedilie departed from

Tatalicoya.

thence. Hee came to another towne called Tatalicoya ; hee carried with him the cacique thereof, which guided him to

Cayas.

Cayas. When hee came to Cayas, and saw the towne scat- tered, hee thought they had told him a lie, and that it was not the province of Cayas, because they had informed him that it was well inhabited. He threatned the cacique, charging him to tell him where hee was; and he, and other Indians which were taken neere about that place, affirmed that this was the towne of Cayas, and the best that was in that countrie; and that though the houses were distant the one from the other, yet the ground that was inhabited was great, and that there was great store of people, and many fields of maiz. This towne was called Tanico. He pitched his campe in the best part of it, neere unto a river. ^{Tanico.}

The same day that the Governour came thither, he went a league farther with certaine horsemen, and without finding any people; hee found many skinnes in a pathway, which the cacique had left there, that they might bee found, in token of peace. For so is the custome in that countrie.

CHAPTER XXVI.

How the Governour discovered the province of Tulla, and what happened unto him.

The Governor rested a moneth in the province of Cayas. In which time the horses fattened and thrived more then in other places in a longer time, with the great plentie of maiz and the leaves thereof, which I thinke was the best that hath been seene, and they dranke of a lake of very hot water, and somewhat brackish, and they dranke so much, that it swelled in their bellies when they brought them from the watering. A lake of hot and somewhat brackish water. Untill that time the Christians wanted salt, and there they made good store, which they carried along with them. The Store of salt made at Cayas. Indians doe carrie it to other places to exchange it for skinnes and mantles. They make it along the river, which,

when it ebbeth, leaveth it upon the upper part of the sand.
And because they cannot make it, without much sand mingled
with it, they throw it into certaine baskets, which they have
for that purpose, broad at the mouth, and narrow at the
bottom, and set it in the aire upon a barre, and throw water
into it, and set a small vessell under it, wherein it falleth.
Being strained and set to boile upon the fire, when the water
is sodden away, the salt remaineth in the bottome of the pan.
On both sides of the river the countrie was full of sowne
fields, and there was store of maiz.

The Indians durst not come over where wee were ; and
when some of them shewed themselves, the souldiers that saw
them called unto them ; then the Indians passed the river,
and came with them where the Governor was. He asked
them for the cacique. They said that he remained quiet,
but that he durst not shew himselfe. The Governour presently sent him word, that he should come unto him, and
bring him a guide and an interpretour for his journie, if he
made account of his friendship ; and if he did not so, he
would come himselfe to seeke him, and that it would bee
the worse for him. Hee waited three daies, and seeing he
came not, he went to seeke him, and brought him prisoner
with one hundred and fifty of his men. He asked him,
whether hee had notice of any great cacique, and which way
the countrie was best inhabited. Hee answered, that the
best countrie thereabout was a province toward the south, a
day and an halfes journie, which was called Tulla ; and that
he could give him a guide, but no interpretour, because the
speech of that countrie was different from his, and because
he and his ancestors had alwaies warres with the lords of
that province ; therefore they had no commerce, nor understood one anothers language.

Immediately the Governour, with certaine horsemen and
fifty footemen, departed toward Tulla, to see if the countrie
were such as hee might passe through it with all his com-

Tulla.

panie : and as soone as he arrived there, and was espied of
the Indians, the countrie gathered together, and as soone as
fifteen or twenty Indians could assemble themselves, they
set upon the Christians ; and seeing that they did handle
them shrewdly, and that the horsemen overtooke them when
they fled, they gat up into the tops of their houses, and
sought to defend themselves with their arrowes ; and being
beaten downe from one, they gat up upon another. And
while our men pursued some, others set upon them another
way. Thus the skirmish lasted so long, that the horses were
tired, and they could not make them runne. The Indians
killed there one horse, and some were hurt. There were
fifteen Indians slaine there, and forty women and boies were
taken prisoners. For whatsoever Indian did shoot at them,
if they could come by him, they put him to the sword.

The Governour determined to returne toward Cayas before
the Indians had time to gather a head ; and presently that
evening, going part of the night to leave Tulla, he lodged
by the way, and the next day came to Cayas ; and within
three daies after he departed thence toward Tulla with all
his companie. He carried the cacique along with him ; and
among all his men, there was not one found that could
understand the speech of Tulla. He staied three daies by
the way, and the day that he came thither, he found the
towne abandoned, for the Indians durst not tarrie his comming. But as soone as they knew that the Governour was in
Tulla, the first night about the morning watch, they came in
two squadrons two severall waies, with their bowes and
arrowes, and long staves like pikes. As soone as they were
descried, both horse and foot sallied out upon them, where
many of the Indians were slaine, and some Christians and
horses were hurt ; some of the Indians were taken prisoners,
whereof the Governour sent sixe to the cacique, with their
right hands and noses cut off ; and sent him word, that if he
came not to him to excuse and submit himselfe, that hee

The Governour commeth againe to Tulla with all his companie.

Indians have their right hands and noses cut off.

would come to seeke him, and that hee would doe the like
to him, and as many of his as hee could find, as hee had
done to those which hee had sent him, and gave him three
daies respit for to come. And this he gave them to understand by signes, as well as hee could, for there was no interpretour.

At the three daies end, there came an Indian laden with
Oxe hides oxe hides. He came weeping with great sobs, and comming
to the Governour cast himselfe downe at his feete. He tooke
him up, and he made a speech, but there was none that understood him. The Governour by signes commanded him
to returne to the cacique, and to will him to send him an
interpretor, which could understand the men of Cayas. The
Oxe hides. next day came three Indians laden with oxe hides; and
within three daies after came twenty Indians, and among
thcm one that understood them of Cayas: who, after a long
oration of excuses of the cacique, and praises of the Governour, concluded with this, that he and the other were come
thither on the caciques behalfe, to see what his lordship
would command him to doe, for he was readie at his commandement. The Governour and all his companie were verie
glad; for in no wise could they travell without an interpretour. The Governour commanded him to be kept safe,
and bad him tell the men that came with him, that they
should returne to the cacique, and signifie unto him, that he
pardoned him for that which was past, and thanked him
much for his presents and interpretour, which he had sent
him, and that he would bee glad to see him, and that he
shuld come the next day to talke with him. After three

The cacique
of Tulla. daies, the cacique came, and eighty Indians with him: and
Many oxe
hides, with
wooll on
them as soft
as sheepes
wool.—Go-
mara Histor.
Gener., cap.
215. Many
oxen toward
the north. himselfe and his men came weeping into the camp, in token
of obedience and repentance for the errour passed, after the
manner of that countrie. He brought a present of many
oxe hides; which, because the countrie was cold, were verie
profitable, and served for coverlets, because they were very

soft, and wolled like sheepe. Not farre from thence toward the north were many oxen. The Christians saw them not, nor came into the countrie where they were, because those parts were evill inhabited, and had small store of maiz where they were bred. The cacique of Tulla made an oration to the Governour, wherein he excused himselfe, and offered him his countrie, subjects, and person. As well this cacique as the others, and all those which came to the Governour on their behalfe, delivered their message or speech in so good order, that no oratour could utter the same more eloquentlie.

<small>The great eloquence of the Indians.</small>

CHAPTER XXVII.

How the Governour went from Tulla to Autiamque, where he passed the winter.

The Governour enformed himselfe of all the countrie round about; and understood, that toward the west was a scattered dwelling, and that toward the south-east were great townes, especially in a province called Autiamque, tenne daies journie from Tulla; which might be about eighty leagues: and that it was a plentifull countrie of maiz. And because winter came on, and that they could not travell two or three moneths in the yeere for cold, waters, and snow: and fearing, that if they should stay so long in the scattered dwelling, they could not be susteined; and also because the Indians said, that neere to Autiamque was a great water, and according to their relation the Governour thought it was some arme of the sea: and because he now desired to send newes of himselfe to Cuba, that some supplie of men and horses might be sent unto him (for it was above three yeeres since Donna Isabella,

<small>A winter of two or three moneths.</small>

which was in Havana, or any other person in Christendome,
had heard of him, and by this time he had lost two hundred
and fifty men, and one hundred and fifty horses) he determined to winter in Autiamque ; and the next spring, to goe
to the sea cost, and make two brigantines, and send one of
them to Cuba, and the other to Nueva Espanna, that that
which went in safetie, might give newes of him : hoping with
the goods which he had in Cuba, to furnish himselfe againe,
and to attempt the discovery and conquest toward the west ;
for he had not yet come where Cabeça de Vaca had been.
Thus having sent away the two caciques of Cayas and Tulla,
he tooke his journie toward Autiamque.   Hee travelled five

Quipana,
five daies
journie from
Tulla.
daies over very rough mountaines, and came to a towne
called Quipana, where no Indians could be taken for the
roughnesse of the countrie : and the towne being betweene
hilles, there was an ambush laid, wherewith they tooke two
Indians, which told them, that Autiamque was sixe daies
journie from thence, and that there was another province
toward the south, eight daies journie off, plentifull of maiz,

Guahate.
and very well peopled, which was called Guahate.   But because Autimaque was neerer, and the most of the Indians
agreed of it, the Governour made his journie that way.

Anoixi.
In three daies he came to a towne called Anoixi.   He sent
a captaine before with thirty horsemen, and fifty footemen,
and tooke the Indians carelesse : hee tooke many men and
women prisoners.   Within two daies after the Governour

Catamaya.
came to another towne, called Catamaya, and lodged in the
fields of the towne.   Two Indians came with a false message
from the cacique to know his determination.   Hee bad them
tell their lord, that hee should come and speake with him.
The Indians returned and came no more, nor any other
message from the cacique.   The next day the Christians
went to the towne, which was without people : they tooke

Autiamque,
sixe daies
journie from
Quipana.
as much maiz as they needed.   That day they lodged in a
wood, and the next day they came to Autiamque.   They

found much maiz laid up in store, and french beanes, and walnuts, and prunes, great store of all sorts. They tooke some Indians, which were gathering together the stuffe which their wives had hidden. This was a champion countrie, and well inhabited. The Governour lodged in the best part of the towne, and commanded presently to make a fense of timber round about the campe, distant from the houses, that the Indians might not hurt them without by fire. And measuring the ground by pases, hee appointed every one his part to doe according to the number of Indians which he had: presently the timber was brought by them; and in three daies there was an inclosure made of very hie and thicke posts thrust into the ground, and many railes laid acrosse. Hard by this towne passed a river, that came out of the pro- A river. vince of Cayas; and above and beneath it was very well peopled. Thither came Indians on the caciques behalfe with a present of mantles and skinnes; and an halting cacique, subject to the lord of Autiamque, lord of a towne called Tietiquaquo, came many times to visit the Governour, and Tietiquaquo. to bring him presents of such as hee had. The cacique of Autiamque sent to know of the Governour, how long time hee meant to stay in his country? And understanding that he meant to stay above three daies, he never sent any more Indians, nor any other message, but conspired with the lame cacique to rebell. Divers inrodes were made, wherein there were many men and women taken, and the lame cacique among the rest. The Governour, respecting the services which he had received from him, reprehended and admonished him, and set him at libertie, and gave him two Indians to carrie him in a chaire upon their shoulders. The cacique of Autiamque desiring to thrust the Governour out of his countrie, set spies over him. And an Indian comming one night to the gate of the inclosure, a souldier that watched espied him; and stepping behind the gate, as he came in he gave him such a thrust, that he fell downe; and so he carried him to the Governour : and as hee asked him wherefore he came, not being able to speake, hee fell downe dead. The night following, the Governour commanded a souldiour to give the alarme, and to say that he had seene Indians, to see how ready they would be to answere the alarme. And hee did so sometimes, as well there as in other places, when he thought that his men were carelesse, and reprehended such as were slacke. And as well for this cause, as in regard of doing their dutie, when the alarme was given, every one sought to be the first that should answere.

Great providence.

They staied in Autiamque three moneths, with great plentie of maiz, french beanes, walnuts, prunes, and conies : which untill that time they knew not how to catch. And in Autiamque the Indians taught them how to take them : which was, with great sprindges, which lifted up their feete from the ground : and the snare was made with a strong string, whereunto was fastened a knot of a cane, which ran close about the neck of the conie, because they should not gnaw the string. They tooke many in the fields of maiz, especiallie when it freesed or snowed. The Christians staied there one whole moneth, so inclosed with snow that they went not out of the towne ; and when they wanted firewood, the Governour with his horsemen going and comming many times to the wood, which was two crossebow shot from the towne, made a pathway, whereby the footemen went for wood. In this meane space, some Indians which went loose, killed many conies with their gives[1] and with arrowes. These conies were of two sorts, some were like those of Spaine, and the other of the same colour and fashion, and as big as great hares, longer, and having greater loines.

Three moneths abode in Autiamque.

Frost and snow.
A moneth of snow.

Conies of two sorts.

[1] The Portuguese word "armadilhas", here rendered "gives", should have been "snares".

CHAPTER XXVIII.

How the Governour went from Autiamque to Nilco, and from thence to Guacoya.

Upon Monday the sixt of March 1542, the Governour de- March 6, 1542.
parted from Autiamque to seeke Nilco, which the Indians
said was neere the great river, with determination to come to
the sea, and procure some succour of men and horses: for he
had now but three hundred men of warre, and fortie horses,
and some of them lame, which did nothing but helpe to make
up the number: and for want of iron they had gone above a
yeere unshod: and because they were used to it in the plaine
countrie, it did them no great harme.   John Ortiz died in The death of John Ortiz,
Autiamque; which grieved the Governour very much: be- and the great misse of him,
cause that without an interpretour hee feared to enter farre being their interpretour.
into the land, where he might be lost.   From thence forward
a youth that was taken in Cutifa-Chiqui did serve for interpretour, which had by that time learned somewhat of the
Christians language.   The death of John Ortiz was so
great a mischiefe for the discovering inward, or going out of
the land, that to learne of the Indians, that which in foure
words hee declared, they needed a whole day with the youth:
and most commonly hee understood quite contrarie that
which was asked him: whereby it often happened that the
way that they went one day, and sometimes two or three daies,
they turned backe, and went astray through the wood here
and there.   The Governour spent ten daies in travelling from
Autiamque to a province called Ayays; and came to a towne that Ayays.
stood neere the river that passeth by Cayas and Autiamque. A river.
There hee commanded a barge to be made, wherewith he
passed the river.   When he had passed the river, there fell
out such weather, that foure daies he could not travell for Great snow about the
snow.   As soone as it gave over snowing, he went three daies 20th of March.

journey through a wildernesse, and a countrie so low, and so full of lakes and evill waies, that hee travelled one time a whole day in water, sometimes knee deepe, sometimes to the stirrup, and sometimes they swamme. He came to a towne

Tutelpinco. called Tutelpinco, abandoned, and without maiz: there passed

A great lake. by it a lake, that entred into the river, which carried a great streame and force of water. Five Christians passing over it in a periagua,[1] which the Governour had sent with a captaine, the periagua overset : some tooke hold on it, some on the trees that were in the lake. One Francis Sebastian, an honest man of Villa Nova de Barca Rota, was drowned there.

The Governour went a whole day along the lake seeking passage, and could finde none, nor any way that did passe to the other side. Comming againe at night to the towne, hee found two peaceable Indians, which shewed him the passage, and which way hee was to goe. There they made of canes

Rafts where-with they passed the lake. and of the timber of houses thatched with canes, rafts, where-with they passed the lake. They travelled three daies, and

Tianto. came to a towne of the territorie of Nilco, called Tianto. There they tooke thirtie Indians, and among them two principall men of this towne. The Governour sent a captaine with horsemen and footemen before to Nilco, because the Indians might have no time to carrie away the provision. They

Three or fowre great townes. passed through three or foure great townes; and in the towne where the cacique was resident, which was two leagues from the place where the Governour remained, they found many Indians, with their bowes and arrowes, in manner as though they would have staied to fight, which did compasse the towne ; and as soone as they saw the Christians come neere

---

[1] A Spanish word, more correctly spelt "piragua", meaning a ferry-boat: the word used in the original Portuguese is "almadia", derived from the Arabic root "ada", to pass, or to transport over a river. It is a small skiff, or canoe, used for crossing lakes and small streams, and also for fishing. Those used in Morocco are called *maadia*, and are commonly made of a kind of bull rush strongly bound together, which grows on the banks of the lakes of the country ; and they are generally navigated by one man.

them without misdoubting them, they set the caciques house
on fire, and fled over a lake that passed neere the towne,
through which the horses could not passe.

The next day, being Wednesday the 29 of March, the ^{March 29.}
Governour came to Nilco : he lodged with all his men in the ^{Nilco.}
caciques towne, which stood in a plaine field, which was inhabited for the space of a quarter of a league : and within a
league and halfe a league were other great townes, wherein ^{Verie great towne.}
was great store of maiz, of french beanes, of walnuts, and
prunes.   This was the best countrie that was seen in Florida, ^{The best countrie of}
and had most store of maiz, except Coça and Apalache. ^{Florida.}
There came to the campe an Indian accompanied with others,
and in the caciques name gave the Governour a mantle of
marterns skinnes, and a cordon of perles.   The Governour ^{Marterns skinnes.}
gave him a few small margarites, which are certaine beades ^{A cordon of perles.}
much esteemed in Peru, and other things, wherewith he was
very well contented.   He promised to returne within two
daies, but never came againe ; but on the contrarie the Indians came by night in canoes, and carried away all the maiz
they could, and made them cabins on the other side of the
river in the thickest of the wood, because they might flee if
wee should goe to seeke them.   The Governour, seeing hee
came not at the time appointed, commanded an ambush to be
laid about certaine store-houses neere the lake, whither the
Indians came for maiz : where they tooke two Indians, who
told the Governour, that hee which came to visit him, was
not the cacique, but was sent by him under pretence to spie
whether the Christians were carelesse, and whether they determined to settle in that country or to goe forward.   Presently the Governour sent a captaine with footmen and horsemen over the river ; and in their passage they were descried
of the Indians, and therefore he could take but tenne or
twelve men and women, with whom hee returned to the
campe.   This river, which passed by Nilco, was that which ^{A river fall-}
passed by Cayas and Autiamque, and fell into Rio Grande, ^{ing into Rio Grande.}

or the great river, which passed by Pachaha and Aquixo, neere unto the province of Guachoya : and the lord thereof came up the river in canoes to make warre with him of Nilco. On his behalf there came an Indian to the Governour and said unto him, that he was his servant, and prayed him so to hold him, and that within two daies hee would come to kisse his lordships hands : and at the time appointed he came with some of his principal Indians, which accompanied him, and with words of great offers and courtesie hee gave the Governour a present of many mantles and deeres skinnes. The Governour gave him some other things in recompense, and honoured him much. Hee asked him what townes there were downe the river ? Hee answered that he knew none other but his owne : and on the other side of the river a province of a cacique called Quigalta. So hee tooke his leave of the Governour and went to his owne towne.

Within fewe daies the Governour determined to goe to Guachoya, to learne there whether the sea were neere, or whether there were any habitation neere, where hee might relieve his companie, while the brigantines were making, which he meant to send to the land of the Christians. As he passed the river of Nilco, there came in canoes Indians of Guachoya up the streame ; and when they saw him, supposing that he came to seeke them to doe them some hurt, they returned downe the river, and informed the cacique thereof : who, with all his people, spoiling the towne of all that they could carrie away, passed that night over to the other side of Rio Grande, or the great river. The Governour sent a captaine with fiftie men in sixe canoes downe the river, and went himselfe by land with the rest. Hee came to Guachoya upon Sunday the 17 of Aprill : he lodged in the towne of the cacique, which was inclosed about, and seated a crossebow shot distant from the river. Here the river is called Tamaliseu ; and in Nilco, Tapatu ; and in Coça, Mico ; and in the port or mouth, Ri.

Guachoya.

Foure names of Rio Grande.

CHAPTER XXIX.

Of the message which the Governour sent to Quigalta, and of the answere which he returned, and of the things which happened in this time.

As soone as the Governour came to Guachoya, hee sent John Danusco, with as many men as could goe in the canoes, up the river. For when they came downe from Nilco, they saw on the other side the river new cabins made. John Danusco went and brought the canoes loden with maiz, French beanes, prunes, and many loaves made of the sub- stance of prunes. That day came an Indian to the Gover- nor from the cacique of Guachoya, and said, that his lord would come the next day. The next day they saw many canoes come up the river, and on the other side of the great river they assembled together in the space of an houre; they consulted whether they should come or not; and at length concluded to come, and crossed the river. In them came the cacique of Guachoya, and brought with him manie Indians, with great store of fish, dogges, deeres skinnes, and mantles. And as soone as they landed, they went to the lodging of the Governour, and presented him their gifts; and the cacique uttered these words:

Mightie and excellent lord, I beseech your lordship to pardon mee the errour which I committed in absenting my-selfe, and not tarrying in this towne to have received and served your lordship; since, to obtaine this opportunitie of time, was, and is, as much as a greate victorie to me. But I feared that which I needed not to have feared, and so did that which was not reason to do. But as haste maketh waste, and I removed without deliberation; so, as soone as I thought on it, I determined not to follow the opinion of the foolish,

Many loaves made of prunes.

which is, to continue in their errour ; but to imitate the wise
and discreet in changing my counsell, and so I came to see
what your lordship will command me to doe, that I may serve
you in all things that are in my power.

The Governour received him with much joy, and gave
him thankes for his present and offer. He asked him, whether
hee had any notice of the sea? Hee answered, no; nor of
any townes downe the river on that side : save that two
leagues from thence was one towne of a principall Indian, a
subject of his ; and on the other side of the river, three daies
journey from thence downe the river, was the province of
Quigalta, which was the greatest lord that was in that
countrie. The Governour thought that the cacique lied unto
him, to rid him out of his owne townes, and sent John Danusco
with eight horsemen downe the river to see what habitation
there was, and to informe himselfe if there were any notice
of the sea. Hee travelled eight daies, and at his returne hee
said, that in all that time he was not able to go above fourteen or fifteen leagues, because of the great creekes that
came out of the river, and groves of canes, and thicke woods,
that were along the bancks of the river, and that hee had
found no habitation. The Governour fell into great dumps
to see how hard it was to get to the sea ; and worse, because
his men and horses every day diminished, being without
succour to sustaine themselves in the country ; and with that

thought he fell sick. But before he tooke his bed, hee sent
an Indian to the cacique of Quigalta, to tell him that hee
was the childe of the sunne ; and that all the way that hee
came, all men obeyed and served him, that he requested him
to accept of his friendship, and come unto him, for he would
be very glad to see him ; and in signe of love and obedience,
to bring something with him of that which in his countrie
A most
wittie and
stout an-
swere of the
cacique of
Quigalta. was most esteemed. The cacique answered by the same
Indian :

That whereas he said he was the child of the sunne, if he

would drie up the river he would beleeve him : and touching
the rest, that hee was wont to visit none; but rather that all
those of whom he had notice did visit him, served, obeyed and
paid him tributes willingly or perforce : therefore, if hee
desired to see him, it were best he should come thither : that
if hee came in peace, he would receive him with speciall good
will ; and if in warre, in like manner hee would attend him
in the towne where he was ; and that for him or any other
hee would not shrinke one foote backe.

By that time the Indian returned with this answere, the
Governour had betaken himselfe to bed, being evill handled
with fevers, and was much aggrieved that he was not in case
to passe presently the river and to seeke him, to see if he
could abate that pride of his, considering the river went now
very strongly in those parts; for it was neere halfe a league
broad and sixteen fathomes deep, and very furious, and
ranne with a great current; and on both sides there were
many Indians; and his power was not now so great but that
hee had need to helpe himselfe rather by slights then by
force. The Indians of Guachoya came every day with fish,
in such numbers that the towne was full of them. The
cacique said, that on a certaine night hee of Quigalta would
come to give battell to the Governour; which the Governour imagined that he had devised to drive him out of his
countrey, and commanded him to bee put in hold; and that
night and all the rest there was good watch kept. Hee asked
him wherefore Quigalta come not? He said that hee came,
but that he saw him prepared, and therefore durst not give
the attempt; and hee was earnest with him to send his captaines over the river, and that he would aide him with many
men to set upon Quigalta. The Governour told him that as
soone as he was recovered, himselfe would seeke him out.
And seeing how many Indians came daily to the towne, and
what store of people was in that countrie, fearing they should
all conspire together and plot some treason against him; and

R

because the towne had some open gaps which were not made
an end of inclosing, besides the gates which they went in
and out by ; because the Indians should not thinke he feared
them, he let them all alone unrepaired, and commanded the
horsemen to be appointed to them and to the gates ; and all
night the horsemen went the round, and two and two of
every squadron rode about, and visited the skouts that were
without the towne in their standings by the passages, and
the crossebowmen that kept the canoes in the river. And
because the Indians should stand in feare of them, hee determined to send a captaine to Nilco, for those of Guachoya
had told him that it was inhabited ; that by using them
cruelly, neither the one nor the other should presume to
assaile him ; and hee sent Nunnez de Tovar with fifteene
horsemen, and John de Guzman, captaine of the footmen,
with his companie in canoes up the river.

The cacique of Guachoya sent for many canoes and many
warlike Indians to goe with the Christians ; and the captaine
of the Christians, called Nunnez de Tovar, went by land
with his horsemen, and two leagues before he came to Nilco
hee staied for John de Guzman, and in that place they passed
the river by night : the horsemen came first, and in the
morning by breake of day in sight of the towne they lighted
upon a spie, which, as soone as he perceived the Christians,
crying out amaine, fled to the towne to give warning. Nunnez de Tovar and his companie made such speed, that before
the Indians of the towne could fully come out, they were
upon them : it was champion ground that was inhabited,
which was about a quarter of a league. There were about
five or sixe thousand people in the towne ; and, as many
people came out of the houses, and fled from one house to
another, and many Indians came flocking together from all
parts ; there was never a horseman that was not alone among
many. The captaine had commanded that they should not
spare the life of any male. Their disorder was so great, that

Five or sixe
thousand
people in
Nilco.

there was no Indian that shot an arrow at any Christian.
The shreekes of women and children were so great, that they
made the eares deafe of those that followed them. There
were slaine an hundred Indians, little more or lesse; and
many were wounded with great wounds, whom they suffered
to escape, to strike a terror in the rest that were not there.
There were some so cruell and butcher-like, that they killed
old and young, and all that they met, though they made no
resistance; and those which presumed of themselves for their
valour, and were taken for such, brake through the Indians,
bearing downe many with their stirrops and brests of their
horses, and some they wounded with their lances, and so let
them goe; and when they saw any youth or woman they
tooke them, and delivered them to the footmen. These
mens sinnes, by God's permission, lighted on their own
heads, who, because they would seeme valiant, became cruell,
shewing themselves extreme cowards in the sight of all men,
when as most neede of valour was required, and afterward Chap. 37.
they came to a shameful death. Of the Indians of Nilco
were taken prisoners fourescore women and children, and
much spoile. The Indians of Guachoya kept back before
they came at the towne, and staied without, beholding the
successe of the Christians with the men of Nilco. And when
they saw them put to flight, and the horsemen busie in killing of them, they hastened to the houses to rob, and filled
their canoes with the spoile of the goods, and returned to
Guachoya before the Christians; and wondring much at the
sharpe dealing which they had seene them use toward the
Indians of Nilco, they told their cacique all that had passed
with great astonishment.

CHAPTER XXX.

Of the death of the Adelantado Fernando de Soto : and how Luys Moscoso de Alvarado was elected Governour in his stead.

The Governour felt in himselfe that the houre approched wherein hee was to leave this present life, and called for the kings officers, captaines, and principall persons, to whom he made a speech, saying :

That now he was to goe to give an account before the presence of God of all his life past : and since it pleased Him to take him in such a time, and that the time was come that he knew his death, that he His most unworthie servant did yeeld Him many thankes therefore ; and desired all that were present and absent (whom he confessed himselfe to be much beholding unto for their singular vertues, love, and loyaltie, which himselfe had well tried in the travels which they had suffered, which alwaies in his mind he did hope to satisfie and reward, when it should please God to give him rest, with more prosperitie of his estate), that they would pray to God for him, that for His mercie He would forgive him his sinnes, and receive his soule into eternall glorie : and that they would quit and free him of the charge which hee had over them, and ought unto them all, and that they would pardon him for some wrongs which they might have received of him. And to avoid some division, which upon his death might fall out upon the choice of his successour, he requested them to elect a principall person, and able to governe, of whom all should like well ; and when he was elected, they should sweare before him to obey him : and that he would thanke them very much in so doing ; because the griefe that he had would somewhat be asswaged, and the paine that he felt, because he left them in so great confusion, to wit, in leaving them in a strange countrie, where they knew not where they were.

Baltasar de Gallegos answered in the name of all the rest. And first of all comforting him, he set before his eies how short the life of this world was, and with how many troubles and miseries it is accompanied, and how God shewed him a singular favor which soonest left it: telling him many other things fit for such a time.   And for the last point, that since it pleased God to take him to himselfe, although his death did justly grieve them much, yet as wel he, as al the rest ought of necessitie to conforme themselves to the will of God. And touching the Governour which he commanded they should elect, he besought him, that it would please his lordship to name him which he thought fit, and him they would obey. And presently he named Luys de Moscoso de Alvarado, his captaine generall.   And presently he was sworne by all that were present and elected for Governour.   The next day, being the 21 of May, 1542, departed out of this life, the valorous, virtuous, and valiant captaine, Don Fernando de Soto, Governour of Cuba, and Adelantado of Florida; whom fortune advanced, as it useth to doe others, that hee might have the higher fal.   He departed in such a place, and at such a time, as in his sicknesse he had but little comfort: and the danger wherein all his people were of perishing in that countrie, which appeared before their eies, was cause sufficient, why every one of them had need of comfort, and why they did not visit nor accompanie him as they ought to have done.   Luys de Moscoso determined to conceale his death from the Indians, because Ferdinando de Soto had made them beleeve that the Christians were immortall, and also because they tooke him to be hardie, wise, and valiant: and if they should know that he was dead, they would bee bold to set upon the Christians, though they lived peaceablie by them. In regard of their disposition, and because they were nothing constant, and beleeved all that was told them, the Adelantado made them beleeve, that he knew some things that passed in secret among themselves, without their knowledge, how, or in

The death of Don Ferdinando de Soto, the 21 of May, 1542, at Guacoya.

A wittie
stratagem.
what manner he came by them : and that the figure which
appeared in a glasse, which he shewed them, did tell him
whatsoever they practised and went about; and therefore
neither in word nor deed durst they attempt any thing that
might bee prejudiciall unto him.

As soone as he was dead, Luis de Moscoso commanded to
put him secretly in an house, where hee remained three daies :
and remooving him from thence, commanded him to bee buried
in the night at one of the gates of the towne within the wall.
And as the Indians had seene him sick, and missed him, so
did they suspect what might bee. And passing by the place
where hee was buried, seeing the earth mooved, they looked
and spake one to another. Luys de Moscoso understanding
of it, commanded him to be taken up by night, and to cast a
great deale of sand into the mantles, wherein he was winded
up, wherein hee was carried in a canoe, and throwne into the
middest of the river. The cacique of Guachoya inquired for
him, demanding what was become of his brother and lord,
the Governour. Luys de Moscoso told him, that he was gon
to heaven, as many other times hee did ; and because hee was
to stay there certaine daies, hee had left him in his place.
The cacique thought with himself that he was dead; and
commanded two young and well-proportioned Indians to be
brought thither ; and said, that the use of that countrie was,
This is also
the custome
of the old
Tartars.
when any lord died, to kill Indians to wait upon him, and
serve him by the way : and for that purpose by his commandement were those come thither : and prayed Luys de
Moscoso to command them to be beheaded, that they might
attend and serve his lord and brother. Luys de Moscoso
told him, that the Governour was not dead, but gone to
heaven, and that of his owne Christian souldiers he had taken
such as he needed to serve him, and praied him to command
those Indians to be loosed, and not to use any such bad custome from thenceefoorth. Straightway hee commanded them
to be loosed, and to get them home to their houses. And one of

them would not goe; saying, that hee would not serve him that without desert had judged him to death, but that hee would serve him as long as hee lived, which had saved his life.

Luys de Moscoso caused all the goods of the Governour to be sold at an outcrie:[1] to wit, two men slaves, and two women slaves, and three horses, and seven hundred hogges. For every slave or horse they gave two or three thousand ducats: which were to be paied at the first melting of gold or silver, or at the division of their portion of inheritance. And they entred into bonds, though in the countrie there was not wherewith, to pay it within a yeere after, and put in sureties for the same. Such as in Spaine had no goods to bind, gave two hundred ducats for an hog, giving assurance after the same manner. Those which had any goods in Spaine, bought with more feare, and bought the lesse. From that time forward, most of the companie had swine, and brought them up, and fed upon them; and observed Fridaies and Saturdaies, and the evenings of feasts, which before they did not. For sometimes in two or three moneths they did eate no flesh, and whensoever they could come by it, they did eate it.

Seven hundred hogges.

CHAPTER XXXI.

How the Governour, Luys de Moscoso, departed from Guachoya, and went to Chaguate; and from thence to Aguacay.

Some were glad of the death of Don Ferdinando de Soto, holding for certaine that Luys de Moscoso (which was given to his ease) would rather desire to be among the Christians at rest, then to continue the labours of the warre in subduing and discovering of countries, whereof they were alreadie

---

[1] *i.e.* an auction :
        " The goods of this poor man sold at an outcry,
        His wife turn'd out of doors."—
                (Massinger's " City Madam", act I, sc. 3.)

wearie, seeing the small profit that insued thereof. The
Governour commanded the captaines and principall persons
to meet, to consult and determine what they should doe.
And being informed what peopled habitation was round
about, he understood that to the west the countrie was most
inhabited, and that downe the river beyond Quigalta was
uninhabited, and had little store of food. He desired them
all, that everie one would give his opinion in writing, and
Their gene-
rall resolu-
tion to tra-
vell by land
westward. set his hand to it: that they might resolve by generall consent, whether they should goe downe the river, or enter
into the maine land. All were of opinion, that it was best
to go by land toward the west, because Nueva Espanna was
that way; holding the voyage by sea more dangerous, and
of greater hazard, because they could make no ship of any
strength to abide a storme, neither had they master, nor
pilot, compasse, nor chart, neither knew they how farre the
sea was off, nor had any notice of it; nor whether the river
did make any great turning into the land, or had any great
fall from the rocks, where all of them might be cast away.
And some which had seene the sea chart, did find, that from
the place where they were by the sea coast to Nova Espanna,
might be four hundred leagues, little more or lesse, and said,
that though they went somewhat about by land in seeking
a peopled countrie, if some great wildernesse which they
could not passe did not hinder them, by spending that sommer
in travell, finding provision to passe the winter in some
peopled countrie, that the next sommer after they might
come to some Christian land, and that it might fortune, in
their travell by land, to find some rich countrie, where they
might doe themselves good. The Governour, although
he desired to get out of Florida in shorter time, seeing the
inconveniences they laid before him, in travelling by sea,
determined to follow that which seemed good to them all.

The fifth of
June. On Monday the fifth of June, he departed from Guachoya.
The cacique gave him a guide to Chaguate, and staied at

home in his owne towne.   They passed through a province
called Catalte : and having passed a wildernesse of sixe daies ^{Catalte.}
journie, the twentieth day of the moneth he came to Chaguate. ^{Chaguate.}
The cacique of this province had visited the Governour, Don
Ferdinando de Soto, at Autiamque, whither he brought him
presents of skinnes, and mantles, and salt.   And a day before
Luys de Moscoso came to his towne, we lost a Christian that
was sicke ; which hee suspected that the Indians had slaine.
Hee sent the cacique word, that he should command his
people to seeke him up, and send him unto him, and that he
would hold him, as he did, for his friend : and if he did not,
that neither he, nor his, should escape his hands, and that
hee would set his countrie on fire.   Presently the cacique
came unto him, and brought a great present of mantles and
skinnes, and the Christian that was lost, and made this speech
following :

*Right excellent lord, I would not deserve that conceit which
you had of me, for all the treasure of the world.   What inforced me to goe to visit and serve the excellent Lord Governour your father in Autiamque, which you should have remembred, where I offered myselfe with all loyaltie, faith, and
love, during my life to serve and obey him ?   What then
could be the cause, I having received favours of him, and
neither you nor he having done me any wrong, that should
moove me to doe the thing which I ought not ?   Beleeve this
of mee, that neither wrong, nor any worldly interest, was able
to make me to have done it, nor shall be able to blind me.
But as in this life it is a naturall course, that after one
pleasure, many sorrowes doe follow : so by your indignation,
fortune would moderate the joy, which my heart conceiveth
with your presence ; and that I should erre, where I thought
surest to have hit the marke, in harboring this Christian
which was lost, and using him in such manner as he may
tell himselfe, thinking that herein I did you service, with
purpose to deliver him unto you in Chaguate, and to serve*

s

you to the uttermost of my power. If I deserve punishment for this, I will receive it at your hands, as from my lord, as if it were a favour. For the love which I did beare to the excellent Governour, and which I beare to you, hath no limit. And like as you give me chastisement, so will you also shew me favour. And that which now I crave of you is this, to declare your will unto me, and those things wherein I may bee able to doe you the most and best service.

The Governour answered him, that because he did not find him in that towne, hee was incensed against him, thinking he had absented himselfe, as others had done : but seeing he now knew his loyaltie and love, he would alwaies hold him as a brother, and favour him in all his affaires. The cacique went with him to the towne where he resided, which was a daies journie from thence. They passed through a

A smal towne. smal town, where there was a lake, where the Indians made

Salt made of salt springs of water. salt : and the Christians made some one day while they rested there, of a brackish water, which sprang neere the towne in ponds like fountaines. The Governour staied in Chaguate sixe daies. There he was informed of the habitation that was toward the west. They told him, that three daies journie from thence was a province called Aguacay. The day that he departed from Chaguate, a Christian, called Francisco de Guzman, the base sonne of a gentleman of Sivill, staied behind, and went to the Indians, with an Indian woman which he kept as his concubine, for feare he should be punished for gaming debts, that he did owe. The Governor had travelled two daies before he missed him ; hee sent the cacique word to seeke him up, and to send him to Aguacay, whither he travelled : which hee did not performe. From the cacique of Aguacay, before they came into the countrie, there met him on the way fifteen Indians with a present of skinnes, fish,

Aguacay. and rosted venison. The Governour came to his towne on Wednesday, the fourth of Julie. He found the towne without people, and lodged in it : he staied there about a day ;

during which, he made some roades, and tooke many men and women. There they had knowledge of the South Sea. Here there was great store of salt made of sand, which they gather in a vaine of ground like peeble stones. And it was made as they make salt in Cayas.

Knowledge of the South Sea.

Store of salt made.

CHAPTER XXXII.

How the Governour went from Aguacay to Naguatex, and what happened unto him.

The same day that the Governour departed from Aguacay, he lodged in a small towne subject to the lord of that province. The campe pitched hard by a lake of salt water, and that evening they made some salt there. The day following hee lodged betweene two mountaines in a thinne grove of wood. The next day hee came to a small towne called Pato. The fourth day after his departure from Aguacay he came to the first habitation of a province called Amaye. There an Indian was taken, which said, that from thence to Naguatex was a day and a halfes journey, which they travelled, finding all the way inhabited places. Having passed the peopled countrie of Amaye, on Saturday, the 20 of Julie, they pitched their campe at noone betweene Amaye and Naguatex, along the corner of a grove of very faire trees. In the same place certaine Indians were discovered, which came to view them. The horsemen went out to them, and killed six, and tooke two; whom the Governour asked, wherefore they came? They said, to know what people hee had, and what order they kept; and that the cacique of Naguatex, their lord, had sent them; and that he, with other caciques which came to aide him, determined that day to bid him battell. While they were occupied in these questions and answeres, there

A smal towne.

Salt made here.

Pato.

Amaye.

Julie 20.

came many Indians by two waies in two squadrons ; and when
they saw they were descried, giving a great crie, they assaulted
the Christians each squadron by it selfe ; but seeing what
resistance the Christians made them, they turned their backes
and betooke themselves to flight, in which many of them lost
their lives ; and most of the horsemen following them in chase,
carelesse of the camp, other two squadrons of Indians, which
lay in ambush, set upon the Christians that were in the campe,
which also they resisted, who also had their reward as the
first.   After the flight of the Indians, and that the Christians
were retired, they heard a great noise a crossebow shot from
the place where they were.   The Governour sent twelve
horsemen to see what it was.   They found sixe Christians,
foure footmen and two horsemen, among many Indians ; the
horsemen defending the footmen with great labour.   These
being of them that chased the first two squadrons, had lost
themselves, and, comming to recover the campe, fell among
those with whom they were fighting ; and so they, and those
that came to succour them, slew many of the Indians, and
brought one alive to the campe, whom the Governour examined, who they were that came to bid him battell.   He
told him, that they were the cacique of Naguatex, and of
Amaye, and another of a province called Hacanac, a lord of
great countries and many subjects ; and that the cacique of
Naguatex came for captaine and chiefest of them all.   The
Governour commanded his right arme and nose to be cut
off, and sent him to the cacique of Naguatex, charging him
to tell him, that the next day hee would bee in his countrey
to destroy him ; and if hee would withstand his entrance,
hee should stay for him.

Hacanac.

That night he lodged there, and the next day hee came
to the habitation of Naguatex, which was very scattering :
he inquired where the caciques chiefe towne was ? They
told him that it was on the other side of a river that passed
thereby.   Hee travelled thitherward, and came unto it ; and

Naguatex.

A river.

on the other side hee saw many Indians, that taried for him,
making shew as though they would defend the passage.
And because hee knew not whether it could bee waded, nor
where the passage was, and that some Christians and horses
were hurt, that they might have time to recover, he determined to rest certaine daies in the towne where he was.   So
hee pitched his campe a quarter of a league from the river,
because the weather was very hot, neere unto the towne, in August.
a thinne grove of very faire and hie trees, neere a brookes
side; and in that place were certaine Indians taken, whom
hee examined, whether the river were wadeable or no ?
They said, yea, at some times, and in some places.   Within
ten daies after, he sent two captaines with fifteene horsemen
a peece upward and downe the river, with Indians to shew
them where they should goe over, to see what habitation was
on the other side; and the Indians withstood them both,
defending the passage of the river as farre as they were able,
but they passed in despite of them; and on the other side They passe
of the river they saw great habitation, and great store of the river.
victuals, and with these newes returned to the camp.

CHAPTER XXXIII.

*How the cacique of Naguatex came to visite the Governour, and how the
Governour departed from Naguatex and came to Nondacao.*

The Governour sent an Indian from Naguatex, where hee
lay, to command the cacique to come to serve and obey him,
and that hee would forgive him all that was past; and if he
came not, that he would seeke him, and give him such punishment as he had deserved for that which he had done
against him.   Within two daies the Indian returned, and

said that the cacique would come the next day; which, the same day when he came, sent many Indians before him, among whom there were some principall men : hee sent them to see what countenance they found in the Governour, to resolve with himselfe whether hee should goe or not. The Indians let him understand that he was comming, and went away presently; and the cacique came within two houres, accompanied with many of his men : they came all in a ranke one before another on both sides, leaving a lane in the middest, where hee came. They came where the Governour was, all of them weeping after the manner of Tulla, which was not farre from thence toward the east. The cacique made his due obedience, and this speech following :

Right high and mightie lord, whom all the world ought to serve and obey, I was bold to appeare before your lordship, having committed so heinous and abominable an act, as only for me to have imagined, deserved to be punished ; trusting in your greatnes, that although I deserve to obtaine no pardon, yet for your owne sake only you will use clemencie toward me, considering how small I am in comparison of your lordship ; and not to think upon my weaknesses, which to my griefe and for my greater good, I have knowne. And I beleeve that you and yours are immortall ; and that your lordship is lord of the land of nature, seeing that you subdue all things, and they obey you, even the very hearts of men. For when I beheld the slaughter and destruction of my men in the battell, which, through mine ignorance, and the counsell of a brother of mine, which died in the same, I gave your lordship, presently I repented me in my heart of the error which I had committed, and desired to serve and obey you ; and to this end I come, that your lordship may chastise and command mee as your owne.

The Governour answered him, that he forgave him all which was past ; that from thenceforth hee should do his dutie, and that he would hold him for his friend, and that he

Tulla not far from Naguatex, eastward.

would favour him in all things. Within foure daies hee departed thence, and comming to the river he could not passe, The river growne unpassable in August at Naguatex. because it was growne very bigge; which seemed to him a thing of admiration, being at that time that it was, and since it had not rained a moneth before. The Indians said, that it increased many times after that manner without raining in all the countrie. It was supposed, that it might bee the tide Conjectures of a sea to the northward. that came into it. It was learned that the flood came alway from above, and that the Indians of all that countrie had no knowledge of the sea. The Governour returned unto the place where he had lodged before: and understanding within eight daies after that the river was passeable, he departed. He passed over and found the towne without people: he A towne. lodged in the field, and sent the cacique word to come unto him, and to bring him a guide to goe forward. And some daies being past, seeing the cacique came not, nor sent any bodie, hee sent two captaines sundrie waies to burne the Townes burned, townes, and to take such Indians as they could finde. They burnt great store of victuals, and took many Indians. The cacique seeing the hurt that he received in his countrie, sent six principall Indians with three men for guides, which knew the language of the countrie, through which the Governour was to passe. Hee departed presently from Naguatex, and within three daies journey came to a towne of foure or five houses, which belonged to the cacique of that province, which is called Nissoone; it was evill inhabited and had Nissoone. little maiz. Two daies journey forward the guides which guided the Governour, if they were to goe westward, guided him to the east; and sometimes went up and downe through very great woods out of the way. The Governour commanded them to bee hanged upon a tree: and a woman that they tooke in Nissoone guided him, and went backe againe to seeke the way. In two daies he came to another miserable towne, called Lacane; an Indian was taken in that place, Lacane. that said, that the countrie of Nondacao was a countrie of Nondacao.

great habitation, and the houses scattering the one from the
other, as they use to bee in mountains, and had great store
of maiz. The cacique came with his men weeping, like them
of Naguatex : for this is their use in token of obedience : hee
made him a present of much fish, and offered to doe what he
would command him.   Hee tooke his leave, and gave him a
guide to the province of Soacatino.

———————

CHAPTER XXXIV.

*How the Governour went from Nondacao to Soacatino and Guasco, and
passed through a desert, from whence, for want of a guide and
an interpretour, he returned to Nilco.*

The Governour departed from Nondacao toward Soacatino,
and in five daies journie came to a province called Aays.
The Indians which inhabited it, had no notice of the Christians : but as soone as they saw that they entred into their
country, they assembled themselves : and as they came together fifty or one hundred, they came foorth to fight : while
some fought, others came and charged our men another way,
and while they followed some, others followed them.   The
fight lasted the greatest part of the day, till they came to their
towne.   Some horses and men were wounded, but not to any
hurt of their travelling : for there was no wound that was
dangerous.   There was a great spoile made of the Indians.
That day that the Governour departed from thence, the Indian that guided him said, that in Nondacao he had heard
say, that the Indians of Soacatino had seene other Christians,
whereof they all were very glad : thinking it might be true,
and that they might have entred into those parts by Nueva
Espanna ; and that if it were so, it was in their owne hand
to goe out of Florida, if they found nothing of profit : for

Aays.

A towne.

they feared they should lose themselves in some wildernes.
This Indian led him two daies out of the way. The Governour commanded to torture him. He said, that the cacique of
Nondacao, his lord, had commanded him to guide them so,
because they were his enemies, and that hee was to doe as
his lord commanded him. The Governour commanded him
to be cast to the dogs: and another guided him to Soacatino, Soacatino.
whither hee came the day following. It was a verie poore
countrie; there was great want of maiz in that place. Hee
asked the Indians, whether they knew of any other Christians. They said, that a little from thence toward the south
they heard they were. He travelled twenty daies through a Twenty daies
travell to-
countrie evill inhabited, where they suffered great scarcitie ward the
south.
and trouble. For that little maiz which the Indians had,
they had hidden and buried in the woods, where the Christians, after they were well wearied with their travell, at the
end of their journie went to seeke by digging what they
should eat. At last, comming to a province that was called
Guasco, they found maiz, wherewith they loaded their horses, Guasco :
here they
and the Indians that they had. From thence they went to found some
Turkie
another towne called Naquiscoça. The Indians said, they stones, and
mantles of
had no notice of any other Christians. The Governour cotton wooll.
Chap. 35.
commanded to torment them. They said, that they came Naquiscoça.
first to another lordship, which was called Naçacahoz, and Naçacahoz.
from thence returned again to the west, from whence they
came.

The Governour came in two daies to Naçacahoz: some
women were taken there : among whom there was one, which
said, that she had seene Christians, and had been taken by
them, and had run away. The Governour sent a captaine
with fifteen horsemen to the place where the woman said
she had seene them, to see if there were any signe of horses,
or any token of their being there. After they had gone three
or foure leagues, the woman that guided them said, that all

T

that she had told them was untrue. And so they held all
the rest that the Indians had said, of seeing Christians in the
land of Florida. And, because the countrie that way was
poore of maiz, and toward the west there was no notice of
They return-
ed to Guasco. any habitation, they returned to Guasco.

The Indians told them there, that ten daies journie from
thence toward the west, was a river called Daycao, whither
they went sometimes a hunting and killing of deere; and
that they had seene people on the other side, but knew not
what habitation was there. There the Christians tooke such
maiz as they found and could carrie, and going ten daies
The river of
Daycao, journie through a wildernesse, they came to the river which
which seem-
eth to be the Indians had told them of. Ten horsemen, which the
Rio del Oro.¹ Governour had sent before, passed over the same, and went
in a way that led to the river, and lighted upon a companie
of Indians that dwelt in verie little cabins; who, as soone as
they saw them, tooke themselves to flight, leaving that which
they had: all which was nothing but miserie and povertie.
The countrie was so poore, that among them all there was
not found halfe a peck of maiz. The horsemen tooke two
Indians, and returned with them to the river, where the
Governour staied for them. He sought to learne of them
what habitation was toward the west. There was none in
the camp that could understand their language. The Governour assembled the captaines and principall persons to deter-

¹ The "Rio del Oro" is placed in Ortelius's map of Florida (Theatrum
orbis terrarum, 1570) midway between the "Rio del Spirito Santo", i.e., the
Mississippi, and the "Rio Escondido", which is probably the "Rio Bravo
del Norte"; but it is difficult to determine which of the several rivers
within that space may be referred to. The reader will have already observed that under the name of Florida are included countries lying far
beyond the tract at present bearing that designation. This name indeed
was originally, though vaguely, applied by the Spaniards to that part
of the United States lying between the ocean and the Appalachian
mountains, and extending east and west from about the Savannah river
as far as Texas.

mine, with their advice, what they should doe. And the most part said, that they thought it best to returne backe to Rio Grande, or the great river of Guachoya; because that in Nilco and thereabout was store of maiz; saying, that they would make pinaces that winter, and the next sommer passe down the river to the seaward in them, and comming to the sea they would goe along the coast to Nueva Espanna. For though it seemed a doubtfull thing and difficult, by that which they had already alleaged, yet it was the last remedie they had. For by land they could not goe for want of an interpretour. And they held, that the countrie beyond the river of Daycao, where they were, was that which Cabeça de Vaca mentioned in his relation, that he passed of the Indians, which lived like the Alarbes,[1] having no setled place, and fed upon tunas[2] and rootes of the fields, and wilde beasts that they killed; which, if it were so, if they should enter into it, and finde no victuals to passe the winter, they could not chuse but perish. For they were entred alreadie into the beginning of October; and if they staied any longer, they were not able to returne for raine and snowes, nor to sustaine themselves in so poore a countrey. The Governour (that desired long to see himselfe in a place where hee might sleepe his full sleep, rather then to conquer and governe a countrie where so many troubles presented themselves) presently returned back that same way that he came.

No travelling by land without an interpretour.

---

[1] *i.e.* the Arabs.

[2] The Indian fig, or prickly pear—*Cactus opuntia.*

CHAPTER XXXV.

How they returned to Nilco, and came to Minoya, where they agreed to
make ships to depart out of the land of Florida.

When that which was determined was published in the
campe, there were many that were greatly grieved at it; for
they held the sea voyage as doubtfull, for the evill meanes
they had, and of as great danger as the travelling by land;
and they hoped to finde some rich countrie before they came
to the land of the Christians, by that which Cabeça de Vaca
had told the emperour; and that was this, that after hee had
found clothes made of cotton wooll, hee saw gold and silver,
and stones of great value. And they had not yet come
where hee had been. For untill that place hee alwaies
travelled by the sea coast; and they travelled farre within
the land; and that going toward the west, of necessitie they
should come where hee had been. For he said, that in a
certaine place he travelled many daies, and entred into the
land toward the north. And in Guasco they had alreadie
found some Turkie stones[1] and mantles of cotton wooll, which
the Indians signified by signes that they had from the west;
and that holding that course, they should draw neere to the
land of the Christians. But though they were much discon-
tented with it, and it grieved many to goe backward, which
would rather have adventured their lives and have died in
the land of Florida, then to have gone poore out of it: yet
were they not a sufficient part to hinder that which was
determined, because the principall men agreed with the
Governour. And afterward there was one that said, hee
would put out one of his owne eyes to put out another of
Luis de Moscoso, because it would grieve him much to see
him prosper; because as well himself as others of his friends

(marginal notes:)
Gold, silver, and precious stones, in Florida.

Turkie stones, and mantles of cotton wooll, found in Guasco.

[1] Turquoises.

had crossed that which hee durst not have done, seeing that within two daies hee should leave the government.

From Daycao, where now they were, to Rio Grande, or the Great River, was a hundred and fifty leagues, which unto that place they had gone westward. And by the way as they returned backe they had much adoe to find maiz to eate, for where they had passed the countrey was destroyed, and some little maiz that was left the Indians had hidden. The townes which in Naguatex they had burned (whereof it repented them) were repaired againe, and the houses full of maiz. This countrie is well inhabited and plentifull. In that place are vessels made of clay, which differ very little from those of Estremoz, or Monte-mor. In Chaguate the Indians by commandement of the cacique came peaceably, and said, that the Christian which remained there would not come. The Governour wrote unto him, and sent him inke and paper, that he might answere. The substance of the words of the letter was, to declare unto him his determination, which was, to goe out of the land of Florida, and to put him in remembrance that he was a Christian, that hee would not remaine in the subjection of infidels; that hee pardoned him the fault which he had done in going away to the Indians; that hee should come unto him, and if they did stay him, that hee would advertise him thereof by writing. The Indian went with the letter, and came again without any more answere, then on the back side his name and his seale, that they might know he was alive. The Governour sent twelve horsemen to seeke him; but he, which had his spies, so hid himselfe, that they could not find him. For want of maiz, the Governour could not stay any longer to seeke him.

Hee departed from Chaguate, and passed the river by Aays; going downe by it, hee found a towne called Chilano, which as yet they had not seen. They came to Nilco, and found so little maiz as could not suffice till they made their

150 leagues betweene the river of Daycao, and Rio Grande.

Naguatex.

Fine earthen vessels.

Chaguate.

Aays.
Chilano.

Nilco.

ships; because the Christians, being in Guachoya in the seede time, the Indians, for feare of them, durst not come to sow the grounds of Nilco; and they knew not thereabout any other countrie where any maiz was; and that was the most fruitfull soile that was thereaway, and where they had most hope to finde it. Every one was confounded, and the most part thought it bad counsell to come backe from the river of Daycao, and not to have followed their fortune, going that way that went over land. For by sea it seemed impossible to save themselves, unlesse God would worke a miracle for them; for there was neither pilot nor sea-chart; neither did they know where the river entred into the sea; neither had they notice of it; neither had they any thing wherewith to make sailes; nor any store of enequem, which is a grasse whereof they make okam, which grew there: and that which they found, they saved to calke the pinaces with-all; neither had they any thing to pitch them withall; neither could they make ships of such substance, but that any storme would put them in great danger; and they feared much it would fall out with them, as it did with Pamphilo de Narvaez, which was cast away upon that coast: and above all other it troubled them most, that they could finde no maiz; for without it they could not bee sustained, nor could doe any thing that they had neede of. All of them were put to great confusion. Their chiefe remedy was to commit themselves to God, and to beseech Him that He would direct them the way that they might save their lives. And it pleased Him of His goodnesse, that the Indians of Nilco came peaceablie, and told them, that two daies journey from thence, neere unto the Great River, were two townes, whereof the Christians had no notice, and that the province was called Minoya, and was a fruitfull soile; that, whether at this present there was any maiz or no, they knew not, because they had warre with them; but that they would be very glad, with the favour of the Christians, to goe and spoyle them. The

Governour sent a captaine thither with horsemen and footmen, and the Indians of Nilco with him. Hee came to
Minoya, and found two great townes seated in a plaine and
open soile, halfe-a league distant, one in sight of another,
and in them he tooke many Indians, and found great store
of maiz. Presently he lodged in one of them, and sent word
to the Governour what hee had found; wherewith they were
all exceeding glad. They departed from Nilco in the beginning of December, and all that way, and before from Chilano,
they endured much trouble; for they passed through many
waters, and many times it rained with a northren winde,
and was exceeding cold, so that they were in the open field
with water over and underneath them; and when at the end
of their daies journey they found drie ground to rest upon,
they gave great thanks to God. With this trouble almost
all the Indians that served them died. And after they were
in Minoya, many Christians also died; and the most part
were sicke of great and dangerous diseases, which had a
spice of the lethargie. At this place died Andrew de Vasconcelos, and two Portugals of Elvas, which were very neere
him, which were brethren, and by their surname called
Sotis. The Christians lodged in one of the townes, which
they liked best, which was fensed about, and distant a quarter of a league from the great river. The maiz that was in
the other towne was brought thither, and in all it was
esteemed to bee six thousand hanegs or bushels. And there
was the best timber to make ships that they had seene in all
the land of Florida ; wherefore all of them gave God great
thankes for so singular a favour, and hoped that that which
they desired would take effect, which was, that they might
safely bee conducted into the land of the Christians.

*Minoya.
Two great
townes.*

*The begin-
ning of De-
cember.*

*Raine, with
northern
wind, ex-
ceeding cold.*

*The death of
Andrew Vas-
concelos.*

CHAPTER XXXVI.

*How there were seven brigandines builded, and how they departed from
Minoya.*

As soone as they came to Minoya, the Governor commanded them to gather all the chaines together, which everie
one had to lead Indians in ; and to gather al the yron which
they had for their provision, and al the rest that was in the
camp, and to set up a forge to make nailes, and commanded
them to cut downe timber for the brigandines.   And a
Portugall of Ceuta, who, having bin a prisoner in Fez, had
learned to saw timber with a long saw, which for such pur-
poses they had carried with them, did teach others, which
helped him to saw timber.   And a Genowis, whom it pleased
God to preserve (for without him they had never come out
of the countrie : for there was never another that could make
ships but hee), with foure or five other Biscaine carpenters,
which hewed his plancks and other timbers, made the brigandines.   And two calkers, the one of Genua, the other of
Sardinia, did calke them with the tow of an hearb like hempe,
whereof before I have made mention, which there is named
enequen.   And because there was not enough of it, they
calked them with the flaxe of the countrie, and with the
mantles, which they ravelled for that purpose.   A cooper
which they had among them fell sicke, and was at the point
of death: and there was none other that had any skill in that
trade.   It pleased God to send him his health ; and albeit
he was verie weake, and could not labour, yet fifteen daies
before they departed, he made for every brigandine two
halfe hogsheads, which the mariners call quarterets, because
foure of them hold a pipe of water.   The Indians which
dwelt two daies journie above the river, in a province called

Enequen is
an herbe like
hempe.

Flaxe of the
countrie.

Taguanate, and likewise those of Nilco and Guacoya, and others their neighbours, seeing the brigandines in making, thinking, because their places of refuge are in the water, that they were to goe to seeke them, and because the Governour demanded mantles of them, as necessarie for sailes, came many times, and brought many mantles, and great store of fish. And for certaine it seemed that God was willing to favour them in so great necessitie, mooving the minds of the Indians to bring them: for to goe to take them they were never able. For in the towne where they were, as soone as winter came in, they were so inclosed and compassed with water, that they could go no farther by land then a league and a league and an half. And if they would goe farther, they could carrie no horses, and without them they were not able to fight with the Indians, because they were many; and so many for so many on foote they had the advantage of them by water and by land, because they were more apt and lighter, and by reason of the disposition of the countrie, which was according to their desire for the use of their warre. They brought also some cords, and those which wanted for cables were made of the barkes of mulberrie trees. They made stirrops of wood, and made ankers of their stirrops. In the moneth of March, when it had not rained a moneth before, the river grew so big, that it came to Nilco, which was nine leagues off: and on the other side the Indians said, that it reached other nine leagues into the land. In the towne where the Christians were, which was somewhat high ground, where they could best goe, the water reached to the stirrops. They made certaine rafts of timber, and laid manie boughes upon them, whereon they set their horses, and in the houses they did the like. But seeing that nothing prevailed, they went up to the lofts; and if they went out of the houses, it was in canoes, or on horseback in those places where the ground was hiest. So they were two moneths,

Taguanate, two daies journey above Minoya.

The great use of horses.

Mulberrie trees.

The mightie increasing of the river for two moneths space, to wit, all March and Aprill.

and could doe nothing, during which time the river decreased not.

The Indians ceased not to come unto the brigantines as they were wont, and came in canoes. At that time the Governour feared they would set upon him. Hee commanded his men to take an Indian secretly of those that came to the towne, and to stay him till the rest were gone : and they tooke one. The Governour commanded him to bee put to torture, to make him confesse whether the Indians did

The grand conspiracie of the Indians against the Christians.
practise any treason or no. Hee confessed that the caciques of Nilco, Guachoya, and Taguanate, and others, which in al were about twenty caciques, with a great number of people, determined to come upon him; and that three daies before, they would send a great present of fish to colour their great treason and malice, and on the verie day they would send

Note well.
some Indians before with another present. And these, with those which were our slaves, which were of their conspiracie also, should set the houses on fire, and first of all possesse themselves of the lances which stood at the doores of the houses; and the caciques with all their men should bee neere the towne in ambush in the wood, and when they saw the fire kindled, should come and make an end of the conquest.

Thirtie Indians of the cacique of Guachoya have their right hands cut off.
The Governour commanded the Indian to be kept in a chaine, and the selfe same day that he spake of, there came thirty Indians with fish. Hee commanded their right hands to be cut off, and sent them so backe to the cacique of Guachoya, whose men they were. He sent him word, that he and the rest should come when they would, for he desired nothing more, and that hee should know that they thought not any thing which he knew not before they thought of it. Hereupon they all were put in a very great feare. And the caciques of Nilco and Taguanate came to excuse themselves ; and a few daies after came he of Guachoya, and a principal Indian and his subject said, he knew by certaine information, that the caciques of Nilco and Taguanate were agreed

to come and make warre upon the Christians. As soone as the Indians came from Nilco, the Governour examined them, and they confessed it was true. Hee delivered them presently to the principall man of Guachoya, which drew them out of the towne and killed them. Another day came some from Taguanate, and confessed it likewise. The Governour commanded their right hands and noses to be cut off, and sent them to the cacique, wherewith they of Guachoya remained very well contented; and they came oftentimes with presents of mantles, and fish, and hogs, which bred in the countrie of some swine that were lost by the way the last yeere. As soone as the waters were slaked, they perswaded the Governour to send men to Taguanate. They came and brought canoes, wherein the footemen were conveied downe the river, and a captaine with horsemen went by land; and the Indians of Guachoya, which guided him till they came to Taguanate, assaulted the towne, and took many men and women, and mantles, which, with those that they had alreadie, were sufficient to supplie their want.

The brigandines being finished in the moneth of June, the Indians having told us that the river increased but once a yeere, when the snowes did melt, in the time wherein I mentioned it had alreadie increased, being now in sommer, and having not rained a long time, it pleased God that the flood came up to the towne to seeke the brigandines, from whence they carried them by water to the river; which, if they had gone by land, had been in danger of breaking and splitting their keeles, and to bee all undone; because that for want of iron the spikes were short, and the planckes and timber were very weake. The Indians of Minoya, during the time that they were there, came to serve them (being driven thereunto by necessity), that of the maiz which they had taken from them, they would bestow some crummes upon them. And because the countrie was fertill, and the people used to feed of maiz, and the Christians had gotten all

The right hands and noses of traitours cut off.

Hogges in Florida.

Taguanate taken.

June.

The river increaseth but once a yeere, when the snowes doe melt in March and Aprill.

A miraculous accident.

from them that they had, and the people were many, they
were not able to sustaine themselves.   Those which came to
the towne were so weake and feeble, that they had no flesh
left on their bones ; and many came and died neere the towne
for pure hunger and weakenesse. The Governour commanded
upon grievous punishments to give them no maiz.   Yet,
when they saw that the hogges wanted it not, and that they
had yeelded themselves to serve them, and considering their
miserie and wretchednes, having pity of them, they gave
them part of the maiz which they had.   And when the time
of their embarkment came, there was not sufficient to serve
their owne turnes.   That which there was, they put into the
brigandines, and into great canoes tied two and two together.
They shipped twenty-two of the best horses that were in the
camp, the rest they made dried flesh of ; and dressed the
hogges which they had in like manner.   They departed from
Minoya the second day of Julie, 1543.

CHAPTER XXXVII.

*As the Christians went downe the great river on their voyage, the Indians
of Quigalta did set upon them, and what was the successe thereof.*

The day before they departed from Minoya, they determined to dismisse al the men and women of the countrie,
which they had detained as slaves to serve them, save some
hundred, little more or lesse, which the Governour embarked,
and others whom it pleased him to permit.   And because
there were many men of qualitie, whom he could not deny
that which he granted to others, he used a policy, saying,
that they might serve them as long as they were in the river,
but when they came to the sea, they must send them away

for want of water, because they had but few vessels. He
told his friends in secret, that they should carrie theirs to
Nueva Espanna. And all those whom hee bare no good will
unto (which were the greater number), ignorant of that which
was hidden from them, which afterward time discovered,
thinking it inhumanitie for so little time of service, in reward
of the great service that they had done them, to carrie them
with them, to leave them slaves to other men out of their
owne countries; left five hundred men and women; among 500 slaves
left in the
whom were many boies and girls, which spake and under- countrie.
stood the Spanish tongue. The most of them did nothing
but weepe, which mooved great compassion; seeing that all
of them with good will would have become Christians, and
were left in state of perdition. There went from Minoya They saile
downe Rio
three hundred and twenty-two Spaniards, in seven brigan- Grande from
Minoya 17
dines, well made, save that the plankes were thin, because daies before
they came to
the nailes were short, and were not pitched, nor had any the mouth
thereof.
decks to keep the water from comming in. In stead of decks
they laid planks, whereon the mariners might runne to trim
their sailes, and the people might refresh themselves above
and below. The Governour made his captaines, and gave to
every one his brigandine, and took their oth and their word,
that they would obey him, untill they came to the land of
the Christians. The Governour tooke one of the brigandines
for himself, which he best liked. The same day that they
departed from Minoya, they passed by Guachoya, where the
Indians tarried for them in canoes by the river. And on the
shore, they had made a great arbour with boughes; they
desired him to come on shore, but he excused himselfe, and
so went along. The Indians in their canoes accompanied
him; and comming where an arme of the river declined on
the right hand, they said, that the province of Quigalta was
neere unto that place, and importuned the Governour to set
upon him, and that they would aide him. And because they
had said, that he dwelt three daies journie downe the river,

the Governour supposed that they had plotted some treason
against him, and there left them; and went downe with the
greatest force of the water. The current was very strong,
and with the helpe of ores, they went very swiftly. The
first day they landed in a wood on the left hand of the river,
and at night they withdrew themselves to the brigandines.
The next day they came to a towne, where they went on
shore, and the people that was in it durst not tarrie. A
woman that they tooke there being examined, said, that that
towne belonged to a cacique named Huasene, subject to
Quigalta, and that Quigalta tarried for them below in the
river with many men. Certaine horsemen went thither, and
found some houses, wherein was much maiz. Immediately
more of them went thither and tarried there one day, in which
they did beate out, and tooke as much maiz as they needed.
While they were there, many Indians came from the nether
part of the river, and on the other side right against them,
somewhat carelessly set themselves in order to fight.

 The Governour sent in two canoes the crossebowmen that
he had, and as many more as could goe in them. They ran
away, and seeing the Spaniards could not overtake them,
they returned backe, and tooke courage; and comming
neerer, making an outcrie, they threatened them; and as
soone as they departed thence, they went after them, some
in canoes, and some by land along the river; and getting
before, comming to a towne that stood by the rivers side,
they joyned altogether, making a shew that they would tarrie
there. Everie brigandine towed a canoe fastened to their
sternes for their particular service. Presently there entred
men into everie one of them, which made the Indians to flie,
and burned the towne. The same day they presently landed
in a great field, where the Indians durst not tarrie. The
next day there were gathered together an hundred canoes,
among which were some that carried sixty and seventy men;
and the principall mens canoes had their tilts, and plumes

The second day.

Huasene.

Another day.

A town burned.

The third day.
A fleete of an hundred faire and great canoes.

of white and red feathers for their ensignes ; and they came
within two crossebow shot of the brigandines, and sent three
Indians in a small canoe with a fained message, to view the
manner of the brigandines, and what weapons they had.
And comming to the side of the Governours brigandine, one
of the Indians entred, and said :

*That the cacique of Quigalta, his lord, sent him his com-
mendations, and did let him understand, that all that the
Indians of Guachoya had told him concerning himselfe was
false, and that they had incensed him, because they were his
enemies ; that he was his servant, and should find him so.*

The Governour answered him, that he beleeved all that he
said was true, and willed him to tell him, that he esteemed
his friendship very much. With this answer they returned
to the place where the rest in their canoes were waiting for
them ; and from thence all of them fell downe, and came
neere the Spaniards, shouting aloud, and threatning of them.
The Governour sent John de Guzman, which had been a
captaine of footemen in Florida, with fifteen armed men in
canoes, to make them give way. As soone as the Indians
sawe them come towards them, they divided themselves into
two parts, and stood still till the Spaniards came nie them ;
and when they were come neere them, they joyned together on
both sides, taking John de Guzman in the middest, and them
that came first with him, and with great furie borded them:
and as their canoes were bigger, and many of them leaped into
the water to stay them, and to lay hold on the canoes of the
Spaniards, and overwhelme them ; so presently they over-
whelmed them. The Christians fell into the water, and with
the weight of their armour sunke downe to the bottome ; and
some few, that by swimming or holding by the canoe could have
saved themselves, with oares, and staves, which they had, they
strooke them on the head and made them sinke. When they of
the brigandines saw the overthrow, though they went about to
succour them, yet through the current of the river they could

not goe backe. Foure Spaniards fled to the brigandine that was neerest to the canoes ; and only these escaped of those that came among the Indians. They were eleven that died there ; among whom John de Guzman was one, and a sonne of Don Carlos, called John de Vargas ; the rest also were persons of account, and men of great courage. Those that escaped by swimming, said, that they saw the Indians enter the canoe of John de Guzman at the sterne of one of their canoes,[1] and whether they carried him away dead or alive, they could not certainly tell.

Eleven Spaniards drowned.
The death of John de Guzman.

CHAPTER XXXVIII.

Which declareth how they were pursued by the Indians.

The Indians, seeing that they had gotten the victorie, tooke such courage, that they assaulted them in the brigandines, which they durst not doe before. They came first to that brigandine wherein Calderon went for captaine, and was in the rerewarde, and at the first volie of arrowes they wounded twenty-five men. There were only foure armed men in this brigandine ; these did stand at the brigandines side to defend it. Those that were unarmed, seeing how they hurt them, left their oares and went under the deck ; whereupon the brigandine began to crosse, and to goe where the current of the streame carried it. One of the armed men seeing this, without the commandement of the captaine, made a footman to take an oare and stirre the brigandine, hee standing before him and defending him with his target. The Indians came no neerer then a bowshot, from whence they offended and were not offended, receiving no hurt ; for

Twenty-five Spaniards wounded.

The great use of large targets.

---

[1] " Os que nadando escaparam disseram que aos Indios vieram ẽtrar cõ Joam de Guzmam pella popa de hũa almadia sua," etc.

in every brigandine was but one crossebow, and those which wee had were very much out of order, so that the Christians did nothing else but stand for a butte to receive their arrowes. Having left this brigandine they went to another, and fought with it halfe an houre; and so from one to another they fought with them all. The Christians had mattes to lay under them, which were double, and so close and strong, that no arrow went thorow them. And as soone as the Indians gave them leisure, they fensed the brigandines with them. And the Indians seeing that they could not shoote levell, shot their arrowes at random up into the aire, which fell into the brigandines and hurt some of the men; and not therewith contented, they sought to get to them which were in the canoes with the horses. Those of the brigandines environed them to defend them, and tooke them among them. Thus seeing themselves much vexed by them, and so wearied that they could no longer endure it, they determined to travell all the night following, thinking to get beyond the countrie of Quigalta, and that they would leave them; but when they thought least of it, supposing they had now left them, they heard very neere them so great outcries, that they made them deafe, and so they followed us all that night and the next day till noone, by which time we were come into the countrie of others, whom they desired to use us after the same manner: and so they did.

Strong mats a good defence against arrowes.

Another province.

The men of Quigalta returned home; and the other in fiftie canoes fought with us a whole day and a night; and they entred one of the brigandines that came in the rereward by the canoe which she had at her sterne, and tooke away a woman which they found in it, and afterward hurt some of the men of the brigandines. Those which came with the horses in the canoes, being wearie with rowing night and day, lingered behind; and presently the Indians came upon them, and they of the brigandines tarried for them. The Governour resolved to goe on shore and to kill

x

the horses, because of the slow way which they made because
of them. As soone as they saw a place convenient for it,
Dried horse-
flesh for
food. they went thither and killed the horses, and brought the
flesh of them to drie it aboord. Foure or five of them
remained on shore alive : the Indians went unto them after
the Spaniards were embarked. The horses were not acquainted with them, and began to neigh, and runne up and
downe in such sort, that the Indians, for feare of them, leaped
into the water, and getting into their canoes went after the
brigandines, shooting cruelly at them. They followed us
that evening and the night following till the next day at
tenne of the clocke, and then returned up the river. Pre-
A smal
towne. sently, from a small towne that stood upon the river, came
seven canoes, and followed us a little way downe the river,
shooting at us ; but seeing they were so few that they could
doe us but little harme, they returned to their towne. From
thence forward, untill they came to the sea, they had no
They sailed
17 daies
downe the
river, which
is about 250
leagues. encounter. They sailed downe the river seventeene daies,
which may be two hundred and fifty leagues journey, little
more or lesse ; and neere unto the sea the river is divided
into two armes ; each of them is a league and an halfe broad.

CHAPTER XXXIX.

*How they came unto the sea : and what happened unto them in all
their voiage.*

Halfe a league before they came to the sea, they came to
anker to rest themselves there about a day ; for they were
very weary with rowing, and out of heart. For by the space
of many daies they had eaten nothing but parched and sod-

den maiz; which they had by allowance every day, an head-
peece ful by strike[1] for every three men. While they rode
there at anker, seven canoes of Indians came to set upon
those which they brought with them. The Governour commanded armed men to go aboord them, and to drive them
farther off. They came also against them by land through a
thick wood and a moorish ground, and had staves with very
sharp forked heads made of the bones of fishes, and fought
very valiantly with us, which went out to encounter them.
And the other that came in canoes with their arrowes staied
for them that came against them, and at their comming, both
those that were on land and those in the canoes wounded
some of us. And seeing us come neere them, they turned
their backs, and like swift horses among footemen gat away
from us, making some returnes, and reuniting themselves
together, going not past a bow shot off; for in so retiring they
shot, without receiving any hurt of the Christians. For though
they had some bowes, yet they could not use them; and brake
their armes with rowing to overtake them. And the Indians
easily in their compasse went with their canoes, staying and
wheeling about as it had been in a skirmish; perceiving that
those that came against them could not offend them. And
the more they strove to come neere them, the more hurt they
received. As soone as they had driven them farther off,
they returned to the brigandines. They staied two daies
there, and departed from thence unto the place where the
arme of the river entreth into the sea. They sounded in
the river neere unto the sea, and found forty fathoms water.
They staied there. And the Governour commanded al and
singular persons to speake their minds touching their voiage,
whether it were best to crosse over to Nueva Espanna, com-
mitting themselves to the hie sea, or whether they should

---

[1] A strike, or strickle, is an instrument used for scraping off the surface
of a measure of grain to a level with the top. The original word is
arrasado, i. e., rased or smoothed.

keepe along the coast. There were sundry opinions touching this matter; wherein John Danusco, which presumed much, and tooke much upon him in the knowledge of navigation and matters of the sea, although hee had but little experience, mooved the Governour with his talke; and his opinion was seconded by some others. And they affirmed, that it was much better to passe by the hie sea, and crosse the gulfe, which was three of foure parts the lesser travell; because in going along the coast, they went a great way about, by reason of the compasse which the land did make. John Danusco said, that he had seene the sea card, and that from the place where they were, the coast ran east and west unto Rio de las Palmas; and from Rio de las Palmas to Nueva Espanna from north to south; and therefore in sailing alwaies in sight of land would bee a great compassing about and spending of much time; and that they would be in great danger to be overtaken with winter before they should get to the land of the Christians; and that in ten or twelve daies space, having good weather, they might bee there in crossing over. The most part were against this opinion, and said, that it was more safe to go along the coast, though they staied the longer, because their ships were very weake and without decks, so that a very little storme was enough to cast them away; and if they should be hindred with calmes, or contrarie weather, through the small store of vessels which they had to carrie water in, they should likewise fall into great danger; and that although the ships were such as they might venture in them, yet having neither pilot nor sea card to guide themselves, it was no good counsell to crosse the gulfe. This opinion was confirmed by the greatest part, and they agreed to go along the coast. At the time wherein they sought to depart from thence, the cable of the anker of the Governours brigandine brake, and the anker remained in the river. And albeit they were neere the shore, yet it was so deepe that the divers diving many times could never find it, which caused great sadnes in the Governour, and in all those that went with him in his brigandine. But with a grindstone which they had, and certaine bridles which remained to some of the gentlemen and men of worship which had horses, they made a weight which served instead of an anker.

The 18 of July, they went foorth to sea with faire and prosperous weather for their voiage. And seeing that they [1] were gone two or three leagues from the shore, the captaines of the other brigandines overtooke them, and asked the Governour wherefore he did put off from the shore? and that if he would leave the coast, he should say so; and he should not do it without the consent of all; and that if hee did otherwise, they would not follow him, but that every one would doe what seemed best unto himselfe. The Governour answered, that hee would doe nothing without their counsell, but that hee did beare off from the land to saile the better and safer by night; and that the next day when time served, he would returne to the sight of land againe. They sailed with a reasonable good wind that day and the night following, and the next day till evening song, alwaies in fresh water; whereat they wondred much, for they were verie farre from land. But the force of the current of the river is so great, and the coast there is so shallow and gentle, that the fresh water entreth farre into the sea. That evening on their right hand they saw certaine creekes, whither they went, and rested there that night: where John Danusco with his reasons wonne them at last, that all consented and agreed to commit themselves to the maine sea, alleaging, as he had done before, that it was a great advantage, and that their voyage would be much shorter. They sailed two daies, and

Marginal notes: They landed the 30 of May 1539. Chap. 7, they went foorth to sea July 18, 1543.

Fresh water almost two daies sailing in the sea.

The coast shallow.

Certaine creekes where they rested a night.

---

[1] *i. e.,* the Governour and John Danusco. The passage in the original stands thus: " Ho Gouernador & coelle Joã Danusco cõ seus bragantins ao mar se meterā, & todos os seguirā; & vēdo q' de trr'a duas ou tres legoas desuiados estavā, os capitães dos outros bragantins os alcāçaram," etc.

when they would have come to sight of land, they could not, for the winde blew from the shore. On the fourth daie, seeing their fresh water began to faile, fearing necessitie and danger, they all complained of John Danusco and of the Governour that followed his counsell : and every one of the captaines said, that they would no more goe from the shore, though the Governour went whither he would. It pleased God that the winde changed, though but a little, and at the end of foure daies after they had put to sea, being alreadie destitute of water, by force of rowing they got within sight of land, and with great trouble recovered it, in an open roade. That evening the winde came to the south, which on that coast is a crosse winde, and drave the brigandines against the shore, because it blew very hard, and the anchors were so weake that they yeelded and began to bend. The Governour commanded all men to leape into the water, and going between them and the shore, and thrusting the brigandines into the sea as soone as the wave was past, they saved them till the winde ceased.

An open roade.

CHAPTER XL.

How they lost one another by a storme, and afterward came together in a creeke.

In the bay where they rode, after the tempest was past, they went on shore, and with mattockes which they had, they digged certaine pits, which grew full of fresh water, where they filled all the cask which they had. The next day they departed thence, and sailed two daies, and entred into a creeke like unto a poole, fenced from the south winde which then did blow and was against them ; and there they

Fresh water is commonlie found by digging in the sands on the sea side.

staied foure daies, not being able to get out; and when the
sea was calme they rowed out. They sailed that day, and
toward evening the winde grew so strong that it drave them
on the shore, and they were sorie that they had put foorth
from the former harbour; for as soone as night approched, a
storme began to rise in the sea, and the winde still waxed
more and more violent with a tempest. The brigandines
lost one another; two of them, which bare more into the sea,
entred into an arme of the sea, which pearced into the land *An arme of the sea.*
two leagues beyond the place where the other were that night.
The five which staied behinde, being alwaies a league and
halfe a league the one from the other, met together, without
any knowledge the one of the other, in a wilde roade, *A wild roade.*
where the winde and the waves drove them on shore; for
their anchors did streighten and came home; and they could
not rule their oares, putting seven or eight men to every oare,
which rowed to seaward: and all the rest leaped into the
water, and when the wave was past that drave the brigandine
on shore, they thrust it againe into sea with all the diligence and might that they had. Others, while another wave
was in comming, with bowles laved out the water that came
in overboord. While they were in this tempest, in great
feare of being cast away in that place, from midnight forward
they endured an intollerable torment of an infinite swarme *A swarme of grievous moskitoes.*
of moskitoes which fell upon them, which, as soone as they
had stung the flesh, it so infected it, as though they had bin
venemous. In the morning the sea was asswaged and the
wind slaked, but not the muskitoes; for the sailes which
were white seemed blacke with them in the morning. Those
which rowed, unlesse others kept them away, were not able
to row. Having passed the feare and danger of the storme,
beholding the deformities of their faces, and the blowes which
they gave themselves to drive them away, one of them laughed
at another. They met all together in the creek where the
two brigandines were, which outwent their fellowes. There

was found a skumme, which they call copee, which the sea
casteth up, and it is like pitch, wherewith in some places
where pitch is wanting they pitch their ships: there they
pitched their brigandines. They rested two daies, and then
eftsoones proceeded on their voyage. They sailed two daies
more, and landed in a bay or arme of the sea, where they
staied two daies. The same day that they went from thence,
sixe men went up in a canoe toward the head of it, and could
not see the end of it. They put out from thence with a south
winde, which was against them; but because it was little, and
for the great desire they had to shorten their voyage, they
put out to sea by force of oares, and for all that made very
little way with great labour in two daies, and went under the
lee of a small island into an arme of the sea, which compassed
it about. While they were there, there fell out such weather,
that they gave God many thankes, that they had found out
such an harbour. There was great store of fish in that place,
which they tooke with nets which they had, and hookes.
Heere a man cast an hooke and a line into the sea, and tied
the end of it to his arme, and a fish caught it, and drew him
into the water unto the necke; and it pleased God that hee
remembred himselfe of a knife that he had, and cut the line
with it. There they abode fourteene daies; and at the end
of them it pleased God to send them faire weather, for
which with great devotion they appointed a procession, and
went in procession along the strand, beseeching God to
bring them to a land where they might serve him in better
sort.

CHAPTER XLI.

How they came to the river of Panuco in Nueva Espanna.

In all the coast wheresoever they digged, they found fresh water: there they filled their vessels, and the procession being ended, embarked themselves, and going alwaies in sight of the shore, they sailed sixe daies. John Danusco said that it would doe well to beare out to seaward, for he had seene the sea card, and remembred that from Rio de las Palmas forward the coast did runne from north to south, and thitherto they had runne from east to west; and in his opinion, by his reckoning, Rio de las Palmas could not be farre off from where they were. That same night they put to sea, and in the morning they saw palme leaves floting, and the coast, which ranne north and south: from midday forward they saw great mountaines, which untill then they had not seene; for from this place to Puerto de Spiritu Santo, where they first landed in Florida, was a very plaine and low countrey; and therfore it cannot be descried, un- lesse a man come very neere it. By that which they saw, they thought that they had overshot Rio de Palmas that night, which is sixty leagues from the river of Panuco, which is in Nueva Espanna. They assembled all together, and some said it was not good to saile by night, lest they should overshoot the river of Panuco; and others said, it was not well to lose time while it was favourable, and that it could not be so neere that they should passe it that night: and they agreed to take away halfe the sailes, and so saile all night. Two of the brigandines, which sailed that night with all their sailes, by breake of day had overshot the river of Panuco without seeing it. Of the five that came behind, the first that came unto it was that wherein Calderan was

Sixe daies sailing.

Floting of palme leaves.

Great moun- taines.

All the north side of the Gulfe of Mexico is verie low land, save in this one place.

Y

captaine. A quarter of a league before they came at it, and
before they did see it, they saw the water muddie, and knew
it to be fresh water; and comming right against the river,
they saw, where it entred into the sea, that the water brake
upon a shold. And because there was no man there that
knew it, they were in doubt whether they should goe in, or
goe along, and they resolved to goe in; and before they
came unto the current, they went close to the shore, and
entred into the port; and as soone as they were come in,
they saw Indian men and women apparelled like Spaniards,
whom they asked in what countrey they were? They an-

The river of Panuco; the towne fif-teen leagues from the mouth of the river.
swered in Spanish, that it was the river of Panuco, and that
the towne of the Christians was fifteen leagues up within the
land. The joy that all of them received upon these newes
cannot sufficiently be expressed, for it seemed unto them
that at that instant they were borne again. And many went
on shore and kissed the ground, and kneeling on their knees,
with lifting up their hands and eyes to heaven, they all ceased
not to give God thankes.

Those which came after, as soone as they saw Calderan
come to an anchor with his brigandine in the river, presently
went thither, and came into the haven. The other two
brigandines which had overshot the place, put to sea to
returne backe to seeke the rest, and could not doe it, because
the winde was contrarie and the sea growne; they were
afraid of being cast away, and recovering the shore they cast
anchor. While they rode there a storme arose, and seeing
that they could not abide there, much lesse endure at sea,
they resolved to runne on shore; and as the brigandines
were but small, so did they draw but little water; and where
they were it was a sandie coast. By which occasion the force
of their sailes drave them on shore, without any hurt of
them that were in them. As those that were in the port of
Panuco at this time were in great joy, so these felt a double
griefe in their hearts, for they knew not what was become

of their fellowes, nor in what countrey they were, and feared
it was a countrey of Indian enemies. They landed two
leagues below the port; and when they saw themselves out
of the danger of the sea, every one tooke of that which he
had as much as he could carrie on his backe; and they travelled up into the countrey, and found Indians, which told
them where their fellowes were, and gave them ·good entertainement, wherewith their sadnes was turned into joy, and
they thanked God most humbly for their deliverance out of
so many dangers.

CHAPTER XLII.

*How they came to Panuco, and how they were received of the
inhabitants.*

From the time that they put out of Rio Grande to the sea,
at their departure from Florida, until they arrived in the They arrived in the
river of Panuco, were fifty-two daies. They came into the river of Panuco, 1543,
river of Panuco the 10 of September 1543. They went up Septem. 10.
the river with their brigandines. They travelled foure daies;
and because the wind was but little, and many times it served
them not, because of the many turnings which the river
maketh, and the great current, drawing them up by towing,
and that in many places; for this cause they made very little
way, and with great labour; and seeing the execution of
their desire to be deferred, which was to come among Christians, and to see the celebration of divine service, which so
long time they had not seene, they left the brigandines with
the mariners, and went by land to Panuco. All of them
were apparrelled in deeres skins, tanned and died blacke,
to wit, cotes, hose, and shooes. When they came to Panuco,

presently they went to the church to pray and give God thankes that so miraculousely had saved them.

The townesmen, which before were advertised by the Indians, and knew of their arrival, caried some of them to their houses, and entertained them whom they knew and had acquaintance of, or because they were their countrimen. The Alcalde mayor tooke the Governour home to his house, and commanded al the rest, as soone as they came, to be lodged six and six, and ten and ten, according to the habilitie of every townesman. And all of them were provided for by their hostes of many hennes and bread of maiz, and fruites of the countrie, which are such as be in the isle of Cuba, whereof before I have spoken.

The towne of Panuco may containe above seventy families; the most of their houses are of lime and stone, and some made of timber, and all of them are thatched. It is a poore countrie, and there is neither gold nor silver in it; the inhabitants live there in great abundance of victuals and servants. The richest have not above five hundred crownes rent a yeere, and that is in cotten clothes, hennes, and maiz, which the Indians, their servants, doe give them for tribute. There arrived there of those that came out of Florida, three hundred and eleven Christians. Presently, the Alcalde mayor sent one of the townsmen in post to advertise the viceroy, Don Antonio de Mendoça, which was resident in Mexico, that of the people that went with Don Ferdinando de Soto to discover and conquer Florida, three hundred and eleven men were arrived there: that seeing they were imploied in his majesties service, he would take some order to provide for them; whereat the viceroy and all the inhabitants of Mexico wondred. For they thought they were miscarried, because they had travelled so farre within the maine land of Florida, and had no newes of them for so long a time; and it seemed a wonderfull thing unto them how they could save themselves so long among infidels, without any

The description of Panuco.

1 Chris- ansarrived Panuco.

fort, wherein they might fortifie themselves, and without any other succour at all. Presently the viceroy sent a warrant, wherein hee commanded, that whithersoever they sent, they should give them victuals, and as many Indians for their cariages as they needed; and where they would not furnish them, they might take those things that were necessarie perforce, without incurring any danger of law. This warrant was so readilie obeyed, that by the way, before they came to the townes, they came to receive them with hennes and victuals.

CHAPTER XLIII.

Of the favour which they found at the hands of the Viceroy, and of the inhabitants of the citie of Mexico.

From Panuco to the great citie Temistitan Mexico,[1] is sixty leagues, and other sixty from Panuco to the Port de Vera Cruz, where they take shipping for Spaine, and those that come from Spaine do land to go for Nueva Espanna. These three townes stand in a triangle; to wit, Vera Cruz to the south, Panuco to the north, and Mexico to the west, sixty leagues asunder. The countrie is so inhabited with Indians, that from towne to towne, those which are farthest, are but a league and halfe a league asunder. Some of them that came from Florida staied a moneth in Panuco to rest themselves, others fifteene daies, and every one as long as he listed; for there was none that shewed a sower countenance

---

[1] " Gram cidade de Mestitam Mexico" in the original. The ancient name of the city of Mexico was properly *Tenochtitlan*. Cortes, in his third Despatch to the Emperor Charles the Fifth, calls it the great city of Temixtitan—" la gran ciudad de Temixtitan", and applies the name Mexico to the province. Bernal Diaz, in his *Conquista de la Nueva España*, ch. 88, speaks of it as " the great city of Tenustitlan Mexico".

to his guests, but rather gave them any thing that they had, and seemed to be grieved when they took their leave; which was to be beleeved. For the victuals, which the Indians doe pay them for tribute, are more than they can spend; and in that towne is no commerce; and there dwelt but few Spaniards there, and they were glad of their companie. The Alcalde mayor divided all the Emperours clothes which he had (which there they pay him for his tribute) among those that would come to receive them. Those which had shirts of maile left were glad men, for they had a horse for one shirt of maile. Some horsed themselves; and such as could not (which were the greatest part) tooke their journie on foote; in which they were well received of the Indians that were in the townes, and better served then they could have been in their owne houses, though they had been well to live. For if they asked one hen of an Indian, they brought them foure; and if they asked any of the countrie fruit, though it were a league off, they ran presently for it. And

This is the manner of China, to carrie men in chaires. if any Christian found himself evill at ease, they carried him in a chaire from one towne to another.

In whatsoever towne they came, the cacique, by an Indian which carried a rod of justice in his hand, whom they call Tapile, that is to say, a sergeant, commanded them to provide victuals for them, and Indians to beare burdens of such things as they had, and such as were needfull to carrie them that were sick. The viceroy sent a Portugall twenty leagues from Mexico, with great store of sugar, raisons of the sunne, and conserves, and other things fit for sicke folkes, for such as had neede of them; and had given order to cloth them all at the Emperours charges. And their approch being knowne by the citizens of Mexico, they went out of the towne to receive them; and with great courtesie, requesting them in favour to come to their houses, every one carried such as hee met home with him, and clothed them every one the best they could; so that he which had the meanest apparrell it cost above thirty ducats. As many as were willing to come to the viceroyes house he commanded to be apparelled, and such as were persons of qualitie sate at his table; and there was a table in his house for as many of the meaner sort as would come to it; and he was presently informed who every one was, to shew him the courtesie that he deserved. Some of the conquerors did set both gentlemen and clownes at their owne table, and many times made the servant sit cheeke by cheeke by his master; and chiefly the officers and men of base condition did so, for those which had better education did enquire who every one was, and made difference of persons; but all did what they could with a good will, and every one told them whom they had in their houses, that they should not trouble themselves, nor thinke themselves the worse to take that which they gave them; for they had bin in the like case, and had bin relieved of others, and that this was the custome of that countrey. God reward them all, and God grant that those which it pleased Him to deliver out of Florida and to bring againe into Christendome, may serve Him; and unto those that died in that countrey, and unto all that beleeve in Him and confesse His holy faith, God for His mercie sake grant the kingdome of heaven. Amen.

CHAPTER XLIV.

Which declareth some diversities and particularities of the land of Florida; and the fruites, and beasts, and fowles that are in that countrie.

From the port de Spiritu Santo, where they landed when they entred into Florida, to the province of Ocute, which may bee four hundred leagues, little more or lesse, is a verie plaine countrie, and hath many lakes and thicke woods, and

Port de Spiritu Santo is in 29 degrees ¼ on the west side of Florida.

in some places they are of wild pine-trees ; and is a weake soile: there is in it neither mountaine nor hill. The countrie of Ocute is more fat and fruitfull ; it hath thinner woods, and very goodly meadows upon the rivers. From Ocute to Cutifachiqui may be one hundred and thirty leagues : eighty leagues thereof are desert, and have many groves of wild pine-trees. Through the wildernesse great rivers doe passe. From Cutifachiqui to Xuala, may be two hundred and fifty leagues : it is al an hilly countrie. Cutifachiqui and Xuala stand both in plaine ground, hie, and have goodly medows on the rivers. From thence forward to Chiaha, Coça, and Talise, is plaine ground, dry, and fat, and very plentifull of maiz. From Xuala to Tascaluça may be two hundred and fifty leagues. From Tascaluça to Rio Grande, or the great river, may be three hundred leagues : the countrie is low, and full of lakes. From Rio Grande forward, the countrie is hier and more champion, and best peopled of all the land of Florida. And along this river from Aquixo to Pacaha, and Coligoa, are one hundred and fifty leagues : the countrie is plaine, and the woods thinne, and in some places champion, very fruitfull and pleasant. From Coligoa to Autiamque are two hundred and fifty leagues of hillie countrie. From Autiamque to Aguacay may be two hundred and thirty leagues of plaine ground. From Aguacay to the river of Daycao one hundred and twenty leagues, all hillie country.

From the port de Spiritu Santo unto Apalache they travelled from east to west and northwest. From Cutifachiqui to Xuala from south to north. From Xuala to Coça from east to west. From Coça to Tascaluça, and to Rio Grande, as far as the provinces of Quizquiz and Aquixo from east to west. From Aquixo to Pacaha to the north. From Pacaha to Tulla from east to west : and from Tulla to Autiamque from north to south, to the province of Guachoya and Daycao.

Marginal notes:
Ocute. Cutifachiqui.
Xuala.
Chiaha, Coça, and Talise.
Tascaluça.
Rio Grande.
Aquixo.
Coligoa.
Autiamque.
Aguacay.
Pagina 72.[1]

---

[1] Page 74 of the present edition.

The bread which they eate in all the land of Florida is of
maiz, which is like course millet.   And this maiz is common Maiz.
in all the islandes and West Indies from the Antiles forward.
There are also in Florida great store of walnuts, and plummes, Walnuts,
mulberries, and grapes.   They sow and gather their maiz mulberries,
every one their severall crop.   The fruites are common to
all : for they grow abroad in the open fields in great abundance, without any neede of planting or dressing.   Where
there be mountaines, there be chestnuts : they are somewhat Chestnuts.
smaller then the chestnuts of Spaine.   From Rio Grande
westward, the walnuts differ from those that grow more east-
ward : for they are soft, and like unto acornes : and those Soft walnuts eastward from Rio Grande.
which grow from Rio Grande to Puerto del Spiritu Santo
for the most part are hard ; and the trees and walnuts in Hard walnuts westward from Rio Grande.
shew like those of Spaine.   There is a fruit through all the
countrie which groweth on a plant like ligoacan,[1] which the
Indians doe plant.   The fruit is like unto peares riall :[2] it A peare riall.
hath a verie good smell, and an excellent taste.   There
groweth another plant in the open field, which beareth a
fruit like unto strawberries, close to the ground, which hath Strawberries.
a verie good taste.   The plummes are of two kindes, red and Plummes of two kinds.
gray, of the making and bignesse of nuts, and have three or
foure stones in them.[3] These are better then all the plummes
of Spaine, and they make farre better prunes of them.   In
the grapes there is onlie want of dressing ; for though they
bee big, they have a great kirnell.   All other fruits are very
perfect, and lesse hurtfull then those of Spaine.

There are in Florida many beares, and lyons,[4] wolves, Beasts.
deere, dogges, cattes, martens, and conies.

There be many wild hennes as big as turkies, partridges Fowles.
small like those of Africa, cranes, duckes, pigeons, thrushes,
and sparrowes.   There are certaine blacke birds[5] bigger than

---

[1] Ligoacan :—*Lignum Guaiacum?*
[2] Pears royal.
[3] *Prunus chicasa* and *P. hiemalis.*
[4] See note at p. 97.
[5] Perhaps the winter cow-bird—*Molothrus pecoris.*

z

sparrows, and lesser then stares. There are gosse hawkes, falcons, ierfalcons, and all fowles of prey that are in Spaine.

The Indians are well proportioned. Those of the plaine countries are taller of bodie and better shapen then those of the mountaines. Those of the inland have greater store of maiz, and commodities of the countrie, then those that dwell upon the sea coast. The countrie along the sea coast is barren and poore, and the people more warlike. The coast runneth from Puerto del Spiritu Santo to Apalache, east and west: and from Apalache to Rio de las Palmas from east to west: from Rio de las Palmas unto Nueva Espanna from north to south. It is a gentle coast, but it hath many sholdes, and great shelves of sand.

Deo gratias.

--- ---- -------

This Relation of the discoverie of Florida was printed in the house of Andrew de Burgos, Printer and Gentleman of the house of my Lord Cardinall the Infante.

It was finished the tenth of Februarie in the
yeere one thousand, five hundred, fiftie
and seven, in the noble and most
loyall citie of
Evora.

FINIS.

APPENDIX.

APPENDIX.

A RELATION OF WHAT TOOK PLACE DURING
the expedition of Captain Soto; with particulars
concerning the nature of the country through
which he passed.

BY LUIS HERNANDEZ DE BIEDMA.[1]

HAVING arrived at the port of Baya-Honda,[2] we landed   <small>Baya-
Honda.</small>
six hundred and twenty men and two hundred and twenty-
three horses.   This operation was scarcely effected, when we
were informed by one of the Indians who had been captured,
that there was a Christian in the country who had accompanied the expedition of Panfilo de Narvaez; messengers
were despatched in quest of this person, who was with a
cacique living eight leagues distant from the harbour.   We
fell in with him on the way, for he was already coming to
meet us.   As soon as the cacique had learnt that we had

[1] This Biedma presented the above Relation to the King (Charles V) in
person, in his council of the Indies, assembled in 1544; as appears by a
decision, wherein it is stated that he accompanied Fernando de Soto in
quality of Factor to his majesty.   (*Note by Muñoz.*)

[2] That the port called Baya-Honda here and at page 174, is Espiritu
Santo Bay, is evident from the concurrent testimony of the Portuguese
author, and of Garcilaso de la Vega.   The latter, indeed, describes the
bay of Espiritu Santo in so many words as "una bahia honda y buena",—
a deep and good bay.   Hence it is possible that this name also was given
to it at the time by the Spaniards, and if so, Biedma is the only narrator who has informed us of the fact.   In the absence of the original
Spanish, we are unable to detect whether any error has crept into the
translation.

landed, he enquired of this Christian whether he wished to go in search of us, and upon his replying in the affirmative, he was sent by the cacique in company with nine Indians. He was naked like them; in his hand he carried a bow and arrows, and his body was painted like theirs. When the Christians perceived them, they supposed that they were natives who had come for the purpose of being spies on our troops, and accordingly marched to attack them; but the Indians fled over a neighbouring hill. The horsemen having overtaken them, gave an Indian a thrust with a lance, and the Christian also narrowly escaped with his life, for he spoke our language very imperfectly, having almost forgotten it; but it occurred to him to call upon our Lady, which circumstance assured us of his being a Christian. We conducted him to the Governor with great delight; he had been twelve years among these Indians, spoke their language, and had so accustomed himself to it, that he passed upwards of four days with us without being able to speak two words consecutively: to every word in Spanish, he added four or five in the language of the Indians: this continued until he had regained the use of our language. He was so ignorant of the country, that he knew not even by hearsay of what was twenty leagues distant. In fact, from the first moment, he told us that there was no gold in the country.

We all left the port of Baya-Honda for the purpose of penetrating into the interior, with the exception of twenty-six horsemen and sixty foot soldiers, who remained to guard the harbour until they should receive the Governor's orders to join him. We marched at first in a westerly direction, and then north-east; we had notice of a cacique, who, according to the report of the Indians, received tribute from all Hurripacuxi the natives: he was called Hurripacuxi, and lived about twenty leagues from the coast. From this place we continued our march, crossing swamps and rivers, for the distance of from fifteen to twenty leagues. We wished to repair

to a town, concerning which the Indians related marvellous
things: amongst others, they pretended that when the inhabitants shouted, they caused the birds which were flying in
the air to fall down. We came to this place, which was
called Etocale, and was but a small village. We found in Etocale.
it some provisions; namely, maize, beans, and little dogs,
which afforded no small relief to our party, who were famish-
ing. We stayed here seven or eight days, during which
several excursions were made in order to capture some
Indians, who might serve us as guides into the province of
Apalache, concerning which place there was much talk in
the country. We caught three or four, but the most skilful
of them only knew the country to the distance of two leagues
round the village. We departed, taking the direction towards
New Spain, and marching ten or twelve leagues from the
coast. In the course of five or six days we passed through
some hamlets, and then entered a village of moderate size,
named Aguacalecuen; all the Indians had taken refuge in Aguacale-cuen.
the woods. We stayed here five or six days in the hope of
taking some Indians to serve us as guides. Ten or twelve
women were captured, one of whom said that she was the
daughter of the cacique: this induced the cacique himself
to come to us in a friendly manner: he promised to give us
some interpreters and guides, so that we might continue our
march, but this promise he did not keep. We were obliged
to take him along with us. After marching for six or seven
days, we fell in with one hundred and fifty Indians, armed
with bows and arrows, who came out against us with the
intention of carrying off the cacique; we killed some of
them, and took the others prisoners. Amongst these were
some natives who had a knowledge of the interior; but on
this subject they told the grossest falsehoods. We crossed a A river.
river which ran through a province called Veachile, and on Veachile.
the opposite shore we found some villages, which, although
deserted, contained all that we wanted, namely, provisions.

Aguile. We left there for a village called Aguile, situated on the borders of the province of Apalache, which is separated from the first-named place by a river, over which we threw a bridge, formed upon a great number of boats fastened one A river. to another; we crossed the river with considerable difficulty, for the Indians who were drawn up on the shore defended the passage: as soon, however, as we reached the opposite Ivitachuco. side, they withdrew into a neighbouring village called Ivita-chuco, where they remained until we came in sight of the place. As soon as they saw us approach, they set fire to the village and fled.

Apalache. The province of Apalache contains a great number of villages, but provisions are scarce. The province to which Yustaga. we were going was called Yustaga. We arrived at a village Iniahico. named Iniahico. On reaching this place, we thought that it was time to obtain some intelligence of those who had remained at the harbour, and to give them news of ourselves; for it was our intention now to penetrate so far into the interior, that it would be no longer possible for us to communicate with them, and we had already travelled one hundred and ten leagues from the spot where we had left them. The Governor accordingly sent orders for them to join us.

The sea. Departing hence, we went in search of the sea, which was nine leagues distant from the village where we now were. We came to the place on the coast where Panfilo de Narvaez had constructed vessels; we recognised the spot where the forge had been set up, and we saw a great number of bones of horses. The Indians told us that other Christians had built barques at this place. Juan de Anasco made several marks of recognition upon the trees along the sea shore. He had received the Governor's orders to proceed in search of the soldiers who had remained at the harbour, and to make them come by land to the village where we were, whilst they (i.e., his own party) were to return by sea in two brigantines and a caravel, which they were to bring up to the province of

Apalache. In the mean time we were to wait at the place where we were now staying. Juan de Añasco sent the party by land, and he himself came by sea as the Governor had directed him. He encountered great dangers, for he observed that this coast was not such as he had viewed it from the land. In sailing, he did not recognize the spots which he had passed, for the shore was edged with small shallow creeks, where the water rose high at full tide, but at the ebb it remained perfectly dry. We built a pirogue, which put out to sea two leagues every day in order to watch for the arrival of the brigantines, and point out to them the spot where they ought to land. God granted a safe arrival to those who were expected both by sea and land.

As soon as the brigantines had arrived, the Governor gave orders for them to set sail again and search out a near harbour on the east side, to reconnoitre the coast and to see if the land came to a termination. The cavalier Francisco Maldonado, of Salamanca, embarked in the brigantines, sailed along the coast, put into all the bays and rivers that he saw, until he reached a river, the entrance into which was easy, A river. and which afforded a good harbour. There was an Indian village situate on the sea shore, and divers of the inhabitants came out to traffick with him; one of these natives he took, and then returned to where we were stationed, after having spent two months in this expedition. We found the time of our sojourn very long, owing to the reports that we had heard respecting the interior. When Maldonado arrived, the Governor told him that we were going in quest of that country, which, according to the Indians, was situate upon another sea: he ordered Maldonado to proceed to Cuba with the brigantines, on board of which was the Governor's wife, Doña Isabella de Bobadilla,[1] and afterwards to bring them

---

[1] In the absence of the original document, we can scarcely doubt that there is some mistake here either in the Spanish or the translation; for both the Portuguese author (*ante* pp. 24 and 111) and Garcilaso de la Vega

back as far as the river Saint Esprit (Espiritu Santo), whither we should repair, if in six months' time he heard no news of us. The brigantines sailed for Cuba, and we resumed our march towards the north, in order to verify the statements of the Indians. We travelled during five days in the midst

A broad and rapid river. of a desert, and at length came upon a broad and very rapid river, over which we could not construct a bridge owing to the force of the current: we made, however, a canoe, in which we crossed to the other side. We entered a province

Acapachiqui called Acapachiqui, where there was plenty of provisions for the sustenance of the Indians; we perceived some villages, but as the country was covered with extensive marshes, we could not reconnoitre all of them: we noticed also that in this country the houses of the Indians were differently constructed from those we had hitherto seen, being dug out of the earth, and having the appearance of caves; whilst all those previously observed had been covered with palm branches and straw. We continued our march, and came in

Two rivers. sight of two rivers, over which we were obliged to construct bridges with pine trees lashed together, as we were wont to do on these occasions. We arrived at a province called

Otoa. Otoa, in which we found a very large village, the most ccnsiderable that we had yet seen; from thence we passed on to other villages of the same province, which might be distant a two days' march; we captured some Indians, who had no suspicion of us, nor had they been apprised of our arrival; others offered to come into our service, on condition that we should deliver up those of their tribes whom we had seized. The Governor consented to this, for they would not have been made prisoners if we had not had absolute need of guides and interpreters.

agree that Doña Isabel de Bobadilla had been left at Cuba ; and in the corresponding passage in Garcilaso, it is distinctly stated that Maldonado was sent with the brigantines to *visit* Doña Isabel :—" Pocos dias despues de la venida de Diego Maldonado, le mandò el Governador, fuese à la Habana con los dos vergantines, que tenia à su cargo, y visitase à Doña Isabel de Bobadilla," etc.—*La Florida del Inca*, p. 102 ; edit. 1723.

We spent five or six days in passing through this province, which is called Chisi. These Indians treated us Chisi.
as well as their poverty allowed them; we then marched
three days without finding a habitation, and at length entered a province called Altapaha. We discovered there a Altapaha.
river, which did not flow towards the south, like those we had
A river.
already passed; but it came from the east, and fell into the
sea on the side where the licentiate Lucas d'Aillon had
landed; this circumstance gave us more confidence in what
the Indian had stated, and we were persuaded that all the
lies which they had told us were truths. This province was
well peopled, and all the inhabitants came to offer their services. The Governor having made some enquiries of them
respecting the province of Cafitachyque, whither we were
going, they answered that it was impossible for us to reach it,
as there was no road leading to it, neither were there any
provisions to be procured on the way; and that we should all
perish from hunger. We set forward nevertheless, and came
into the territories of the caciques named Ocute and Cofoqui; Ocute.
they supplied us with provisions, and told us that if we
Cofoqui.
wished to make war upon the Queen of Cafitachyque, they
would furnish us with everything necessary for the journey,
but they gave us to understand that there was no road
thither; that they held no communication with each other,
because hostilities were going on; that they only saw each
other when they were engaged in fighting from time to time,
which they did always secretly and in ambush; and that it took
from twenty to twenty-two days to reach there, during which
they subsisted altogether on herbs and parched maize which
they carried with them. Seeing, however, that we were
determined upon going, they gave us eight hundred Indians
to carry our provisions and baggage, as well as guides,
who immediately took an easterly direction, and in this
way we marched for three days. The Indian who deceived
us said that in three days he would conduct us thither;

at the expiration of which, we began to perceive the falsity of this man; nevertheless the Governor continued to follow the route taken, because he had a foreboding (which indeed eventually came to pass) of the great want that we should have to endure. After three days we reached some huts; the Indians were already bewildered, and knew no longer what road to take; the Governor went in advance in order to search for one, but returned in despair at his ill success. We then proceeded half a league, until we came to a large river, when we were necessitated for the first time to eat the swine that we brought along with us; each man received for his allowance a pound of flesh, which was boiled in water without salt or anything to season it. The Governor sent a party to seek out a road in two opposite directions. One person proceeded up the river at the north-north-east side, and another descended it in the direction of south-south-east. He allowed ten days to each in going and returning, and directed them to give notice if they should discover any villages or a road. The explorer, who went towards the south-south-east, returned in four days with the news that he had found a small hamlet and some provisions; he brought three or four Indians, who spoke with the man who had deceived us; they understood each other, which was no small satisfaction to us, considering the extreme scarcity of interpreters in this country. They confirmed the lies which that Indian had told us, and we believed them because he made himself very easily understood by these Indians. We all set out in company immediately, to go and await the arrival in that small village of the messenger who had been on the other side; we remained there four or five days until we were all once more assembled; we found about fifty fanegas (bushels) of maize, a small quantity of meal of roasted maize, numerous mulberry trees loaded with mulberries, and some wild fruits.

A large river.

Cofitachyque.

We departed for the village of Cofitachyque, which

was two days' march from this hamlet, and situated on
the banks of a river which we supposed to be that of Saint
Helena, whither the licentiate Ayllon had gone. When
we arrived there, the Queen sent to us one of her nieces,
who was carried in a litter by Indians, and appeared to
possess considerable authority; she gave us to understand
that she was well pleased at our arrival, and that she would
give us all that was in her power. She presented the Governor with a necklace of pearls of five or six rows, procured
for us canoes to pass the river, and assigned the half of the
village for our quarters. After having been in our company
three or four days, she escaped into the forest; the Governor
caused search to be made after her, but without success; he
then gave orders to break open a temple erected in this village, wherein the chiefs of the country were interred. We
took out of it a vast quantity of pearls, which might amount
to six or seven arrobas,[1] but they were spoiled by having
been underground. We found also buried there a couple of
hatchets for felling wood, of Spanish manufacture, a chaplet
made of the seeds of the wild olive, and several small pearls
similar to those which are brought from Spain to barter with
the Indians. We supposed that they had procured all these
articles in trafficking with the party which had accompanied
the licentiate Ayllon. According to the report of these
Indians, the sea was distant thirty leagues; we likewise learnt
from them that Ayllon's company had penetrated only a
short distance into the interior, that they had nearly always
followed the sea-coast, until the death of Ayllon, and that his
companions had destroyed each other, not being able to agree
in the choice of a leader. A great number died of starvation,
as we were informed by one of the soldiers who had remained
in the country. Out of six hundred men who had landed
with Ayllon, only fifty-seven escaped: this great loss was

*The sea dis-
tant thirty
leagues.*

---

[1] An arroba is a Spanish weight of twenty-five pounds.

mainly attributable to the shipwreck of a large vessel laden with provisions.

We remained in the village of this queen ten or eleven days, after which we agreed to go and explore the country and search for provisions, of which we had but very little left : we had to find subsistence for the Indians, the Christians, and the horses. We set forward with all expedition, taking the direction of the north. We marched during eight days through a poor country, in which few provisions were found, and came to a province called Xuala, which was thinly inhabited, because the soil is very barren ; we found however some huts of Indians in the mountains. We ascended to the source of the great river whose course we had followed, and which we believed to be that of Saint Esprit (Espiritu Santo) ; we entered a village called Guasuli, where we were presented with several dogs and a little maize, for there was only a small quantity in the place. We continued our march during four days, and at length reached a village called China, where there was plenty of provisions ; it is built on one of the islands of the river of Saint-Esprit, which are numerous and considerable close to its source. We found for the first time in this province fortified villages ; the Indians make here a great quantity of nut oil ; we remained twenty-six or twenty-seven days in order to rest the horses, which from want of food had become excessively wearied. We pursued our course along the banks of the river, and reached another province called Costehe, the villages of which are also built upon the islands of the river ; we afterwards entered the province of Coca, which is one of the best we have met with in Florida. The cacique came out to meet us ; he was carried in a litter, and attended by a numerous suite, the procession presenting the appearance of a fête. A great number of villages are subject to this cacique. The next morning all the Indians escaped ; we took the cacique, that we might compel him to give us Indians to carry our

Marginal notes:

Xuala.

The great river, supposed to be that of Espiritu Santo. Guasuli.

China.

Costehe.

Coca.

baggage, and we remained several days until he had furnished them.   In this province we found plums similar to Plums and
those of Spain, and a considerable number of wild vines, vines.
which produced excellent grapes in abundance.

Leaving the village, we shaped our course west and south-
west.   During five or six days we met with villages belonging to this cacique, at length we reached another province
called Italisi.   The inhabitants having fled, we proceeded to Italisi.
seek for them.   Some Indians came to us ; the Governor
told them to summon the cacique, who came and presented us
with twenty-six or twenty-seven women, some deer-skins,
and other things.   Quitting this village, we proceeded towards the south in the direction of New Spain.   We passed
through several villages, and arrived at another province
called Faszaluza, the cacique of which was an Indian of a sta- Faszaluza.
ture so immense that he was universally believed to be a giant ;
he quietly awaited us in his village. On our arrival, we showed
him all sorts of courteous attentions, and got up a tournament
and horse-racing for his diversion, but he appeared to
take very little interest in them. We at length asked him to
procure for us some Indians to carry our baggage, to which
he replied that he was not accustomed to serve anybody, but
on the contrary he made every one serve him. The Governor
gave orders to prevent his returning home, and to keep
him prisoner. This Indian was greatly exasperated at thus
seeing himself detained in our power; and this was the cause
of the treachery which he committed in the sequel. He told
us that he could give us nothing in this place, but that if we
repaired to another village called Mavila, which belonged to
him, he would there supply us with what we had asked of
him. Having set out for this village, we found a large river A large
which we supposed to be that which falls into the bay of river.
Chuse ; we learnt that the vessels of Narvaez had arrived
there in want of water, and that a Christian named Teodoro
and an Indian had remained among these Indians : at the

same time they showed us a dagger which had belonged to
the Christian. We employed two days in constructing rafts
for the passage of the river, during which the Indians killed
a Christian, who was one of the Governor's own guard. The
Governor being greatly displeased, treated the cacique very
roughly, and told him that he would have him burnt alive if
he did not deliver up the murderers; the cacique replied
that he would give them up to us at Mavila. This Indian
cacique had a great number of natives under his orders; he
had always near his person a man whose duty it was to keep
off the flies; another behind him carried a large umbrella
made of feathers to protect him from the rays of the sun.

Mavila.   We arrived at Mavila at nine o'clock in the morning; it was
a small village built on a plain, surrounded by walls and very
strong. There had been some cabins outside the enclosure,
but all of these the Indians had demolished in order that the
ground might be perfectly clear. Some of the chiefs came to
meet us, and told the Governor through the interpreter, that
he might take up his quarters either on the plain or in the
village, whichever he preferred, and that in the evening we
should receive some carriers. The Governor, thinking it
best to enter the village in their company, gave orders
accordingly, and we followed the Indians. We conversed
with them amicably, for we saw only three or four hundred;
but there were at least five thousand concealed in the houses
of the village. They gave us a cordial welcome, commenced
their dances and their exercises, and in order the more completely to deceive us, they introduced fifteen or twenty
women, who capered before us. After they had danced for
some time, the cacique arose and entered one of the houses.
The Governor sent to order him to come out; he replied that
he would not. The captain of the guard to the Governor entered to compel obedience, but perceiving in the interior of
the house a vast number of warriors, all on their guard, he
judged it more prudent to withdraw and to leave the cacique

there; he then reported to the Governor how he had seen
those houses full of Indians armed with bows and arrows,
and ready to commit some treachery. The Governor called
to another cacique who was passing by, but this man likewise refused to come. One of the gentlemen who was standing near, caught him by the arm to lead him, but the man
made a movement, and disengaged himself from his hold,
whereupon the gentleman drew his sword, and struck at him
a blow which cut off his arm. The Indian had no sooner
received this wound, than all the rest began to discharge
their arrows at us from the interior of the houses, through
the numerous loopholes which they had made, whilst others
attacked us from the outside. As we were completely thrown
off our guard, having considered them as friends, we sustained such considerable loss that we were obliged to
retreat out of the village, leaving behind all the baggage
which the Indians had carried, in the place where they had
unloaded it. Directly they perceived us on the outside,
they closed the gates of the village, and began to beat their
drums, display their flags, and set up a great shouting;
they then opened our trunks and packages, and from the top
of the walls exhibited to our view the property which they
had made themselves masters of. As soon as we had left the
village, we mounted our horses, and surrounded the walls,
in order to prevent the Indians from coming out. The
Governor made sixty or eighty of our men, all well armed,
dismount, and ordered us to divide into four squadrons, and
to go and attack the village in as many different places.
The first who should enter, had orders to set fire to the
houses, so as to prevent the besieged from doing us any
injury. The horsemen, and the other soldiers who were not
armed, were directed to guard the exterior of the village, and
to take care that no Indian escaped. We put our plan into
execution, entered the place, and set fire to the houses. A
great number of Indians were burnt, but all our baggage

B B

became a prey to the flames. Not a thing belonging to us remained. We fought the whole day till the evening without a single Indian asking for quarter; they defended themselves like furious lions; all of them perished, some by the sword, others by the fire; whilst those who endeavoured to escape were killed by thrusts from the lance. When night came, there remained no more than three Indians, who were guarding the twenty women they had brought out to dance; they placed these women in front of them, who crossed their hands, and made signs to the Christians as though asking to be taken; they then withdrew, and the three Indians discharged their arrows at us; we killed two of them, and the one now left, not willing to yield, climbed a tree which was upon the wall, unstrung his bow, fastened the cord round his neck and hanged himself.

On that day the Indians killed more than twenty of our men, and upwards of two hundred and fifty were wounded; we received more than six hundred and sixty arrowshots. During the night we dressed the wounds of our men with the fat of the dead Indians. No other medicine remained for our use, all that we possessed having been burnt in the affray. We stayed here twenty-seven or twenty-eight days, in order to recruit our strength. God permitted us all to escape. We took the women and made them tend those who were most seriously wounded. We learnt from the natives that we were distant upwards of forty leagues from the sea; we were very anxious for the Governor to proceed thither, that we might obtain tidings of the brigantines; but he would not venture, it being already the middle of November and the weather very cold. It was advisable to seek a country in which to winter, where there would be no want of provisions, for there was a scarcity in the place we now were staying at; we accordingly pursued our route towards the north, and marched ten or twelve days, suffering excessively from cold, and from the passage of

Forty leagues from the sea.

rivers which we were obliged to ford ; at length we reached
an extensive and fertile province, where we might pass the
winter until the extremity of the cold was over ; for more
snow falls in this country than in Spain.

This province was called Chicaza ; the Indians attempted to Chicaza.
defend the passage of a river, which we had to cross ; we made A river.
a halt of three days, at the expiration of which we passed over
in a canoe that we had constructed. All the Indians fled into
the forest. Seven or eight days afterwards, messengers from
the cacique came to the Governor, and said that their master
intended to come and offer his services to him and all his company. The Governor received them favorably, and sent word
to the cacique to come, and he would make him numerous presents. The cacique came accordingly, attended by a great many
Indians, who carried him on their shoulders. He presented
us with some little dogs and deer-skins. The cacique stayed
with us, and the other Indians went away ; each day they
came and departed, bringing us many rabbits and whatever
else they could procure in the country. In the night we
surprised some Indians, who, under the pretext of being
friendly, came to see how we slept and kept guard. Having
no suspicion of their designs, we told the cacique that we
should resume our journey on the morrow. He left, and
the same night marched against us. As these Indians knew
the places where we posted our sentinels, three hundred of
them entered the village by twos and fours, carrying fire,
which they had put into small pots so that we might
not perceive them ; and whilst they were making their way
along, another troop was heard shouting their war cries ; but
the former had already set fire to the village. We experienced a great loss, for on this night they killed fifty-seven
of our horses, upwards of three hundred swine, and thirteen
or fourteen men ; but what would appear to be a great miracle
of God, is, that they fled without our offering them the
slightest resistance. If they had persevered in their attack,

our destruction must have been inevitable. We left that place to make our way to a cabin, which might be a league distant; we were told that the Indians intended to march against us in the night, but it pleased God to send a little rain, which was the cause of their not coming.

We were in a very sad plight; a few horses were left, but we had neither saddles, lances, nor bucklers,—all had been burnt. We immediately set to work to make shields, saddles, and lances, as well as we were able. Five days afterwards the Indians sallied out to attack us again; they marched in good order of battle, and assailed us on three sides. As we had been forewarned, we marched to meet them, and put them to flight, after having killed a considerable number, which circumstance, God be praised, prevented their return. We stayed in this place two months, during which time we made saddles, lances, and bucklers, and at length resumed our march towards the north-west.

Alibanio.

We proceeded to the province of Alibanio, where an event occurred to us, such as they say was never witnessed in the Indies. The natives who had in this place neither provisions, women, nor anything else to defend, constructed, in the middle of the road, for the sole purpose of contending with us, a very strong palisade, behind which three hundred warriors posted themselves, determined to die rather than allow us to pass. Directly we made our appearance, some of the Indians came out of the palisade, and threatened us, saying that not one of us should escape alive. As soon as we caught sight of the palisade, and of the warriors who were defending it, we supposed that behind it there were provisions or other valuables. We stood in the greatest need of food, for we knew that we should have to traverse a desert of twelve days' march, during which we should not meet with victuals of any kind. We then formed into a body of forty or fifty men, and divided ourselves into two troops to attack the enemy as soon as a trumpet should give the signal. We carried the palisade, but with the loss of seven or eight men, and twenty-five were wounded; we killed several Indians, and took some prisoners, from whom we learnt that they had constructed this barrier for the express purpose of trying the mastery between us. We found some provisions in the environs, in order to enable us to pass the desert, through which we marched twelve days. ^{A desert} The sick and wounded that we carried caused us considerable trouble. One day, at noon, we entered a village, named Quizquiz, so suddenly, that the Indians had received no ^{Quizquiz.} notice of our arrival, but were at work in their maize fields; we took upwards of three hundred women in the village. These people were wretchedly poor, having only with them some skins and cloaks; it was in this place that we gathered for the first time small nuts of the country, which are superior ^{Small nuts.} to those of Spain. The village is built on the banks of the river Saint-Esprit, and we ascertained from the inhabitants, ^{River Espiritu Santo.} that this, as well as divers others in the immediate neighbourhood, were tributary to the sovereign of Pacaha, who is greatly renowned throughout all the country.

As soon as the Indians knew that we had captured these women, they came as friends to demand them of the Governor, who gave them up, and desired them to let him have some canoes in order to pass the Great River; they promised, but ^{The Great River.} failed to do so, and even collected their forces to make war upon us, and presented themselves before the village in which we were; they did not, however, venture to attack us, but went away. We quitted the village, and proceeded to encamp upon the bank of the river, in order to see how we could pass it. We perceived a number of Indians, with a great many canoes, on the opposite side, ready to dispute our passage. We resolved upon making four large pirogues, each capable of containing sixty or seventy men, and five or six horses; and we spent twenty-seven or twenty-eight days in constructing them. During this time the Indians came out every day at three o'clock in the afternoon in two hundred and fifty canoes,

adorned with handsome flags, and approaching the shore
where we were, they raised their war cries, and discharged as
many arrows at us as they could; they then returned to the
opposite shore. When, however, they saw that our barques
were ready to pass the river, all of them fled and abandoned
the place.

We crossed the river with much order; it was about a
league broad, and the depth from nineteen to twenty fathoms.
On the opposite side we found some excellent villages; we
ascended the current with the intention of repairing to the
province of Pacaha, for it was necessary to take this course in
order to reach there. But before arriving at that province, we
fell in with another sovereign, named Ycasqui, who was at war
with the cacique of Pacaha; he came in a friendly manner to
visit us, and said that he had long heard of us, that he knew
we were men from heaven, on whom their arrows could inflict
no injury, and that on this account he wished not to make
war upon us, but to render us service. The Governor received him courteously, and forbade any person whomsoever
to enter his village, or do him any harm. We encamped in
a plain in sight of this cacique's village, where we rested two
days.

On the day of our arrival, the cacique asked the Governor
to give him a sign by means of which after our departure he
should be enabled to demand assistance during these wars,
and by which his subjects could obtain water, which they
greatly needed for the cultivation of their grounds, as their
children were starving. The Governor ordered his men to
make a large cross of a couple of pine trees, and told the cacique
to return on the next day, when the sign from heaven which
he had asked for would be given to him, and that he believed
he would want for nothing, if he placed implicit faith in it.
The cacique repeated his visit on the following day, and he
then made a long oration, in which he asked why we delayed
so long to give him the sign that he had requested, since he

Ycasqui.

was so well disposed to serve and to follow us; he began to weep bitterly because we did not give it him immediately, and in such a manner as to draw tears from all our eyes at witnessing his devotion, and the fervency with which he sought it. The Governor told him to return with his Indians, and that we should come in the evening to his village, and bring the sign which he was anxious to obtain. In the evening he presented himself with all his Indians, and we marched with them in procession to the village. The caciques of this country are in the habit of erecting, near the houses in which they reside, very high mounds; some, however, have their abodes on the summit of these mounds. It was upon one of these little mountains that we planted the cross. We all repaired thither, and with the greatest devotion fell on our knees to kiss the foot of it. The Indians followed our example, and afterwards brought a great quantity of reeds, with which they constructed a fence round about it.

The same evening we returned to our camp, and on the following morning departed for Pacaha, which was situated Pacaha. higher up; we marched two days, and arrived at a village in the middle of a plain, encompassed by walls and a moat full of water, dug by the hand of man. We approached as near as we could, and when we were quite close, we halted, not daring to enter. As we were turning round, we perceived at one side a vast number of the inhabitants leaving the place. We entered the village without meeting with any opposition. We took a very few Indians, for nearly all of them had already fled; but they were not able to place in safety the little that they possessed, for everything remained in the town. Whilst we stayed outside the walls without daring to enter, we saw a numerous party of Indians behind us, whom we took for warriors coming to the assistance of the village. We marched to meet them, but soon recognized the cacique we had left behind, and with whom we had planted the cross; he had come to render us assistance in

case we stood in need of it; we conducted him into the village. He began by thanking the Governor for the cross
which he had given to him, and said that on the previous day
rain had fallen in abundance; that all his subjects were so
well satisfied, that they intended not to leave us again, but
wished to bear us company. The Governor made him enter
the village, and gave him all that we found there; (for they
esteem as a great treasure a few collars formed of shell fish,
skins of cats and of roebucks;) we gave him likewise a
small quantity of maize that was in the village, and he left
much delighted. We remained in this place in order to see if
we could take the northern route, so as to cross to the South
Sea.

After an abode of twenty-six or twenty-seven days, during
which we made some excursions, we advanced towards the
north-east, as we had been told that in that direction we
should meet with large towns wherein we might take up
A desert. our quarters. We travelled eight days through a desert
covered with very extensive marshes, and where not a tree
was to be seen; we could perceive nought but plains,
where certain herbs grew so high and thick that the horses
could with difficulty pass through them; we afterwards met
with a party of Indians, who lived under tents stitched together, which they carry away with them whenever they
choose; they have at such times only to roll up the covering
of the tent, which an Indian takes charge of, whilst the woman
carries the poles that support it; they construct and remove
these tents with the greatest ease, and consequently being
able to take their houses with them, they change their abodes
very frequently. We ascertained from these Indians that
in the interior there were several tribes like their own,
who were nomadic, and pitched their tents in those places
which were stocked with deer; that they frequented a
marsh where there was an abundant supply of fish; that as
soon as the game had been scared, and they caught no more

fish, they shifted their abode, and transporting their houses on their backs, and every thing they possessed, they betook themselves to some place where they could procure food. The name of this province was Calusi. The natives pay Calusi. little attention to cultivating the soil, but depend entirely on hunting and fishing for subsistence. We returned to Pacaha, where the Governor had remained. We found the cacique, who had come again as a friend, along with the Governor; in the meantime the other cacique, who had kept further behind, and with whom we had planted the cross, arrived; it was a wonderful thing to see the reconciliation of these two hostile caciques. The Governor made them both sit by his side, and one could hardly imagine the pains that each took to obtain the right-hand place.

Finding that there was no possibility of reaching the other The other sea, we returned towards the south. The cacique with whom we had planted the cross, accompanied us. On taking leave of him, we marched in the direction of the other sea, that is to say, towards the south-west, until we reached a province called Quiguata, in which is the largest village that we have Quiguata. seen in Florida; it was situated on one of the arms of the great river. Here we stayed eight or nine days for the purpose of procuring interpreters and guides, intending always to reach the other sea, for the Indians told us that eleven days' march would bring us to a province where they killed oxen, and where we should find interpreters who would conduct us to the sea.

We left with the guides for that province which is called Coligua; there was no beaten track; every evening they led us near to a marsh where we refreshed ourselves, and found abundance of fish. We crossed vast plains, and very high mountains, and at length came quite suddenly upon the town of Coligua, as though we had reached it by a high road. We observed all along the way traces of the passage of Coligua. men; we found a great quantity of provisions in this

C C

country, and a considerable number of ox tails tanned, and others in preparation.   During the route, we made inquiries of the Indians respecting the country we were in search of, and whether there were any village far or near ; but to these inquiries we could never obtain any answer : all they said was, that if we wished to go to any villages, we ought to take the direction of west-south-west.   We accordingly followed the route which the Indians had pointed out, and arrived a some scattered villages which bore the name of Tatil Coya we found there a large river which falls into the Rio Grande ; we learnt that by ascending the first stream we should meet with a considerable province, called Cayas ; we accordingly went to this place, and saw that it was composed of detached villages thickly peopled, where we made some reconnoiterings ; the entire country is covered with mountains.

During an excursion, the cacique and a great number of natives were seized, of whom we made inquiries respecting the country : they replied, that by ascending the river we should find a large province called Tula.   The Governor was desirous of going to see whether it would be possible for us to winter there : he accordingly set out with twenty horsemen, leaving the remainder in the province of Cayas. Before, however, we reached Tula, we passed over steep mountains, and at length entered the village without any notice being given of our arrival ; we set about capturing some Indians, but they defended themselves, and that day wounded nine or ten of our horses and seven or eight Spaniards.   They were so brave that they formed into parties of eight or ten, and rushed upon us like furious dogs ; we killed about thirty or forty of them.

The Governor seeing that we were but few in number, considered that it was not prudent to pass the night in this place ; we accordingly returned by the same route that we had taken.   We crossed a level plain surrounded by the

(marginal notes)
Tatil Coya.

A large river, falling into the Rio Grande.

Cayas.

Tula.

river, after having passed over the mountain, which we feared
might be occupied by the Indians. The next day the
Governor came to the spot where he had left his party, but
the Indians who had been seized had made their escape, and
there were none others in the province whom our interpreter
could understand. The Governor gave orders that all should
get ready to go to that province, and we proceeded thither
without loss of time. We had scarcely arrived on the following day, when we perceived three large troops of Indians
advancing towards us from three different sides. We routed
them after having killed some men, which put an end
to hostilities; two or three days afterwards, they despatched
messengers to us as if to sue for peace, but as we had no
interpreters, we were not able to understand them. We
made them comprehend by signs, that they were to send us
interpreters for the natives whom we intended to visit;
they brought us five or six Indians who understood our
interpreters. They were inquisitive to know who we were,
and what was the object of our journey; we made inquiries after some large province where there might be a
good supply of provisions, for we began to feel severely
the rigour of the winter; they said, that in the direction we were following, they had no knowledge of any very
extensive population. Seeing that no other resource was
left for us, we resumed the route of the south-east, and proceeded to a province called Quipana, which was situated at Quipana.
the foot of very lofty mountains. From thence we turned
towards the east, and crossing those mountains, we descended Mountains.
into a plain, which was inhabited, and appeared favourable
for our plans; not far off was a village where there was
plenty of provisions; it was constructed on the bank of a
large river, which flowed into the great river, along which we
had passed: the province was called Viranque, and here we Viranque.
spent the winter, and suffered so much from the cold and
snow, that we thought we should have perished. The

Christian who was found among the Indians whom Narvaez had visited, and who acted as our interpreter, died at this place.

We departed from this village at the beginning of March, when we supposed that the extremity of the cold was over. We descended the course of the river, on the shores of which we found other provinces well peopled and rich in provisions; at length we reached another province, called Anicoyanque, which appeared to us to be one of the best that we had seen in this country. A cacique whose name was Guachoyanque, came to visit us; his village was situated on the bank of the great river; he was frequently at war with the cacique whom we were leaving. The Governor set out immediately for the village of Guachoyanque in company with the cacique. His village was very well enclosed with walls, and fortified, but there was only a scanty supply of provisions, for the Indians had robbed him of all that he had.

The Governor came to a resolution at this place, in case he should discover the sea, to build some brigantines which might convey intelligence to Cuba that we were alive, and to ask for horses and other things of which we stood in need; he despatched the captain towards the south, with orders to search out some road so as to reach the sea; for notwithstanding the questions which were put to the Indians, no exact knowledge could be obtained as to its existence on this side. He came back and reported that he had not discovered any road by which to cross the vast morasses formed by the great river on this side.

The Governor being in great perplexity of mind, and matters not turning out according to his wishes, fell sick and died, having nominated Luis de Moscoso to succeed him. Not discovering any road for reaching the sea, we determined upon resuming the route towards the west, in the hopes of proceeding by land to Mexico, provided we did not succeed

Anicoyanque.

Guachoyanque.

Soto's death.

in finding in the interior some place where we could remain;
we marched during seventeen days, and arrived at the province of Chavite, where the Indians made abundance of Chavite.
salt; we had no information respecting the north; from
thence we repaired to the province of Aguacay, and three Aguacay.
days more were spent in getting there, taking a direct northerly course.

The Indians told us that we should not meet with any
inhabited country, unless we descended towards the south-east
and south, where we should find villages and provisions; but
on the side to which we were desirous of going, there were only
extensive tracts of sand, without village or any kind of food;
we were consequently forced to turn our steps to that side
which the Indians had pointed out. We next reached a
province called Nisione, and subsequently others called Nan- Nisione.
dacaho and Lacame: the country becoming more and more Nandacaho.
Lacame.
barren, the scarcity of provisions increased; we received
some notice respecting the province of Xuacatino, which we
had been told was considerable; the cacique of Nandacaho
gave us an Indian for a guide who would conduct us into a
country from whence we could no more escape; he led us
then into a wild country through which there was no road,
and finished by telling us, that his master had ordered him
to carry us to a place where we should die of hunger. We
took another guide, who conducted us into the province of
Hais, to which herds of oxen occasionally resorted. As soon Hais.
Oxen.
as the natives saw us enter their territories, they collected
their forces in order to prevent our killing the oxen; they
attacked us with their arrows, which occasioned us some
loss. We left this province for that of Xacatin, which is Xacatin.
surrounded by thick forests; provisions there were scarce;
from thence the Indians conducted us on the east side into
other small villages, which were destitute of provisions; they
pretended to lead us to a country where there were other
Christians; we soon, however, found out that they were

deceiving us, and that they could not have acquired any such knowledge, as they had seen no other Christians but ourselves; but as our course had been so very circuitous, it was possible that they had already seen us pass by. We then took once more the southerly direction, with a firm determination to reach New Spain, or perish in the attempt.

We marched six days in the direction of south-south-east, after which we halted. We sent out a detachment of six horsemen, with orders for them to advance for eight or nine days as far as possible, and to see whether they could not discover some village where we might procure a supply of maize for the journey. They set out accordingly and proceeded as far as they could, and met with some poor Indians who had no houses, but lived in wretched cabins; they cultivated no plants of any kind, but subsisted solely on fish and game; four or five of these natives were taken, but no one could be found who understood their language.

Seeing that we were without interpreters, and without provisions, and that the maize which we had brought began to fail,—in short, that it was impossible so many persons could travel through so poor a country,—we resolved upon returning to the village where the Governor Soto had died, thinking that at that place we should find greater facilities for constructing the vessels in which we might take our departure from the country.

We accordingly retraced our steps to the place where the Governor had died. When we arrived there, we were disappointed in our expectations, for the Indians had carried off all the provisions that were in the village; this compelled us to seek another, with a view of wintering there, and building the vessels. God permitted us to discover two villages most suitable for our purpose; they were situated upon the great river, were fortified, and contained great store of maize. Here we took up our quarters, and set to work to build our vessels. Six months were spent in con-

structing seven brigantines, with the utmost difficulty ; at
length we launched them into the stream, and in truth it was
miraculous that they sailed so well, and did not let in the
water, considering that they were only caulked with the bark
of mulberry trees, and without any pitch.   We took with us
some canoes, into which we put twenty-six horses ; and
we intended, in case we met with a village on the coast
where we could live, to despatch two brigantines with intelligence to the viceroy of New Spain, so that he might send
vessels to seek us.

On the second day, as we were descending the river, forty
or fifty Indian canoes, of a very large size and very light,
approached us; one of these contained eighty warriors, who
kept hovering in our rear, and showering their arrows upon
us ; many of our men looking upon it as a piece of cowardice
not to attack them, took four or five of our small canoes, and
advanced against those of the Indians, who, as soon as they
saw their manœuvres, surrounded them, cut off their retreat,
overturned their canoes, and killed twelve of our best soldiers, without our being able to render them any assistance.   The stream was very rapid, and we had but few oars
on board.

The Indians, emboldened by this success, continued pursuing us until we reached the sea, which lasted nineteen
days. We sustained a heavy loss from them, and had several
of our soldiers wounded.   Perceiving that we had no weapons
which could reach them from a distance—for we had neither
crossbow nor arquebuss remaining, but only a few swords
and bucklers—they had not the least fear of us, but approached very near to discharge their arrows at us.   We
entered the sea by the mouth of the river, which forms a
very large bay.   We sailed during three days and nights in
very fair weather, without perceiving land.   We suspected
that we were in the open sea, but at the expiration of the
above-mentioned time, we took up water which was as fresh

as that of the river, and very good to drink. We discovered some small islands on the west side; towards these we shaped our course, and from that time we continually followed the coast, gathering shell-fish, and searching after anything we might find to eat, till at length we entered the river of Panuco, where we had a welcome reception from the Christians.

Signed, LUIS FERNANDEZ DE BIEDMA.

INDEX.

Martyr (Peter), extracts from, relating to Cabot, viii, ix; on the discovery of Florida, and why so called, x; descriptive of the Indians of Duharhe, xv; relative to Ayllon, xvii

Mavilla, xxxii-xxxv; supposed to have stood on the n. side of the Alabama, and at a place called Choctaw Bluff, xlviii; 74-81, 184-186

Mauvila, xxxii

Mendoça (Don Antonio de), Viceroy of Mexico, 164

Mexico, ancient name of, 165

Micanopy, Fort, xxxix, xl

Minoya, lix, lx, lxiv, 143-149

Mississippi River, called by the Spaniards Rio de Espiritu Santo and Rio Grande; discovered and named by Pineda in 1519, xxiii; crossed by Cabeça de Vaca, xxi, xxiii; Mr. Greenhow's letter respecting, xxiii; four Indian names of, 118; crossed by De Soto's army in 1541, probably within thirty miles of Helena: according to Irving, at the lowest Chickasaw Bluff; and according to M'Culloh, about twenty or thirty miles below the mouth of the Arkansaw River, xxi, lii, 92, 189; described, li, 90-92, 182; the Spaniards descend the river, lx, lxiii, lxiv, 149-154, 199

Mocoço, 32, 33

Monette (Dr. J. W.), his "History of the discovery and settlement of the valley of the Mississippi, xxxvii; route of the Spaniards west of the Mississippi, lii-lx

Moscoso de Alvarado (Luys de), takes the command on the death of Soto, 125, 196

Musquitos, an infinite swarm of, 159

N.

Naçacahoz, 137
Naguatax, lix, 131-135, 141
Nandacaho, xxxii, 197
Napetuca, 39
Naquiscoça, 137
Narvaez (Pamphilo de), his expedition to Florida in 1527-8, xix-xxvi, 11, 20, 38, 43, 142, 176, 183
Natchitoches, lix
Nicalasa, 82
Nilco, xxxii, lviii, lix, 116-123, 141-147
Nisione, xxxii, 197
Nissoone, xxxii, 135
Nondacao, xxxii, 135, 136
Nuttall (Mr. T.), his travels into the Arkansa, xxxvii

O.

Ocali, xxxii; probably in the neighbourhood of Fort King, xxxix
Ochete, 43
Ochile, xxxii, xxxix
Ochlockony River, crossed by the Spaniards, xliv
Ochus, probably either Pensacola, or the entrance of the Mobile, xlii, 45
Ockockona River, xli
Ocute, xxxii, xxxvi, xliv, xlv, 49, 179
Ohahichee Swamp, xlii
Okefenokee River, xl
Orange Lake, xxxix
Oro, Rio del, 138
Ortiz (Juan), the interpreter, 29, 173, 174; death of, at Autiamque, 115, 196
Osachile, conjectured by Fairbanks to be Suwanee Old Town, xl
Oscilla river, xl, xli
Ossachile, xxxii, xl
Otoa, xliv, 178
Ouachita river, lvi

P.

Pacaha, xxxii, 93-103, 191
Pafallaya, 81
Palache, xxxix
Palisema, lvi, 106
Panuco, river and town, 162-164, 200
Paracossi, xxxii, xxxvii, 34, 35
Pato, 131
Patofa, xxxiv, 50
Pearl river, xlix
Pearls, found at Cutifa-Chiqui, 57
Pensacola bay, discovered by Narvaez, xxi, xlii
Piache, 73
Pineda (Alonzo Alvarez de), takes the command of an expedition towards Florida in 1519, and afterwards coasts westward as far as Vera Cruz, xii; discovers the river Mississippi, xxiii
Piragua, meaning of, 116
Ponce de Leon (Juan), discovers and explores Florida, x; account of his voyage and search after the Fountain of Youth, xi
Potano, 37

Q.

Quigalta, 118-121, 150, 153
Quigate, lvi
Quigaute, xxxii, 102-105
Quiguata, xxxii, 193
Quiguate, lv
Quipana, xxxii, 112, 195
Quizquiz, xxxii, li, 89, 189

For EU product safety concerns, contact us at Calle de José Abascal, 56–1°,
28003 Madrid, Spain or eugpsr@cambridge.org.

www.ingramcontent.com/pod-product-compliance
Ingram Content Group UK Ltd.
Pitfield, Milton Keynes, MK11 3LW, UK
UKHW010346140625
459647UK00010B/868